RESEARCH IN
RACE AND
ETHNIC RELATIONS

*Volume 10* • 1997

THE BLACK INTELLECTUALS

# RESEARCH IN RACE AND ETHNIC RELATIONS

## THE BLACK INTELLECTUALS

*Editor:*   RUTLEDGE M. DENNIS
*Department of Sociology*
*George Mason University*

VOLUME 10 • 1997

 **JAI PRESS INC.**

*Greenwich, Connecticut*                    *London, England*

# CONTENTS

## PART IV. PUBLIC INTELLECTUALS

# LIST OF CONTRIBUTORS

Earnest N. Bracey

Department of Political Science
Community College of Southern
    Nevada

Sandra Lee Browning

University of Cincinnati

Rodney D. Coates

Black World Studies
Miami University

W. Avon Drake

Department of Political
    Science
Virginia Commonwealth
    University

Stefano Harney

Department of Social
    Sciences
Pace University

L. Adele Jinadu

Department of Political Science
Lagos State University, Nigeria

John H. Stanfield, II

Department of Sociology
University of California,
    Davis

Doris Wilkinson

Department of Sociology
University of Kentucky

Alford A. Young, Jr.

Department of Sociology
University of Michigan

TO

BABBER (IN MEMORIAM)
IDEE
NITA
LEON P.
BECCA
ABRAHAM

FROM BROTHER, WITH LOVE

# INTRODUCTION:

## W.E.B. DU BOIS AND THE TRADITION
## OF RADICAL INTELLECTUAL THOUGHT

Rutledge M. Dennis

W.E.B. Du Bois outlined the issues and assumptions for an approach to critical and radical intellectual thought in the United States, especially as this thought focuses on race and class. From Du Bois' earliest studies (Du Bois 1896 [1969], 1897, 1899) to the present, race and class, as structural constraints, have continued to frustrate attempts, great and small, to move the society towards greater equity and justice. Thus, Du Bois' role as an intellectual and the distinct manner in which he both thought about and analyzed race and class cause us to return to him for the sharpness and clarity with which he approached the issues. We do so because we believe his unique insights and intellectual tools are of value to contemporary thinkers and scholars who, as they attempt to lasso and corral, and make sociological sense of both racism and classism, often find themselves entangled in knots.

**Research in Race and Ethnic Relations, Volume 10, pages xi-xxiv**
**Copyright © 1997 by JAI Press Inc.**
**All rights of reproduction in any form reserved.**
**ISBN: 0-7623-0275-5**

This paper explores the multifaceted themes in Du Bois' intellectual arsenal which supported his personal quest for meaning in a society which was racially irrational; more importantly, he wanted to use that arsenal to probe this racial irrationality as it negatively affected an oppressed group. An analysis of these themes permit us to understand the methodical manner Du Bois used to survey, study, then, in his manner, purpose methods to surgically remove the cancer of social inequality from the society.

The role of the intellectual and the process of intellectually are crucial elements in Du Bois' approach to radical social change. That this is so is made evident by the extent to which he is cited in the papers presented in this volume. Du Bois himself virtually created, single-handedly, the role of the public intellectual, a role played with much zeal and gusto by two public intellectuals discussed in this volume, James Baldwin and Cornel West. The idea of a public intellectual is contrasted to a non-public intellectual: the academic or ivory tower intellectual.

The legacy of Du Bois as intellectual entails a review of a process by which he begins as an academic intellectual, then is simultaneously both an academic and public intellectual; finally, towards the last third of his life we note an evolution by which the public intellectual completely absorbs the public intellectual. That this occurred can be explained by the immensity of the issues and problems related to race and racial matters which inordinately consumed him on a personal level; these issues and problems also consumed him as one belonging to a larger submerged oppressed group.

Du Bois' concept of the role of the intellectual in any society was initially predicated on several assumptions: that prejudice and discrimination represented concrete concepts and depicted existing attitudes and behavior towards "pariah" groups; that the intellectual class represented a new, and hopefully, evolving radical secular order whose mission it would be to serve as the moral and intellectual conscience for the nation; that a collective social ignorance accounted for much of the manifest hatred and animosity between groups; that ultimately, the force and dedication of the intellectual class would persuade the less enlightened members of the society that it was not in its best interest nor in the larger public interest to ostracize, and mistreat, or exclude groups.

The specific subjects which comprised the core of Du Bois' intellectual legacy will be examined in the remainder of this paper.

One matter of strategic importance, and one permeating this volume, is the similarity of themes broached by Du Bois and those intellectuals who followed him. Indeed, when Du Boisian perspectives are analyzed in-depth one feature is clear: he was able to set the emotional,intellectual, political, and logic standards from which subsequent approaches to minority life in the United States would be measured.

We now examine the specific thematic perspectives within which DuBois'intellectual legacy may be assessed. Section 1 discusses Du Bois' assessment of the role of intellectuals; Section 2 examines Du Bois' public opposition to social injustice; Section 3 analyzes the dynamics of oppressed communities; Section 4 states Du Bois' arguments against Western colonialism and imperialism; Section 5 reviews Du Bois' assessment of organizations and institutions; Section 6 presents an analysis of the importance of scholarship in Du Bois' intellectual legacy; Finally, Section 7 presents Du Bois' assessment of politics as action.

## THE ROLE OF THE INTELLECTUAL

The educated, called The Talented Tenth, occupied the most central position in Du Bois' strategy for social justice and social change. Du Bois was often imprecise in his use of the Tenth: sometimes referring to a cultural "aristocracy"; at other times referring to the educated who would educate future generations; yet at other times, the term is used to characterize those individuals who are not merely educated but have chosen the world of ideas and the elucidation of ideas as the defining feature of their life. It is this last definition which concerns us here.

Du Bois' arguments for what he called a "Revolutionary group" were predicated on these factors: that racial oppression was pervasive and a noose around the necks of blacks in the North as well as in the South; that whites were alternately indifferent and antagonistic to blacks; that the history of cultures and groups was that of leadership by a revolutionary group which provided an impetus to freedom and liberation, and that radical social change could be jumpstarted with such a dedicated radical intellectual class (Du Bois 1897, 1898, 1899, 1903).

The call for an intellectual class to spearhead social change among the outcasts was indeed a "revolutionary" idea: Revolutionary in that Du Bois assumed a certain intellectual and emotional threshold already in existence, one which would greatly facilitate the type of rapid social change he envisioned. That Du Bois expected such greatness and sacrifice from a small enlightened cadre within a newly liberated people attests to several things: his understanding of the existing educational and cultural achievements of this group and his intuitive prescience of the latent skills and talents not yet unearthed in a population existing as he said, "behind a veil."

That Du Bois clearly distinguished between a primarily middle class leadership cadre and one which he characterized as a distinctive intellectual cadre can be seen in the special (and radical) role he envisioned for the Negro Academy, the organizational arm of the intellectual cadre. That such a cadre was necessary was situated in Du Bois' early statements regarding the stages by which an intellectual cadre would study "the Negro Problem": outline the social issues, research the problems, propose solutions to these problems, publicize the findings, and finally, engage in the struggle to enact the necessary social policy.

The consistent thread throughout Du Bois' discussion of the intellectual has been the pragmatism with which he couched problems and solutions. He outlined the scenario in the manner that he did because he believed that approached was both practical and most feasible, and offered the best opportunity to alter an existing social status quo. That his explanation of the role of intellectuals in the struggle for equality did not unfold precisely in the manner he envisioned was a source of great consternation to him later in life: he abandoned the idea of the importance of an intellectual elite in the freedom struggle. This abandonment, however, neither diminishes nor eliminates the concept of the intellectual as one of Du Bois' most important legacies to subsequent generations.

## THE PUBLIC ADVOCATE: WRITINGS AND SPEECHES

In his many writings and public speeches Du Bois, with much zeal, became a one-man crusader against social injustice. These activities moved him into the realm of the public intellectual. As a public intellectual Bois operated as a "truth squad," challenging both the American government and the private sector (business and political) as these institutions adopted and supported policies and programs prejudicial to blacks and other groups. Indeed, one of the key features of the Du Boisian legacy against hate, intolerance, and inequality, was that this opposition, to be effective, had to be public rather than merely private and academic. Hence, a review of where he published his views—scientific journals, newspapers, special reports, and pamphlets—confirms his intent to expound his views in publications directed towards professionals and the lay public. A sampling of the periodicals where he published his views in his first ventures as a public intellectual include the following: *The Voice, Independent, Atlantic Monthly, Horizon, Southern Workman, Harpers, Dial, Bulletin of the United States Department of Labor, Political Science Quarterly, Christian Register, The Moon Illustrated Weekly,* and *Publications of the American Economic Association.*

A sample of the titles of articles published during Du Bois' early years as a public intellectual demonstrate the issues which captured his attention: "The Burden of Negro Schooling," " The Storm and Stress in the Black World," "The Suffrage Fight in Georgia," "The Study of the Negro Problem," "The Spawn of Slavery," "The Problem of Housing the Negro," "Training of the Negro for Social Power," and "Crime and Our Colored Population."

The early speeches and addresses by Du Bois reflected his emerging role as a public intellectual. In this role he methodically and meticulously pealed away the layers of racial myths and irrationalities and railed against a system devoted to perpetuating and justifying the virtual enslavement of blacks. The speeches and addresses were oriented in two directions: messages specifically designed for whites and those specifically designed for blacks: "The Value of Agitation"; "Is Racial Separation Practicable?"; "We Claim Our Rights"; "A Conservation of Races"; "Race Prejudice"; "Disfranchisement"; "The Economic Future of the Negro"; "Address to the Nations of the World."

One of the most important features of the public intellectual as advocate, exemplified by Du Bois, was a willingness to state, in speeches and writings, his special view of the world and a boldness in stating these views unequivocally. His arguments and explanations were stated with great precision, clarity, passion, and objectivity. This role as public advocate and a messenger of social justice was consistent with Du Bois' concept of the role of the intellectual; writings and speeches were the vehicles to distribute the call for a new social and political morality.

# SOCIOLOGY OF OPPRESSED COMMUNITIES

Analysis of the dynamics of oppressed communities was one of Du Bois' central intellectual legacy. His massive urban study, *The Philadelphia Negro* (1899) became a model for urban and community studies, especially those focusing on outcast and marginal groups. These studies were designed to demonstrate the rich cultural, social, and institutional life blacks were able to develop "behind the veil." Indeed, Du Bois' studies of Northern and Southern communities were designed to illustrate the two different sociologies of Black America: one North, born in relative freedom and shaped by the industrial North; the other South, shaped by segregation and intimidation. In his Northern community studies Du Bois (1899, 1901) explored the evolution from slavery; the activities during the Reconstruction; the emergence of Jim Crow Laws, and the growing terrorism in the South in the post-Reconstruction era, and the resulting migration northward. His studies of Southern black communities (Du Bois 1898, 1899, 1903, 1907) was, and had to be, different in tone, and described, not so much the formation of communities, but rather, how already existing communities coped with their tenuous status under constant duress and strains.

The delineation of life within communities behind the veil was a crucial feature of the Du Boisian intellectual legacy. It confirmed the viability of institution-organization formation in black community life; it validated the need to view and interpret minority community formation from values and perspectives which originated from the inner workings of black life rather than only orienting itself to the values and perspectives of the dominant white majority; it sanctioned the view of a black cultural development which was often parallel to, but other times diverging from, mainstream cultural motifs.

For Du Bois, the differing communities of the North and the South did not negate the one feature they had in common: they lived behind a veil of inequality and racial oppression. That Northern oppression was more tempered and civil than the Southern version was not important from Du Boisian perspectives; he was not interested in analyzing degrees of freedom. What did interest him immensely was the manner in which these communities, North and South, creatively circumvented, deflected, and outmaneuvered some aspects of racism while simultaneously building the interstitial networks to sustain communities.

## ANALYSIS OF WESTERN IMPERIALISM
## AND COLONIALISM

Du Bois launch a sustained systematic study and attack of Western values, customs, and power and their consequences for African and Asian people and those Americans from those continents then living in the United States. Beginning with his study of the African slave trade (1896), followed by other studies of Africa (1924, 1930, 1939, 1945, 1960, 1965), Du Bois set the pace for a trenchant critique of the West and it role in the merging of color and servitude. Thus, Du Bois' early statement on the relationship between Africa, Asia, and the West demonstrated an uncanny ability to "see" the future, both national and international: "The problem of the twentieth century is the problem of the color-line,—the relations of the darker to the lighter races of men in Asia and Africa, in America and the islands of the sea."(Du Bois, 1903). For Du Bois, the imperative for attacking colonialism and imperialism was a natural evolution of the universal human quest for freedom and liberty. To assist in this universal quest the progressive, educated, and politically enlightened segment of the society had an obligation to fight on the side of the weak. For Du Bois, the issue was not simply one of political or economic equality, thought this was important. It was also a question of social morality and the quest for a virtuous community where all members of the society, regardless of race or color, would be united in a spirit of mutual obligation and cooperation.

The Du Boisian legacy of an assault on racial practices within the country as well as a critique of European colonialism in Africa and Asia can be discerned in the articles in this volume. Even truer to Du Bois' legacy (see the citations mentioned above) are the assertions by intellectuals, analyzed in this volume, linking the imperial and colonial policies of the European to segregationist and discriminatory policies of both the public and private sectors in the United States. Like Du Bois, those intellectuals who followed him accepted his belief that the public role of the intellectual consisted of the use of their knowledge and relative independence to publicly expose and indict whatever agencies, public or private, national or international guilty of abridging the freedom of others. Before Du Bois, prominent figures like William Highland Garnett, Martin Delaney, and Frederick Douglass were public intellectuals who, unequivocally, publicly, and in print stated their opposition to colonialism, at home and abroad.

Du Bois, like the intellectuals who followed him, had an inner moral imperative to both act against and, if necessary, reject the country of their birth whenever that country appeared committed to an iron-clad policy of social inequality.

## THE ORGANIZATION AS A WEAPON

As he began to realize the magnitude of the problem of inequality and the depth of the ideology of white supremacy, Du Bois very early viewed organizations as important tools in the struggle for social equality. His early advocacy of the importance of the American Negro Academy (1898, 1903) as well as the emphasis he placed on the role of churches, secret societies, beneficial societies, cooperative enterprises, and other institutions in his study of black life in Philadelphia (1899). As he noted then Du Bois 1899, pp. 233-234): "...thoughtful men see that invaluable training and discipline is coming to the race through these organizations, and they encourage the formation of them...it is apparent that the largest hope for the ultimate rise of the Negro lies in this mastery of the art of social life..."

The organization as vehicle for social change existed within two mutually reinforcing frameworks for Du Bois: organizations oriented around the print media—the scientific journal,newsletter, and political and cultural organizations as educational and solidarity agents. The printed media permitted Du Bois to get his message of human liberation to the public. It was a message addressed to blacks and whites, rich and the poor, North and the South,and the very educated and the average educated. He chose the media, the scientific or the lay, which would be most effective in promoting his message. The following journals and newspapers were either founded by Du Bois, headed by Du Bois or were both founded and headed by him: Chief Editor of *Fisk Herald* (1887-1988); Editor of Atlanta University Studies of the Negro Problem (1897-1911); Founder and Editor of *The Moon* (1906); Founder and Editor of *The Horizon* (1907-1910); Editor-in-Chief, Encyclopedia Project of the Negro (1933-1945); Founder and Editor of *Phylon*; Chief Editor: Preparatory Volume: *Encyclopedia of the Negro*, and Editor and Founder of *The Crisis* (1910-1934).

One marvels at the sheer magnitude of Du Bois as organizer in the print media. His skills were duplicated in the political and cultural organizational arenas. Given the history of the Washington-DuBois debate, it is somewhat understandable how and why Du Bois'organizational structures tended to focus on the political. A list of Du Bois' political organizations and affiliations clearly reflected his personal political choices and societal objectives.

They also reflected the vast political divergence between which he gravitated most of his life: Founder and General Secretary of the Niagara Movement (1905-1909); One of the original Founders and Incorporators of the National Association for the Advancement of Colored People—NAACP—(1909); Founder of the Pan African Movement; Organizer of the Pan-African Congresses (1919); Chairman, Council on African Affairs (1949); Chairman, Peace Information Center (1949), and joins the Communist Party of the United States (1961).

Du Bois' orientation to the organizational structures described above was predicated on the idea that organizations represented a degree of power and independence from which the intellectual dissenter could more effectively challenge the system, maintain a steady stream of information and propaganda, and for the structural organizational format, provide a source for new members and the funds to enable the organization to better fight for justice and equality. The breadth and scope of Du Bois' organizational network was astonishing, reflecting both his high energy level and a high level of political intensity. Organizations, both related to media and political structure, enabled Du Bois to coordinate the link between messages presented in media format and messages representing the political ideology of the organization as structure. Du Bois coordinated and effectively linked the media as the organizational messenger and the organization as the fount of ideological wisdom, and at times, organizational purity. The degree to which he often succeeded in challenging the power structure and planning the strategies and tactics for the assorted organizations he founded and directed attested to his intellectual and organizational genius.

## COMMITMENT TO SCHOLARSHIP

Du Bois' scholarship was one of his earliest legacies to contemporary intellectuals. His study of the African slave trade (1896) was the first systematic study of that topic. What was important in Du Bois' study and much, though not all of his subsequent works, was his early adherence to a concept of science and scientific knowledge as approaches to move beyond the subjectivity then so prevalent in the academic world. Though he later questions the value of the much touted scientific approach and ends up rejecting much of that earlier scientific orientation, his earlier studies reflected his compatibility with the then newly emerging idea of science as the guarantor of scientific and social objectivity. His *Philadelphia Negro* (1899) was even more of a landmark study in that it opened the doors to the complexities of urban and community research; it was also radical in that he applied this new scientific knowledge to the first systematic study of an oppressed community. Though Du Bois could not resist the temptation to occasionally editorialize, the study is important because, despite the racial tensions and conflicts of that era, Du Bois as a sociologist placed the Philadelphia community under a microscope just as the scientist in the lab placed the cell under the microscope.

The commitment to scholarship was more than any other single factor motivated by the idea that truth was discernible and more readily captured when scientific methods were used. The logic was as follows: truth was largely hidden by falsehood, thus, the people who exploited and ruled cruelly did so due to imperfect and inadequate knowledge and information. Ergo, if they only knew the truth and the full extent of their injury to others, they would cease and desist from such behavior. Du Bois believed his studies could be effective in several ways: by informing the dominant power structure of the life and values of a subjugated people assist in lessening the hate and animosity towards the oppressed; the information presented could help to demarcate truth from fiction and myth. That this did not work as Du Bois envisioned says nothing about Du Bois' works; rather, the failure of academic studies to alter social views speaks more to the tenacity of deeply rooted ideological indoctrinations. Du Bois believed his studies could persuade whites, lay and professional, to be and act differently towards blacks. It was only later (Du Bois 1940) that he concluded that in the realm of race, social science findings seldom altered prejudicial opinions and values.

Du Bois' disappointments with the heralded scientific approach notwithstanding, he passed on an intellectual legacy of the value of an intellectual inquiry whose origins were not solely rooted in the personal and subjective. He clearly understood that a complex array of data attached to explanations of a people's everyday cultural existence would help unlock the sociological key to the subtle intricacies of black intellectual, cultural, and emotional life; he saw great value in tracing the links between these variables and the situational political and economic forces which shaped the paths and behavior of collective black and white community life in the United States.

Africa and African American life history and culture were rich mines to be tapped in what Du Bois viewed as the black intellectual's quest to make visible the sociologically invisible; this unlocking would free the entire society by de-mystifying race and group differences. This he hoped to do with his community studies, North and South. While the de-mystification process was initially attached mainly his scientific studies, his *Souls of Black Folk* (1903) was intended as a moral (and non-scientific) plea to win the hearts of the white lay and professional populations.

Just as Du Bois used his community studies to re-interpret the social, religious, and cultural strands in black life, his *John Brown* (1909) and *Black Reconstruction* (1935) were used to redefine how class, race, economics, and politics converged to shape the destiny of the American nation. Likewise, his African studies, *The Negro* (1915), *Black Folks: Then and Now* (1939), and *The World and Africa* (1947) were to be, and were, fresh approaches to African history, culture, and contemporary events. Like the community and civil war studies, Du Bois' African books told Western scholars that there was yet another way to interpret data they had been used to seeing and analyzing.

One of the missions of black intellectuals, according to Du Bois, would be that of studying, reassessing, and redefining the ordinary and common place features of African and African American life, those aspects taken for granted, intentionally or unintentionally by European and American scholars; Du Bois sought to give those lives, cultures, and histories new meaning. Only by doing this, he thought, could African people take their rightful place among the people of the world as worthy inheritors of a proud and rich social and cultural legacy.

## THE VALUE OF POLITICAL ACTIVISM

Political activism remained a fixture in Du Bois' life from the earliest stages of his life until the very end. Just as he assessed scholarship and research as activist activities, he likewise viewed the world of politics as a world of action. It would not be, on the other hand, a world devoid of thought, but the thought would be a precursor and a necessary component to action. To Du Bois, politics meant activism; likewise for scholarship. In the Du Boisian world any scholarship was not designed to provide the ammunition for social action and social change was practically worthless. All knowledge was to be used to prompt individuals and groups to reflect on the meaning of the new information, thus, providing the rationale to revise their knowledge base, and hopefully change their values and social behavior. With such a political and social philosophy, it is understandable, given the magnitude of manifest national and international racial oppression throughout his life, why he was greatly disappointed in the inability and unwillingness of individuals, especially those well educated, to behave in a more humane manner towards other human beings. Given the reluctance of individuals and groups to be fair and just, Du Bois' political activism was designed to rally public sentiment towards a greater sense of justice: to rally the oppressed towards the political organizations which offered greater possibilities for racial and class solidarity; also, it was to enlist the dominant groups in the campaign for greater social equity by noting that to do so was in their best interest.

The dualistic and synthetic approaches used by Du Bois to promote this political activism appears at first glance to be intellectually chaotic and inconsistent. How else can one explain the Du Boisian political shifts and dialectics which prompted him to be politically liberal, socialist, Pan-Africanist, and eventually, communist, often simultaneously. One can only surmise that for Du Bois, different social and political situations required different political shifts and orientations. In other words, one should not be foolishly wedded to rigid political dogma; Political theories and values were useful as practical means to accomplish necessary community values and goals. This is no flippant unthinking scattered approach to politics; simply one which seeks its roots and explanations in the actual economic and political suffering of oppressed people. For Du Bois, it was a matter of logically seeking out and affirming the best workable policies and procedures with which to move the society towards greater equity.

When one understands that pragmatic feature of Du Bois' political activism, it makes clear his life-long pragmatic political shifts. We get the gist of his political activism from his autobiography (Du Bois 1968, pp. 438-439): 1910: joins Socialist Party; 1912: supports Woodrow Wilson's campaign; resigns from Socialist Party; 1917-1918: Supports U.S. entry into World War I; fights maltreatment of black troops; leads massive Silent Protest Parade down Fifth Avenue against lynching and jim-crow; 1919; Investigates the treatment of blacks in Europe; 1947: Presents "An Appeal to the World" address to the United Nations to protest racial discrimination in the United States; 1950: Candidate in New York for U.S. Senator on the Progressive Party ticket, and 1961: Joins the Communist Party of the United States.

## CONCLUSION

This chapter has argued that Du Bois created a rich legacy of black intellectual thought; this legacy has been of immense importance to contemporary intellectuals as they sought to navigate the conflicting, and often confusing, array of options and positions to more effectively address the racial and class problematics of life in contemporary societies. As the first in a long line of intellectuals who defined the intellectual role as essentially a public role, Du Bois first had to validate the existence of such a class called intellectuals, then to affirm that blacks, too, could be, and were, intellectuals, based on their education and willingness to engage in the heated public debates centered around social policies on social justice and equality.

In this chapter we acknowledged the Du Boisian assessment of the intellectual role as entailing both *knowledge* and *commitment*. The knowledge would be unearthed through scholarship and social research and would have as its purpose the changing of attitudes and behavior which would enable the society to become more moral; the commitment was personal as well as collective. This commitment would be a logical precursor to a well-thought through political activism.

When Du Bois' entire life, his massive scholarship, research, and political activism (plus the fact that he lived to be 95 years old), are analyzed in their entirety, he presents a daunting challenge to contemporary intellectuals. This is so because, fortunately for blacks and other oppressed groups, Du Bois does not appear to have had much of a private and personal life; his energies appear to flow totally in the eddies of scholarship and political activism. But that is not the main challenge he presents to contemporary thinkers. The greatest challenge to contemporary intellectuals is not to compete with him to cover the vast array of activities as he did. Rather, the difficult challenge may be that of honing in on at least one of the intellectual streams he traveled; to extend his ideas and insights; to use his research ideas as stepping stones for new and radical ideas and themes, and to move, as he did, to have research and scholarship directed towards social policies designed to alleviate social injustice and inequality. Undoubtedly, there are those whose talents may situate them on one or the other side of the research and scholarship/ social and political activism line. Du Bois himself never made the claim that each intellectual had to wade in both waters. He swam in both waters because he wanted to and could. He never said it was a mandatory goal of all intellectuals. He did remind us, however, that we each had an obligation to do something. To him, doing nothing was to abdicate the vaunted intellectual role. This he would have found unforgivable.

## REFERENCES

Du Bois, W.E.B. 1896. *Suppression of the African Slave Trade to the United States of America, 1638-1870*. New York: Longmans, Green, and Co.

_____. 1898a. "The Negroes of Farmville Virginia: A Social Study." *Bulletin of the United States Department of Labor* 3 (January): 1-38.

_____. 1898b. "The Study of the Negro Problems." *Annals of the American Academy of Political and Social Science* 11 (January): 1-23.

_____. 1899a. *The Philadelphia Negro*. Philadelphia: The University of Pennsylvania Press.

_____. 1899b. "The Negro in the Black Belt: Some Social Sketches." *Bulletin of the United States Department of Labor* 4(May): 401-417.

_____. 1901. "The Black North: A Social Study." *New York Times* (November 17, 24, December 1, 8, 15).

_____. 1903. *The Souls of Black Folk*. Chicago: A.C. McClurg and Co.

_____. 1907. *The Negro in the South* (with Booker T. Washington). Philadelphia, PA: George W. Jacobs and Co.

_____. 1909. *John Brown*. Philadelphia. PA: George W. Jacobs.

_____. 1915. *The Negro*. New York: Henry Holt and Co.

_____. 1935. *Black Reconstruction*. New York: Harcourt, Brace and Co.

_____. 1939. *Black Folk: Then and Now*. New York: Henry Holt and Co.

_____. 1947. *The World and Africa*. New York: Viking Press.

_____. 1968. *The Autobiography of W.E.B. Du Bois*. New York: International Publishers.

# PART I

## TOWARDS A THEORY OF BLACK INTELLECTUALS

# THE BLACK INTELLECTUAL AS THE "NEW BLACK"

Rutledge M. Dennis

More than 70 years ago Alain Locke coined a term which he thought reflected an evolving transformation in the sociology of Black American: the emergence of *The New Negro* (1925). Locke's survey of the "New Negro" entailed a description of a "class" in the making: the "old Negro" had not disappeared, and the final form of the "New Negro" had not yet fully surfaced, and that which was discernible was in its infantile stages. What was "sensed" and "perceived" by Locke was a new orientation to self and culture and the desire and need to relate that self (both singular and collective) in new juxtapositions to the larger society. Indeed, the factors conducive to the rise of the "New Negro" were very much evident in the emergence of a Du Boisian "Talented Tenth": the relative freedom possible in the North (compared to the South) and the host of concomitant features accompanying this—the availability of higher and better education, the cross currents of ideas and values in multiethnic urban settings, the opportunities for

Research in Race and Ethnic Relations, Volume 10, pages 3-11
Copyright © 1997 by JAI Press Inc.
All rights of reproduction in any form reserved.
ISBN: 0-7623-0275-5

political participation, and the possibilities for upward occupational and economic mobility. Essentially, the convergence of opportunities and possibilities in such diverse spheres created for the "New Negro," a mood and an atmosphere of "freedom."

Black intellectuals occupy a special position in the American society. The most significant feature of this special position is the role as minority, as Black, with all of the concommittant sociological consequences of this position. The other specialness is that of being intellectuals. However we choose to define this term, and we will here not debate the merits of the divergent definitions possible. This paper proposes a minimalist definition of intellectuals: simply those whose main preoccupations revolve around the exposition of ideas, usually written, and an elaboration and application of such ideas and themes as they assist in defining or demarcating issues and problems in the society. Being either Black or intellectual in America is an enigma in and of itself (see Hofstadter 1963). That one was Black *and* intellectual may be said to entail a double enigma in that it compounded the specialness. The delineation of this specialness and its convergence in the making of a new social type the New Black, comprise the central theme of this paper.

## INTELLECTUALS AND THE QUESTION OF IDENTITY

In a racist society, as demonstrated through the years, education, money, or other material and symbolic status and holdings will not isolate minority groups from negative attitudes and racist behavior. This racism may promote a profound crisis in identity among the powerless because it highlights and accentuates the vast discordance between the substance of democracy and the everyday workings of a society in which race and racial thinking is so inordinately central. However, despite the discordance between the ideal and the reality, the New Black as intellectual does not display the classical Du Boisian dilemma, at least the dilemma as stipulated in one version of Du Bois' "double conscious" theme (see Dennis 1996, pp. 69-90). Rather, the intellectual of today is more self conscious of who he is, what he has been, and what he wishes to be, and how these mesh and interlock with the larger society. This does not in any way connate that identity is a taken-for-granted-factor among intellectuals. Instead, with his own life as a reference point, his reading of history, and his generally vast knowledge of the interlocking features of American life, this new class of intellectuals is more collectively assured, just as individually he is more confident and self- assured. While this confidence and collective assurance neither ignores nor abolish the question of identity, the new intellectual as the New Black does not view the issue of identity in the emotional and eternally split manner that Du Bois did. While placing the question of minority identity within the context of those internal dynamics of minority community life on one hand, on the other hand, the intellectual as the New Black also understands minority identity as a feature of a more general societal power where inequality and group domination prevail.

One variant of the Du Boisian thesis, that one can be both Black and American, is a view accepted by the New Black without reservation. Such a view acknowledges the existence of unique events and situations which shape the sociology of Black life. But that uniqueness, though different, is not seen as pathological. Rather, this difference is seen as one piece of the mosiac comprising the American whole. As Ralph Ellison has so profoundly noted over the years: the socio-cultural streams in African American and European American life have mutually reinforced each other in different ways at different periods in American history (Ellison 1964). That one can be both flies in the face of those whites who desire sole ownership of the American political-cultural legacy. It also flies in the face of many Blacks who view the entire white American legacy as so irreversibly evil and rotten that they do not desire inclusion and view that legacy as eternally white and "The Other." The New Black is not willing to concede to others any vestiges of the American legacy because he knows that, like it or not, he is, and has always been, at the heart of this legacy, whether white Americans desired this or even understood it. He simply is and will be.

Rather than viewing the realm of blackness as the cause for anguish, it is clear that the New Black views identity and the philosophical ramifications of this blackness as a defining feature of his specialness. The insights culled from this "dual identity" may be seen as affording manifold opportunities rather than only the oft repeated curse. This is not to say that the New Black glories in this duality, but that he emphasizes the constructive elements, philosophical and cultural, made possible by his dual identity.

Though problems are not ignored, he neither defines himself as a problem nor does he define himself through and by the problems. Thus, the New Black may loudly proclaim both his Blackness and his Americanness in so much as both continues to be a vast reservior and the well spring of his unique cultural and intellectual creativity.

The juggling of these two sociological identities adds depth and dimensions to intellectual life. For the intellectual as the New Black this duality gives him a greater understanding of the larger and more diverse elements of American life. In such a position the New Black may be in a better position to transcend immediacy and thus forge and propose options, insights and possibilities for social change. If this is true, a case can be made that the New Black, with dual identities, has the potential to be more sober, thoughtful, and insightful than those possessing a single identity. A host of previous Black intellectuals had to confront this very issue in the early decades of this century just as many do today. Many New Blacks studied the works of these earlier intellectuals; this permitted them to place the dual identity in its proper sociological perspectives.

## UNIVERSALISMS AND PARTICULARISMS

Just as the New Black understands the importance of his dual identity and existence, he is likewise opened to another form of duality which encompasses his special world (the particular) and the larger world (the universal). Like his dual identity, the duality of the universal and the particular is not mutually exclusive, but for greater clarification may be analyzed as separate ideas. In reality, a case cannot be made to radically separate the two. In the case of the New Black, the universal themes of human freedom, justice, and democracy as applied to all individuals and groups must pertain and be relevant to particular groups. Like intellectuals of previous generations, Frederick Douglass, Du Bois, Martin Luther King, and many others, their concern and love for their people did not hinder their embrace of the causes of other oppressed groups, that is, the Irish, Asians, and Native Americans. These men were prime exemplars of the merging of the universal and the particular: that Blacks who were concerned about their particular oppression could not be oblivious to the oppression of others. That is, one can focus on one's specialness and simultaneously engage in other universalist themes and struggles.

There are those who may opt precipitately to diminish or even eliminate an orientation towards the specialness of the ethnic enclave under the impression that the nation has reached a stage in race relations whereby the needs of the smaller ethnic enclave can be best expressed and fulfilled by focusing on the universal. The New Black, while recognizing the value of the universal, sees the danger of a premature absorption into the universal. Whereby he may advocate selective absorption, depending upon the particular issues, he believes the time not yet ripe for the wholescale abolition of particular community issues and concerns. More specifically, there are too many examples of the role of race in American society for the New Black to justify dismantling the institutional and organization network Black Americans have had to construct to protect themselves from racial exclusion and terrorism, be it political, economic, or otherwise.

The New Black is sociologically alert enough to know that the particulars relating to the minority enclave cannot exist without the universals. There is also an awareness that the New Black is a universalist in that he understands the importance of attention to the larger whole whether it be that of the metropolitan area, the entire United States, or foreign nations. He is the universalist because he knows that patterns of dependencies and interdependencies which describe Black American realities have parallel shapes and forms in the dependencies and interdependencies of other racial and ethnic groups throughout the world. It is this awareness which ties him to the universal; it is also this knowledge which reminds him of the importance of the specialness of his ethnic specialness and the level of sustained intellectual work (theoretical and practical) yet to be completed. Thus, the New Black is committed to both the universal and the particular and sees no contradiction inherent between the two; the approach is rooted in the fact that both positions may have differing realities, located in time and place. Our New Black as an astute observer attempts to capture, define, and delineate those realities. He is able to do so because he embodies in his person the sociological nuances of each.

## CRITICAL AND ANALYTICAL THINKING

The New Black is critical and analytical and may direct his critical and analytical eye towards his special particularist world within or the larger universalist world without. The New Black, following in the intellectual tradition of Du Bois, Frazier, and Cox, does not hestitate to do both, often simultaneously (Du Bois 1899; Frazier 1957; Cox 1974). With the exception of Frazier who tended to be more critical of the world of the dominated, Du Bois and Cox focused more on the world of the dominator. In their critique of social inequality both directed their sociological eye towards the culture and philosophy of capitalism. This way of approaching the problems of the dominated via a larger almost all encompassing political-economic structure enabled both Du Bois and Cox to fix their gazes beyond the more immediate and obvious, and like Marx, Freud, and Darwin, to sketch a larger historical picture within which the immediate takes shape and form. It is either that format or the format whereby each individual case is analyzed as special in and of itself. This position does not permit a grasp of the whole, hence, our analysis will be eternally partial and incomplete.

Like Du Bois and Cox the New Black understands the importance of a systematic and systemic approach to inequality and is more likely to view the persistence of poverty, racism, colonialism, and imperialism as variants of a larger political-economic system. Hence, the solutions to problems of inequality entail an attack on the existing political-economic system itself, an attack which rebounds in counter-attacks in as much as the system which is bountiful to the dominators is less so to the dominated. Thus, Du Bois and Cox were placed in the position, as the New Black is, of attacking the very system into which they seek entrance. The case can be made, however, that their attacks on the system are designed to reform and alter that system, hence, they anticipate an entrance into a more enlightened system as a result of their criticisms.

The willingness of the New Black to confront the reality of inequality and to engage in the ideological battles surrounding this inequality has special meanings today in contrast to the days of Du Bois and Cox. Both were largely academic and intellectual outsiders, though both spent many years in predominately Black academic institutions. A review of their scholarly works, however, indicates the breadth and scope of their intellectual interests and probes. Such a review is also interesting because it reveals that despite their institutional marginalization both published extensively in mainstream academic and intellectual journals and periodicals; they did not hestitate to take their critical and analytical views into the sanctuaries of the academic establishment. The New Black may not be so marginalized academically or intellectually; he may, in fact, spent much if not all of his professional life within establishment institutions. He does not hesitate, however, to cast a critical and analytical eye on this very system. He is able to do so because, like the discussion on the universal and the particular, the New Black is keenly aware of the larger sociological landscape in which he is a part. Being in the midst of the institutional and organizational world of universalism has meant neither a denial of the particular nor an unwillingness to refrain from a systematic analysis of, and if necessary, an attack on the very universalist system of which he is institutional a part. He does so due to a heightened awareness as he operates within the universalist system that that universalist system is in reality a particularist one, albeit, for a particular group. That is, in the name of universalism special attention is directed towards particular classes and social groups. It is this Orwellian double-speak that the New Black must decipher, analyze, and shatter. The global and structural approaches of Du Bois and Cox provided astute insights into the manner in which a network of capitalist theory, culture, politics, and economics controlled and shaped societies and the particular forms of social and group relations which emerged. The single-minded devotion to capital and capitalism does not mean that the New Black is uncritical towards socialism. He simply confronts and challenges capitalism because it is the system within which he resides, and it is the system which has fostered the type, shape, and form of inequality which he analyzes and criticizes. This appears to be logical and sound, and if the New Black appears revolutionary, it is generally a revolutionary stance, coupled with a variant of reformism, centered within and around the interstices of an existing but imperfect capitalism. The New Black, therefore, attacks the system of inequality because he wants the system to move towards greater social and economic democracy. He therefore debates the issues in speeches and publications in order to realize this goal.

This critical and analytical perspective can be seen as a form of intellectual activism and is a recognition that the journey towards social equality is long and hard; no one individual will live long enough to place all the necessary pieces together before final victory can be declared. In the meantime, each New Black must bring to the intellectual and academic battlefield whatever arsenal he possesses in order to engage in the war. The New Black instinctively understands this and allows and makes room for other New Blacks

to fight the war congruent with their own unique skills and talents.
Whatever the approach, critical and analytical thinking is
paramount.

## CONCLUSION

This paper was a call for and recognition of an emerging new type
of intellectual, the New Black. As can be seen, this New Black has
much in common with many among the Old Black, but there are
distinguishing features between them. Many among the New Blacks
are strategically located within the intellectual and academic
chambers which represent establishment universalism. The New
Black whereby understanding this universalism and accepting many
features of such, does not believe the time is yet ripe to discard the
particularist perspective. In fact, he believes we may never be in the
position to unilaterally abandon all features of the particularist world,
the world of the ethnic enclave, the world of the dominated. In the
case of the intellectuals mentioned in this chapter and mentioned
throughout this volume, this inequality can be best understood and
analyzed by casting a critical and analytical eye on the cultural and
economic system of capitalism since it is the prevailing system which
has had the greatest, and generally, the only impact, on the politica,
culture, and economics of the oppressed group about which he has
chosen to write.

Our discussion has centered on the New Black as a man on the
politically left as opposed to the politically right. This position is in
recognition of the fact that the rise of intellectuals of the right is
generally a relatively new phenomenon in the United States. The
pattern for intellectual thought in the United States has focused on
critical and analytical thinking from those who largely attacked social
inequality. The New Black as I envision him will follow in this
tradition. He will continue to bridge the world of multiple identities
and place his feet in both the universal and the particular. If he can
accomplish the task with skill and astuteness, his success will be
accompanied by success in the social and community arena in as
much as he contributes towards the structural changes needed in all
areas of American life. As Alain Locke so succinctly noted, and this
applies to the New Black, there is something stirring, and what we
see are tendencies which lead us to believe that we are witnessing the

making and molding of a New Black. As we approach the twenty first century, the New Black will have many challenges to test his worth as an individual ans as an intellectual.

## REFERENCES

Cox, O.C. 1976. *Race Relations.* Detroit: Wayne State University.

Dennis, R.M. 1996. "DuBois' Concept of Double Consciousness." In *Research in Race and Ethnic Relations,* Vol. 9, edited by R.M. Dennis. Greenwich, CT: JAI Press.

DuBois, W.E.B. 1899. *The Philadelphia Negro.* Philadelphia, PA: University Publishers. (Reprinted by Schooken Books, 1969.)

Ellison, R. 1964. *Shadow as Act.* New York: Random House.

Frazier, E.F. 1957. *Black Burgeoise.* Glencoe, IL: Free Press.

Hofstader, R. 1963. *Anti-intellectualism in American Life.* New York: Vintage Books.

# BLACK RADICAL SOCIOLOGICAL THINKING

John H. Stanfield, II

A central mission of the Black radical sociological imagination is to recover the African descent origins of change oriented sociological analysis. It has been routine in the canons of the history of sociology and of the other human sciences to trace the tradition of activism in disciplinary crafts to the pens of radical white men and to a lesser extent, women. This has been most clear in the historical and contemporary attention paid to controversial thinkers advocating the use of science to understand and to bring about change. Thus we have reams of studies of the thoughts of Marx, Veblen, Gramsci, Mills, and other radical sociologically oriented intellectuals. Many of the men of social activists traditions have been canonized in the plethora of masters of sociological thought. They are the thinkers in other words that every graduate student in the craft are to at least know by name if not in actual substantive reading.

But, nowhere among the celebrated gods do we find assessments of the life and works of William E. B. Du Bois. It is true that

Research in Race and Ethnic Relations, Volume 10, pages 13-24
Copyright © 1997 by JAI Press Inc.
All rights of reproduction in any form reserved.
ISBN: 0-7623-0275-5

intellectual historians and historically sensitive literary figures have given us extensive insights into Du Bois' life history and vast body of scholarship and social commentary. It is equally true that for a brief moment in the 1970s in a renaissance of Black sociological thought, there was much mention about Du Bois as sociologist. But, he never has been integrated in a serious way into the canons of American and more broadly, western sociological thought.

The exclusion of Du Bois is an uncomfortable chapter in the history of American sociology for a number of reasons. For one thing, it is more than apparent that Du Bois' turn of the century emergence converged quite tragically with the crystallization of sociology as an academic discipline influenced by the ascent of a Jim Crow society and the trendiness of Social Darwinism. The progressivism which influenced the first generation of American sociologists was centered and anchored in a new industrial society which re-fashioned the historically persistent relevance of race through the invention of race centered intellectual crafts and professions. The biological premises of Jim Crow as a public policy and as a way of thinking would serve as the intellectual apparatus which rationalized racialized splits and castes in the organization of the new industrial America. In this sense, Jim Crow would justify the division of labor in schooling which created an under-resourced historically Black college sector which kept ex-slaves in their rural southern places in lower caste rungs while whites could enjoy entry into a more well financed of the new high tech university sector. Jim Crow excluded the consideration of Blacks as intellectuals in the arts, sciences, and literature since being Black and intellectual was considered to be a contradiction in terms.

So, after returning from German post-graduate training, Harvard educated William E. B. Du Bois, a mulatto from New England, found himself locked out of the emerging years of the academic human sciences and history once he attempted to embark on a career. Unlike other brilliant white sociological thinkers of his day who would eventually get recruited by the University of Chicago and other evolving centers of sociology, Du Bois would be reminded of his caste standing during his long life through being relegated to Black institutions, movements, and to periods of under-employment. He would never be able to gain the ear of the most powerful men who would shape the character of sociology and of the other social sciences. This is even though it was Du Bois more so than his white generational counterparts who would do the earliest solid empirical work which would eventually give sociology a unique disciplinary identity. It was Du Bois who through his massive study of the turn of the century Black community would introduce a scientific methodology for understanding issues such as social stratification, community formation, ecological analysis of urban life, survey research, and other principles of sociological analysis. His work preceded that of William I. Thomas the supposed father of community sociology by at least 20 years. In other studies he would offer illustrations of participant-observation well before the Chicago School came on the scene.

It is hard to believe that Du Bois is absent from the pages of classical sociological theory textbooks because his white peers did not know he was around. They knew he existed. The large applied sociology program he organized at turn of the century Atlanta University was the most active research program of its kind in the country. It is hard to believe that Robert E. Park who was working for Booker T. Washington in Tuskegee, Alabama at the same time Du Bois was in Atlanta did not know that his boss's nemesis was in the next state over. And Park certainly did not forget about Du Bois when he joined the Chicago faculty in 1913 where he would professionalize the sociological study of race relations.

What is most intriguing is how Du Bois became a lost figure in American sociological thought with the emergence and domination of the Chicago School after World War I. This had to do for a number of reasons. First and foremost, there was the factor of race. Prior to World War I, the seemingly fixated place of Blacks in the South as portrayed in the collective images constructed and popularized by Booker T. Washington's utterances, made Black people an irrelevant topic in the Mid-western and Eastern academic settings which spawned professional sociology. An examination of sociology textbooks authored by Mid-western and Eastern first generation bears out a tendency to ignore Black experiences. It is no small thing to point out that European immigrants not Blacks were considered to be the most daunting problems northerners were experiencing. As I have written elsewhere, this would change once Black migration from south to north would provoke a racial crisis in cities which would be responded by academic sociologists. It is not surprising to see the study of Blacks as a social problem became a focal point of intellectual attention at Chicago in the aftermath of World War I. The Windy City as it is called was being flooded with a massive influx of southern Black migrants not kindly welcomed in the urban area. Over the course of some 20 years, Park and his colleagues would construct the race cycle paradigm for interpreting the urbanizing Negro problem and would pass it on to their white and Black students who would institutionize the study of race relations and of Black people in particular.

This Chicago perspective on race relations which portrayed Blacks as being in varying levels and degrees of assimilation in a Jim Crow and post-Jim Crow society has influenced generations of sociologists.

The popularity of the study of race relations in academic sociology made it a respectable subfield to invent, professionalize, and control thorough the construction of the race cycle paradigm and the strategic placement of students such as E. Franklin Frazier, Donald Pierson, Andrew Lind, Louis Wirth, and Everett Hughes. It did not hurt that the Chicago Department controlled major media in the field which assured the dominance of the voices of faculty and students.

As in other areas of American intellectual life, when the value of analysis in a field or subfield goes up, the ability of Blacks to gain or maintain access as authorities declines. I am not merely speaking of the ability of Blacks to discuss intellectual issues. It is more deeper than that. I am referring to political and social control over the means of knowledge production which define the contours and contents of textual substance and which determines the construction and advancement of careers. When it became increasingly apparent that something could be gained in terms of career enhancement, the study of Black people shifted from the control of Blacks working in Black institutions and civil rights movements to white academic men and women in distinguished universities with the resources to shape the study of Black people in their own image.

In the process of professionalizing the study of Black people, Du Bois and his significant contributions to the field were either ignored or intentionally overlooked. It was not because his work was superficial or speculative. The problem was that he was Black and thus an embarrassment to those who believed in the white supremacy norms characteristic of the Jim Crow age. How would it had looked to acknowledge that in terms of brain power and productivity, Du Bois towered over his white cohort members—Albion Small, Lester Ward, Charles Cooley, Franklin Giddings, William I. Thomas,

Edward Ross, and last and certainly not least, Robert E. Park? It was more convenient to pretend he did not exist or was not relevant for citation purposes in the major professional sociology journals. It would only be Park's Black students E. Franklin Frazier and Charles S. Johnson who would acknowledge Du Bois' sterling contributions. But they were Black and their studies of Black people have never been considered as important as the words of their white teachers. That is apparent in the fact that it is Robert E. Park rather than Frazier or Johnson who is given credit for professionalizing the study of race relations as seen in his canonization in Lewis Coser's *Masters of Sociological Thought*.

But besides race, Du Bois orientation towards sociology and the human sciences in general made him an obsolete figure by the time the 1930s came around. Du Bois believed like the other members of the first generation of sociologists that the human sciences should be utilized to reform societal ills. That is, the human sciences were not cold, distant exercises in data collection and analysis. They were to be facilitators of societal change.

This DuBosian mandate in the human sciences was not only apparent in the applied sociology program he organized at Atlanta University but also in his establishment of *Crisis* as the journal of the newly organized the National Association for the Advancement of Colored People. Among other things, *Crisis* would become a medium through which Du Bois popularized progressive academic thinking about Black quality of life issues and about race relations. It was a way, in other words, of tearing down the veil between the academy and the community; between Black intellectuals and Black folks in the community.

Du Bois' role as an interpreter of human science evidence to broad public audiences was not much different from that of other members of his generation who wrote for the popular press as well as for the emerging professional journals. Edward Ross offered up his keen ability to express himself in writing to publishing in the eugenic and nativistic popular media of his day.

The 1930s was the time period in which a new generation of sociologists began to search for a quantitative sense of scientific respectability which was devoid of activist agendas. A major part of that search involved making a deliberate move away from the social reformist interests of the founding turn of the century generation. This movement, which Howard Odum described in interesting biographical details in *American Sociology*, would make the entire generation of Du Bois oddities for classical theory buffs only.

It did not help that as Du Bois aged he radicalized. His reformist progressivism of his youthful days would transform into a radical critique of American society in his fifties and sixties. It is doubtful that Du Bois would have been given his professional due if he had remained a progressive reformist through the aging process. It made it even more doubtful he would get a hearing as a Marxist since the sociology establishment was from the beginning anti-Marxist and became even more so as the decades wore on.

The anti-Marxist orientation of American sociology, particularly when it came to Black intellectuals, was more than apparent in the disciplinary tendency to ignore if not destroy the careers of Black Marxist sociologists. It is telling that nowhere in the annuals of conventional American sociological thought is there mention of the flourishing school of Marxist sociologists of race relations between the two world wars. Most of the more important work along Marxist lines were alternatives to liberal Chicago School race relations perspectives on the southern racial caste system.

But, the most enduring example of the conventional hostility towards Black Marxist sociologists was the treatment of Oliver C. Cox. To this day, Oliver Cromwell Cox has a peculiar historical immortality in the annuals of American sociology. Even though his work is read and praised in Europe, it has been ignored or harshly critiqued in the United States. It is not surprising then to find that the longstanding secular holy script of the intellectual history of Black sociologists by James Blackwell and Morris Janowitz (1974) does not consider Cox as a founding figure of Black sociology (along with Du Bois, Frazier, and Johnson) let alone twentieth century American sociology. His contributions are instead relegated to four pages later on in the anthology text in a chapter by Butler Jones (155-158).

There are two reasons why Cox is not well respected in American sociological circles. First, he was a Marxist. Second, he was disloyal to his University of Chicago ala mater in his scathing critiques of the Chicago School of race relations. Cox's magnificent *Race, Caste, and Class* was published in 1948, during the initial phase of the Cold War. *Race, Class, and Caste*, which is an *early* precursor of world-systems theory, is a brilliant comparative analysis of inequality which had no equal in Cox's generation and very few peers since the 1950s. One can imagine that it was due to the stunning breath and depth of this marvelous work by a Negro did not sit very well in a profession which did not take too kindly to independent,creative Black intellectuals. The fact that *Race, Class, and Caste* was premised on Marxist principles probably deepened the aggravation of Cox's White and Black colleagues. This was especially the case since as a response to the Cold War, sociologists were settling into a Parsonian structural functional worldview which conformed to public cultural hostilities towards any ideas which even faintly appeared to be Marxist or Communistic.

Some would say that Cox's prickly personality and physical handicap may have also been factors in his inability to gain respect in American sociological circles. That may have indeed been the case. It has always been the case that personality matters much more than intellectual depth when it comes to the extent to which Blacks are allowed into the back kitchen door of academic sociology. Needless to add, as in most other academic enterprises, sociology has not looked too kindly on scholars who are physically disabled. We have yet to see a blind or a deaf or a wheel chaired person be elected as President of the American Sociological Association and such disabled persons are rarely if ever hired and retained by the most distinguished sociology departments.

Cox's bitterness for being excluded from the inner circle of the Black sociologists of his day was more than apparent in his introduction to Nathan Hare's *The Black Anglo Saxons*. Unknown to Hare, the publisher asked Cox to write an introduction to his book which was supposed to be a sequel to E. Franklin Frazier's *The Black Bourgeoisie*. Hare, who was a prodigy of Frazier, was infuriated that the publisher offered Cox a platform which lead to an attack on his mentor's career. In part, Cox observed that Frazier was entrapped by the evolutionary presumptions and other reactionary ideas of his University of Chicago mentors resulting in his inability to do sobering critiques of racial inequality. Hare responded by accusing Cox of being jealous of Frazier's luminary career.

Perhaps it is indeed the case that it was professional if not personal jealously which provoked Cox to attack his intellectual rival. But, he did have a point. Frazier's mainstream professional career as a sociologist did indeed warp his ability to be a creative intellectual. The evolutionary thinking of his Chicago mentors and their range of ambivalent to hostile attitudes about the social equality of Blacks could not help but reinforce the conservatism Frazier brought to the profession as culture and emotional baggage.

Even though it is true Frazier had his radical moments in private life his eagerness to become an eminent professional sociologist was seen in his willingness to conform to the racial norms of a Jim Crow saturated discipline and academia. This is more than apparent in the professional ideas about Black family and class issues he published in the conventional sociology journals between the two world wars. It has been documented time and time again that the pathological perspectives on such Black experiences issues were very much in keeping with emerging ideas about the social and cultural inferiority of Blacks. Such negative cultural and social notions of Black experiences, which were major preoccupations of the reigning Chicago School of Sociology, were considered to be improvements on traditional biological ideas of Black inferiority. Nevertheless, they still portrayed the problems of Black people in victim terms. As we have seen during the past 25 years, such culture of poverty ideas have found their way into both liberal and conservative public policy arenas.

It is easy to attempt to defend Frazier by arguing that he was a product of his time. That argument holds some water when we assume that everyone writing on the same Black experiences as he held the same beliefs and interpreted data the same way. That simply is not true. There are numerous examples of scholars who published alternative views of Black family issues which take exception to Frazier's pathological interpretations.

For instance, there are the Black family and life-cycle studies of Chicago trained sociologist Charles S. Johnson. In his studies of Blacks in the rural south, Johnson examined the impacts of the collapsing political economy of the plantation south on Black family patterns. In Johnson's frame of reference, Black female headiness was a function of the economy rather than as in the case of Frazier a cause and effect of social pathology. Carter G. Woodson's historical studies of Black families were network descriptions of eminent extended kinship structures. Zora Neale Hurston's folklore and ethnographic work as well as her autobiography centered and empowered the role of Black women in family structures. Cayton and Drake's *Black Metropolis* contextualized Black family issues in networks of community institutions. Ira De A. Reid's *The Negro Immigrant* deracialized the Black box in it's exploration of the nationality and ethnic variation of African descent families and other institutions in the United States. Herskovists African extension work was an attempt to demonstrate how Black American patterns such as family issues were extensions of African cultures.

As much as these different perspectives injected needed complexity into examinations of Black families, it was Frazier's pathological perspective which held sway from the 1930s through the 1970s as the major influence in academic social science and in public policy circles. The tragedy of such historical immortality is that it has placed in concrete Frazier as the founding figure of the culture of poverty perspective on Black family issues. As academic sociologists and other social scientists move away from pathological models, Frazier's work increasingly is viewed as an oddity. We only read Frazier's Black family studies now out of curiosity or to be well read rather than an interest in borrowing his ideas to continue the search for empirical truths.

In the post-1960s, an effort to promote a change oriented, radical Black sociological imagination has failed dismally. The publication of the Joyce Ladner edited volume, *The Death of White Sociology* in the mid-1970s raised a few eyebrows but in the long run, became an ignored text rather than a blueprint to critique and expand the contours of the discipline. Rather than the discipline embracing culturally different perspectives, especially those offering sobering critiques of intellectual racism, discipline gate keepers have preferred to turn to the right. It is no wonder why the most sobering sociology of racism critiques within and outside the academy have come more from journalists and novelists than from the pens of Black sociologists. Discussing racial issues soberly in public is viewed as a risky business to those Black sociologists with career ambitions.

Even when contemporary Black sociologists try their best to be change oriented,their socialization into a discipline stressing cultural assimilation and racism as a reified experience which only through validated measurement tools results in the failure of their effort. If not their methodologies, the norms of a racially conservative discipline makes it difficult for radical minded Black sociologists to find employment in the most prominent departments and universities.

But with that said I will conclude this essay with some thoughts on some essential elements of radical Black sociological thinking for the twenty-first century. I am sketching out these fundamentals of Black radical sociological thinking for guideposts for those Black sociologists who may choose to take a career path of much resistance which involves calling into question some of the most sacred canons of the discipline.

1. *The examination of American capitalism and its globalization.* Outside of Cox, there has not been a Black sociologist who has attempted to offer a comprehensive analysis of the global dynamics of capitalism. Particularly in the Post-Cold War era with its information-based infrastructure, Black sociologists cannot afford to examine Black institutions and communities without understanding the globalization of American capitalism in convergence with other modes of globalized capitalism.

2. *The questioning of the relevance of conventional sociological concepts as applied to Black experiences.* How adequate are conventional sociological terms such as class, family, gender, deviance, community, and identity when applied to Black experiences. When, for instance, when we consider the conventional definition of middle class as being a social strata with invested professional authority in key institutions, to what extent are those we call the Black middle class, really middle class? Are they "something else" we have yet to establish a label for?

3. *Deconstructing race.* Race is not only a myth but it is a lucrative cottage industry in American sociology which needs to be dismantled. Although racial studies have served Black sociologists well, it has also been a ghettoized track that has imprisoned most of us. Through buying into the mythology of race and having it become part of our identify as an area of study, we have contributed to an oversimplified approach to Black experiences. The "Black category box" has glossed over numerous cultural and social distinctions in the Black populations and has done more to reinforce racial stereotyping than offering accurate empirical analyses. Thus, we need to deconstruct race and while doing so disentangle it from the realities of ethnicity, status, culture, gender, and so forth.

4. *Studying ethnicity and culture.* The assimilationist canons which continue to anchor sociological thinking about Black people has distracted attention from the rich cultural and ethnic differences in Black populations. Besides the retention of African cultural attributes from the pre-twentieth century slavery experiences, there is the more significant twentieth and twenty-first century Black ethnic and cultural distinctions created through ethno-regionalism and African descent Caribbean and South American and Black African immigration to the United States. From the standpoint of sociology, we have yet to have

a clear, comprehensive sense of Black ethnic and cultural diversity in identity, status, institutions, and community issues.

5. *White Power and Authority.* We find few Black sociologists studying the power dynamics of White social organizations: institutions, status groups, networks, and communities. It is difficult to understand how, why, and when Black oppression occurs if we do not do sobering studies of the biographies and social organizations of powerful White men and women.

6. *The Critique of the Academy.* Critiquing the American academy has been a tradition among radical thinking White males and females for quite sometime. We have yet to see contemporary Black sociologists working in historically White institutions soberly reflecting about the racialist cultures of the universities and colleges employing them. Meanwhile, the large number of Black scholars in historically White institutions dying in prime age from stress related diseases is enough to tell us that such critiques are well needed.

7. *Activist theory-driven public policy.* The Black sociologists of the twenty-first century who will have the greatest impacts in the academy and in larger society are going to be those who influence public policy through constructing and testing empirically ground theories through being engaged in social activist work. The traditional models of the distant academic claiming to be an activist but never leaving the campus and of the activist who sees no value of using social practices to develop grounded theories to influence public policies are already becoming obsolete in a world demanding creative bridges between the academy and local and international communities.

8. *Becoming multiethnic.* A radical Black sociological perspective in this day and age must be multiethnic in several ways: understanding multiethnic local communities and regions in which Blackness is becoming redefined through dynamics of rich multiethnic demographics; exploring the ways in which patterns of African descent immigration into the United States are creating domestic transnational cultures as well as deepening and expanding the historical transnational character of the nation-state in its global context; and investigating multiple descent identities, institutions, and communities more extensively. Becoming multiethnic also involves deracializing Blackness and exploring the complexities and pluralism of Black African descent ethnicities in Africa, Europe, the Caribbean, and in other parts of the world.

It is not difficult to understand why it is that so few Black sociologists will take the risk to be radical thinking scholars. It is much more easier to take the path of least resistant, meaning viewing race as a real thing to study and to engage in atheoretical policy analysis. It is much more easier for getting career brownie points by remaining by studying Blacks as deficient populations rather than macro studies of White power, authority, and control. It is much easier to ignore if not internalize the pathologies of surrounding academic environments than to probe them and write about them as the critique of the academy as a racialized privileged sector. But somehow or another, we must become aware that the Black sociological thinkers who continue to have the greatest historical immortality are those radical, change-oriented intellectuals who understood that principle stands higher than career considerations, taller than material comforts, and deeper than professional recognition.

It should be noted as a conclusion that until professionally trained Black sociologists find ways to wean themselves from the conservative conventions of the discipline, radical Black sociological thinking will remain in the domain of literary figures, theologians, historians, and musicians. It is a testament to that observation when we consider the fact that the most sobering critiques of pre-World War II American racism came from the pens of Langston Hughes, Richard Wright, Carter G. Woodson, and Ida B. Wells than from Black sociologists holding academic berths. The same can be said in contemporary Black social thought when we consider the work of Cornel West, Henry Louis Gates, Toni Morrison, and Angela Davis who have done much more than Black sociologists in keeping change-oriented issues as they relate to Black people on the public agenda. The dominance of Black humanists in advancing critical to radical sociological thinking about Black experiences does indeed let us know that the absence of such traditions in mainstream professional Black sociological thought has more to do with the conservative conventions of an academic discipline than the inadequacy of sociology as a type of imagination to explore and explain the worlds around us.

# PART II

## RACE, CLASS, AND CAPITALISM

# RACISM AND CAPITALISM:
## THE CRITICAL THEORIES OF OLIVER COX

Doris Wilkinson

## INTRODUCTION

In the company of W.E.B. DuBois (1868-1963), Oliver Cromwell Cox (1901-1974) has been one of the most exciting intellectuals and politically controversial theorists of African lineage in American Sociology in the twentieth century. Yet, minimal coordinated information and constructive indepth analyses exist about his ideas and exceptional substantive contributions to social theory in either the social history or sociological literature. Negating the deliberate omission of the research and explanatory paradigms of this perceptive critical thinker from the annals of sociological thought and the biographical narratives of social scientists, the Caucus of Black Sociologists granted him the ASA DuBois-Johnson-Frazier Award (Smith and Killian 1974). This discussion seeks to document and re-affirm the exceptional scholarship exemplified in his comparative,

Research in Race and Ethnic Relations, Volume 10, pages 27-41
Copyright © 1997 by JAI Press Inc.
All rights of reproduction in any form reserved.
ISBN: 0-7623-0275-5

quantitative and historical studies, theoretical premises, and conceptual models. The influence and contemporary relevance of his thorough examinations of capitalism and racism in social thought, primarily sociology, are also highlighted.

African American intellectuals, like European societal critics and social theorists, have always been shaped by their personal biographies and by the material conditions and cultures of their times. With the exception of Frantz Fanon and DuBois whose life spanned nearly a century, all of the early twentieth century sociological thinkers of African ancestry—E. Franklin Frazier, St. Clair Drake, Charles S. Johnson, and Allison Davis—were products of a similar historical era and economic circumstance. Their views of reality mirrored the specific contexts in which they found themselves interpreting the structural arrangements and contradictions of the American social order, particularly the paradoxes inherent in democracy and capitalism.

As men of African ancestry, each shared fundamental commonalities related to placement and rank in the power hierarchies. This fact enhanced the uniqueness of their incisive dissections of class relations and conflict, the "black-white" dynamic, and the normative character of society at a given historical moment. Adherence to distinctive critical theoretical positions in American sociological inquiry, and their assumptions about the world in which they lived, revealed their life experiences. Understanding the linkages between the social location of a scientist and his or her systems of thought, discloses the value-based nature of theory despite protestations to the contrary.

Coinciding with the questions posed by philosophers and social thinkers throughout history, scholars in America of African descent have continually sought answers to such perplexing macro-level questions as: (1) How is the society arranged and what are the origins of this arrangement? (2) What are the mode of production and hence the form of economic relations and the class structure? (3) What is the meaning of race in a democratic capitalistic economy? (4) What accounts for the evolution of racial ideology and what needs does it serve? (5) What forces serve as catalysts for the transformation of society?

Three basic objectives underly this synopsis and interpretive essay: (1) to restate some premises from selected writings by Oliver Cox, especially in *The Foundations of Capitalism* and in *Race Relations*, (2) to highlight his theoretical position regarding the antecedents of capitalism and racial ideology, and (3) to document the significance of his frame of reference to sociological and social theory—past and present. Criticisms of his ideas, which have been extensive, do not constitute the principal nucleus of this account (Blizzard 1949; Chand 1994; Ghurye 1949; Miles 1980). Instead, documenting the intellectual value of the content of his high quality scholarship to contemporary dialogues on race is a central goal.

## BACKGROUND

Born in Trinidad at the turn of the century, Cox received his undergraduate degree from Northwestern in 1928. As the Depression was waning, he joined the leading department of sociology in the country at the University of Chicago (Faris 1967). Between World War I and World War II, this university served as one of the major institutions for the production of exceptionally talented African American sociologists (Doyle 1937; Frazier 1957; Johnson 1941). From there, he earned both his Masters and Doctorate. Although his intellectual skills and professional interests were cultivated following the entrenchment of "the Chicago school," Cox was not captured by the emphases nor methodological foci of that American sociological "movement." Applying the training acquired and his skillful analytical insights, he emerged as a major translator of the culture and the racialized economic structure. He was also outspoken about the mode of sociology in vogue. For example, he felt that many of the prominent writers about race relations and social stratification such as Robert Park, St. Clair Drake, W. Lloyd Warner, and Allison Davis, if not myopic, were politically conservative in their approach to the complexities of domination and racial separation under a capitalistic democracy (Ethridge and Kopala 1967; Jones 1974; Hurst 1988; Smith and Killian 1974).

A significant indicator of Cox's place within the scholarly community, as Butler Jones noted, was that "he [was] the only one in the group [of major African American sociologists] with broad-based theoretical concerns." Nevertheless, students are unlikely to find him cited or even listed in past and current syllabi for American social theory courses or in the bibliographies of basic theory texts.

Oliver Cox was a contemporary of several eminent American and European social critics, literary figures, and sociologists. These included Charles S. Johnson (1893-1956), Erich Fromm (1900-1980), T.W. Adorno (1903-1969), Richard Wright (1908-1960), Talcott Parsons (1902-1979), E. Franklin Frazier (1894-1962), and St. Clair Drake (1911-1990). He was a young man when the Harlem Renaissance blossomed (1920-1929). In spite of the strategic theoretical course that he would later chart for himself, he was only a few years younger than the bright and productive African American sociologists whom he would have an opportunity to know from the University of Chicago—Johnson and Frazier. Under the influence of the dominant theoretical convictions of their time, they became followers of the Park Chicago School which concentrated on race relations, community structure and such processes as conflict and competition. Cox (1938, 1940, 1945b, 1946, 1971, 1974) chose a separate intellectual path.

An imaginative analyst and outspoken opponent of racism, Cox rejected the Gunnar Myrdal thesis permeating the classic—*An American Dilemma* (see Clayton 1996; Myrdal 1944). He evaluated the treatise on "the American Creed" as a "mystical" commentary about pernicious and historically ingrained racial discrimination. Myrdal and his associates failed to articulate economic forces and the widespread effects of the white power structure. Targeting Frazier's ideas on the same subject for criticism, he argued that the U.S. form of race relations was engulfed in control, domination and the class hierarchy. Consequently, black-white social exchange was situated within the political-class matrix and in economic exploitation.

Concomitantly, he felt that integrity was revealed in how African American social scientists responded to racial dynamics. Acquiescing to prevailing precepts compromised one's own values and beliefs. He viewed E. Franklin Frazier as a spokesman and an apologist for the white controlled status quo. Of Frazier, the first African American to be elected President of the American Sociological Association, Cox said: "He won many prizes and honors, but the exigencies of winning involved his soul and his manhood" (Cox 1965; Hare 1965, p. 13; Smith and Killian 1974, p. 202).

In Cox's theoretical system, the manufacture of racial discrimination was contingent on the white ruling strata's "divide and rule" techniques of control. William Darrity, an economist, offers a limited critique of this aspect of his conceptual model. He contends that "the divide-and-rule argument tends to minimize the agency of white laborers in pursuing their own interests in engaging in discrimination...Cox's analysis of the American class structure tends to be bipolar—capitalists and workers, in all their ethnic and geographic varieties... (Darrity 1996, p. 116). In spite of what he describes as "two shortcomings of this approach," Darrity's own intepretive scheme "situates racial disparity and discrimination in a context that goes beyond Myrdal [and] in the direction charted by Cox" (Darrity 1996, p. 116; Cox 1959, pp. 509-538).

Like most scholars of African heritage in sociology and in other disciplines who have been trained in the country's distinguished institutions, Cox was never given an opportunity to teach outside the south. From 1938-1944, he was a Professor of Economics at Wiley College in Marshall, Texas. He was there when he studied the correlation between the sex ratio and marital status by race (Cox 1940). When he left Texas, he began teaching at Tuskegee where he remained for five years (1944-45). Although in his later years, he taught at Wayne State, his principal position was as a Professor of Sociology at Lincoln university.

## THEORETICAL PERSPECTIVE

Various constructs and axioms have always comprised the diverse theoretical explanations of the economic structure, power matrix, and race relations in American sociology. Cox, a well trained and skillfull social scientist, chose an empirically grounded and rational macro-level approach to describe and interpret the design and operations of economic systems and political cultures. In his studies of U.S. capitalism, race relations, and even women's employment, he was guided by a comparative sociological and historical framework. As expressed earlier, the central questions that underscored his analytic paradigm are as old as those advanced by the contract theorists who appraised the state, collective existence, and the hierarchical aspects of stratification.

The primary intellectual interests of Cox centered on capitalism, class struggle, power, race relations and racial ideology. Social status, the fundamentality of religion, and nationalism were also integral to his perspective. One of the basic postulates derived from his studies pertained to the evolution of capitalism. He reasoned that it was directly correlated with growth in urban populations. In fact, he maintained that "...capitalism grew hand in hand with the rise of unprecedentedly large urban populations..." (Cox 1959, p. 482). As a result, urbanization has historically been both a catalytic force and a parallel process progressing with the spread of the capitalistic mode of economic and social life.

Under capitalism, Cox acknowledged a widespread disdain for "people of color." Flowing from his research as well as his personal experiences, he rationally asserted that the capitalistic ethic was the impetus for racial ideology. Discussing "Venice the Progenitor" in *The Foundations of Capitalism*, he affirmed that "the economic philosophy of capitalism resulted in" contempt for those who were marginalized. A certain outcome from the suppresssion and isolation of a population under capitalism was the growth of "a class of outcasts" (Cox 1959, p. 51). Those who rule do not conceal their feelings of superiority toward the "inferiorized" stratum (Cox 1962, 1964).

In addition, Cox addressed the issue of the composition and vested interests of the ruling class. From his analyses, he found that a capitalistic government is simply "a legislature made up of business leaders or their representatives devoted mainly to promotion of the welfare of the foreign and domestic commerce and industry of a nation" (Cox 1959, p. 481). Further, he found that capitalism, no matter how it was labeled, was commercial. As a result, in capitalistic societies, industry evolved as indispensable to the design of economic and political systems.

> Studies on the rise of capitalism have commonly referred to the phenomena which we have been discussing as "commercial capitalism." In due course, however, we shall attempt to demonstrate that all capitalism is essentially commercial. Industry has an important but peculiar place in capitalist society... Although capitalist peoples strive to include and to monopolize an unlimited number of industries, they usually recognize some one or a relatively few of them as traditionally peculiar to their economic order....It was... in the shipbuilding industry that Venice evinced most clearly the strains of capitalism... (Cox 1959, pp. 75, 76).

One of the salient objectives of capitalists is to purposefully incorporate outsiders—immigrants, aliens, or slaves—for the goal of building the political economy and expanding capitalism's philosophy and control. In a probing description of the germination of this economic form, Cox explained that: "Like all future leading capitalist nations, Venice continually attracted foreign workers. Because of her extensive control of markets, her demand for labor was greater..." (Cox 1959, p. 77). Labor disputes, the accumulation of wealth and power, and demands and agitation by workers were inevitable consequences of capitalistic development. Ultimately, this economic complex, "set in motion by its foreign trade, produced all sorts of consumptive demands at home..." (Cox 1959, p. 78).

Moreover, based on his comprehensive historical and comparative inquiry, Cox demonstrated that the capitalist town or country grows when it augments its economic role in a wider world of complex and underdeveloped regions. Likewise, it is predisposed to decline as opportunity for such expansion recedes or becomes limited. "This is so because capitalist production tends essentially to be geared to foreign market commitments....[The] peculiar economic order...generates rivalry and competitiveness among communities..." As its commercial dimensions intensify, capitialism spreads and incorporates larger "areas of the world within its sphere of influence" (Cox 1959).

What are the structural outgrowths of this spreading mode of production with its associated norms, beliefs, attitudes and social relations? Addressing this matter, Cox construed that the constant searching for new markets and "exploitable resources of the world had transformed foreign economies in principally two ways: (1) by undermining older economic systems and leaving them without a satisfactory substitute; and (b) by gradually replacing the traditional social order [with] a capitalist society" (Cox 1959, pp. 480-481).

Further, Cox theorized that capitalism was the molder or precursor of religious ideologies. His historical work documented that during the transition to this "peculiar economic order," the industrial revolution had a cumulative impact. For with the simultaneous growth of capitalism and industrialization, "greater reliance and faith began to be placed in the efficacy of science and engineering as means of production and economic competition" (Cox 1959, p. 481). Eventually, capitalism's link to other social institutions had to be considered, especially its connection to the church. Modifying the Weberian thesis in *The Protestant Ethic and the Spirit of Capitalism*, (1930), Cox pointed out that the transformation of an economy and society into a capitalistic model necessitated a restructuring of traditional religion. Ultimately, the church would have to appreciate and adapt to the needs of this escalating economic force.

Religion, always a vital concern of human society, had also to be reoriented. The church, as an institution, had to be made to accept the ideology of capitalism in place of that of feudalism. The most obvious way to do this was to nationalize the church. Venice had a high degree of success in this by insisting that her priesthood be Venetian born; Florence and Genoa, partly because of their involvement in the economic and political interests of the Vatican had less success; while Holland and England came late enough to adopt Protestantism, the internationally uncommitted, capitalist variation of Christianity (Cox 1959, p. 482).

With the inescapable outcomes from the reconstruction of the economic base, "a government dominated by business men and a nationalistic church, the foundations of capitalism were laid" (Cox 1959, p. 482). The notion of a centralized ruling or capitalist class and the inevitable reframing of religion revealed a Marxian paradigm, albeit a modified one.

Political and class stratification and leadership comprised key explanatory tools for examining social organization in the writings of Cox (Cox 1950a, pp. 223-227, 1950b, 1962). Nevertheless, Jones (1974) recognized that he was highly critical of the prevailing conceptions. Specifically, Cox "argued that the caste theories failed to distinguish clearly among race, class, and caste as analytic concepts" (Jones 1974, p. 157). Relying on a quasi-Marxian interpretation and mirroring the realities and meanings of his own encounters as a sociologist of African descent, Cox accented the indispensable prerequisites for a viable capitalist economy. For him "the reality is that capitalism requires the continuation of an exploitable class in order to preserve itself" (Jones 1974, p. 157).

With *The Foundations of Capitalism* (1959), Cox presented not only a sociological treatise but a partial economic chronicle, although he indicated that his objective was not to assemble an economic history. He commented that "had that been our design, quite apart from the question of technical competence for such a task, both the method and scope of the essay would have been different" (p. 482). However, he does carefully trace the origins and dimensions of the capitalistic state. Essentially, business men control the government; and a church entrenched in nationalism juxtaposed with the prevailing material philosophy frames social values and norms (Cox 1959, p. 482).

To Cox, capitalism constituted an extraordinary form of economic organization. On the other hand, in the process of shaping an entire culture flowing from its intrinsic ideals, problems such as the consolidation of power, economic pressures on family life, value contradictions, extensive income disparities and pervasive racial animosities came into being. In other words, this economic order produced not only unprecedented institutional arrangements but multiple social uncertainties as well (Cox 1945a, 1946, 1959).

> The capitalist system is indubitably the most powerful and dynamic form of social organization ever created by man...Major social problems of contemporary society are essentially problems of capitalism (1959, p. 1)...To understand the nature of the capitalist system it is necessary to examine the characteristics and the processes of development of medieval and early modern European cities (p. 25)...The national cities were the center of capitalist organization and action; they constituted the true home of capitalists. They succeeded in a very high degree to isolate themselves from feudalism and to develop a distinct system of law and economic order (p. 27).

Every single institution, the values and belief configurations were reshaped as capitalism permeated the entire fabric of European life. Religion thereafter served as an imperative for launching and sustaining the capitalistic motif. That is the germinating "spirit of capitalism" embodied a set of precepts and an explanatory logic that warranted a moral philosophy. "Protestantism undoubtedly was considered a priceless cultural possession..." (Cox 1959, p. 358). Cox reasoned that since religious institutions and political allegiances were inextricably linked, the quest for a national church was predestined. Accordingly, he observed that the capitalistic way of life became inherently restrictive and discriminatory. Expectedly, the attitudes and nationalistic feelings of its adherents were likewise exclusive.

Because Cox, like DuBois, probed the pathos of racism and critiqued white domination, he was marked as a radical sociologist instead of as an intellectual or sound social theorist. Although a pioneer in the systematic study of capitalism and a prolific and thoughtful writer, he predictably became one of the "forgotten Black sociologists." He experienced what many productive scholars of African descent have encountered—rejection, exclusion, stigmatization and even "demonizing"—because they are competent, independent thinkers, and critical commentators on the status quo. Perhaps, he is best known for his first work—a major sociological interpretation of the class structure—*Caste, Class and Race*—published in 1948 for which he received a George Washington Carver award. At the culmination of the 1950s, *The Foundations of Capitalism* (1959) was published. Each writing extended his thesis regarding the qualities and functional needs of a viable capitalistic economy and the theoretical necessity to logically contrast race, class and caste (Cox 1945b).

As the 1960s unfolded and on the threshold of the Civil Rights Revolution, Cox published two books that contained his general principles about the modern expansionistic economy: *Capitalism and American Leadership* (1962) and *Capitalism as a System* (1964). His sustained and high quality scholarship spanned more than a fourth of this century. In 1970, *Caste, Class and Race* was re-issued and a work in his honor—*Race Relations*—was published posthumously (1976).

## RACE PREJUDICE AND AMERICAN CULTURE

One of the most striking aspects of Cox's creative intellectual contributions and his social theories was his discounting the notion that African Americans were members of a caste. In his "Theory of Race Prejudice and Racism," he examined caste and race from a critical perspective. He explored their origins within the framework of capitalism as a global system in Europe and mapped the connection between this economic mode and cultural beliefs.

> What we seek to show is that a certain culture of unparalleled power and sophistication originated and developed in western Europen; and, driven by its unique wealth-producing employment of capital, expanded inexorably over the whole earth, subordinating in its wake all other groups of mankind and more or less supplanting their cultures (Cox 1976, p. 21).

Cox argued that the worldwide encroachment of European capitalism generated an ethos of superiority that was not limited to economic supremacy. Rather, the depictions of European social organization as vibrant and omnipotent were paramount. Blending with the grand shift of an unfolding and expansionistic political economy, the presumption of inferiority of other ways of life, especially the folk customs of the "nonwhite people of the world," became implanted. Stemming from the embedding of capitalism and a ruling capitalist class, race prejudice and racism were spawned. Both emanated from entrenched processes of "societal subordination and reconstruction" in the "feudal culture of Europe" (Cox 1976, p. 21) and the eventual rationalization of slave labor. To fully comprehend the cultivation of slavery and slave labor, one must grasp the essence of this material order.

> The transportation of West Africans to work in the Americas was a clear act of labor recruitment—recognition of this fact need not involve ethical judgments...[Race prejudice] emanates from a powerful, elite interest group which...orients the society on all significant questions...The southern dominant class has had a continuing interest in the maintenance and spread of race prejudice and discrimination—not only in the North but also in other parts of the world (Cox 1976, pp. 22-23).

In developing an empirically testable theory of prejudice and racism, Cox clearly understood the influence of the forces of production in the shaping of attitudes and the interrelations of these with the concentration of power. In a direction that differed from Frazier's dissection of "The Pathology of Race Prejudice" (1927), he outlined the social meanings of racism. Both described the functions of racial prejudice and discrimination as being to isolate "the different"—those who are the targets—to a lower status or rank. They also expressed that members of the dominant sector may not always be cognizant of their ingrained racialized beliefs and predispositions. Regardless of the theorized parallels between racial and caste prejudice, Cox countered that these social realities, as stated earlier, are quite dissmiliar.

A reading of Cox on two prevailing academic questions that are posed for endless debate is instructive. These are: (1) Do races exist? (2) How does race prejudice differ from racism? First, he grasped the essential structural and material reality of race (see Blauner 1971; Cox 1948, 1959, 1976; Fanon 1963; Staples 1972; Wilkinson 1972, 1995; Wilkinson and King 1987; Wilson 1973). Throughout his distinguished career, he documented that it was (and is not) a mythical conception nor merely a psycho-social construction. In discussing economic functions, patterned actions of the capitalist class, political uses and shared sentiments linked to race and concomitantly to racial prejudice, rather than defining the latter as personality flaws or peculiarities, Cox constructed a model for a "sociology of race prejudice." He argued that it was culturally derived and that the racial ideology mirrored modern capitalistic culture.

To the extent that the study of race prejudice is individualized to that extent also it must be regarded as idiosyncratic and thus of little if any particular sociological significance...It is the group that feels, not the individual...[Our] first realization should be that race prejudice is a peculiar socio-political attitude" (Cox 1976, pp. 23-24).

Thus he introduced a sociological theoretical interpretation of race prejudice as an alternative to a psychological one. He considered the material base as the prime source of racialized responses.

Also, Cox delineated the vast distinctions between the social experiences and life histories of European peoples and "people of color." Whites, he observed, do not encounter ingrained and permanently fixed race prejudice. This a fact that remains true today regardless of their gender, class-status, or sexuality. And, there is little likelihood of other nationalities, such as the Japanese, violating European cultures and developing a counter racial belief network. For deeply rooted animosity or pathology accompanies race prejudice to such an extent in the American culture that "attempts to abate it...have generated opposition severe enough to threaten the very stability of the government..." (Cox 1962, p. 141).

If our analysis of the origin and progress of race prejudice is tenable, we may conclude, as a corollay, that white people have scarcely ever been subjected to race prejudice....[No] people of color have been able to develop and maintain such capitalist strength as would overarch and subject whites as a group to that peculiar condition of economic inferiority that spawns race prejudice...[The] chances that other colored nations might develop the crucial economy that could bring whites under their control are becoming more remote (Cox 1976, pp. 23-25).

One feature of race prejudice at the group level is that those who are discriminated against may also hold prejudicial attitudes toward members of their "in-group" or racial population. Cox described this phenomenon in terms of the structural or material derivation rather than within the discourse that relies on psychological reductionism or psychoanalytic models of self-hatred. Given its roots and role in the permanent framing of consciousness, "people of different colored races may become prejudiced against each other." They display not only racial biases against other persons of color but among themselves vis-à-vis the "dominant white culture." However, nationalistic movements renounce such divisive qualities. In order to be successful and to implement movement objectives, "nationalism among peoples of color has been resistant to such a practice" (Cox 1976, p. 25).

Finally, Cox offered a detailed appraisal of the social Darwinian thesis advanced by Herbert Spencer. He disputed the notion of evolution under capitalism where it could be used to rationalize "various stages of [advancing] toward Nordic perfection." Those who comply with the ideology of racism associate biology with morality, intelligence, beauty, health, and accomplishments. He pointed out that this had been an essential feature of the thought systems of public racists from the early Spanish adventurers to Adolf Hitler. "It was Hitler's mission...to demonstrate the cultural prowess of Aryanism" (Cox 1976, pp. 30-31).

Notwithstanding the global or expansionistic nature of white racism, Cox felt that the ideology had not always existed.

Racism, as we know it in modern times, is not merely verbal recognition of physical differences, ethnocentric comparisons among peoples, early mythological speculations about the place of various known peoples in the designs of creation, or invidious remarks by ancient conquerors about the physical and cultural traits of the vanquished (Cox 1976, p. 25).

## CONCLUSION

An exceptionally imaginative thinker, Oliver Cromwell Cox may have been the first truly critical theorist and Marxist trained in sociology in the United States. He enriched immensely the knowledge base of American intellectual thought. Specifically, he framed world systems theory, Americanized Marxian models, critical thinking, and structural interpretations of race prejudice. He was a forerunner in the articulation of the "sociological imagination" and in the use of historical, comparative as well as quantitative methodologies. For these extraordinary accomplishments, Cox deserves a prominent place in all studies of capitalism; race, class, and gender; economic systems and their correlates; the sociology of religion; power, racism and racial conflict; women and work; and the African experience in the Americas.

## REFERENCES

Blackwell, J.E., and M. Janowitz. (eds.). 1974. *Black Sociologists: Historical and Contemporary Perspectives.* Chicago: University of Chicago Press.

Blauner, R. 1972. *Racial Oppression in America*. New York: Harper & Row.

Blizzard, S. 1949. "Caste, Class, and Race: A Study in Social Dynamics," by O.C. Cox (Book Review). *American Sociological Review* 13: 357-358.

Chand, G. 1994. "Capitalism, Democracy and Discrmination—the Rise and Decline of Racism in Cox's 'Caste, Clss and Race.'" *The Review of Black Political Economy* 23 (Fall): 71-93.

Clayton, O. (ed.) 1996. *An American Dilemma Revisited: Race Relations in a Changing World*. New York: Russell Sage.

Cox, O.C. 1938. "Factors Affecting Marital Status of Negroes in the United States." PhD. Dissertation. Chicago: University of Chicago.

————. 1940a. "Sex Ratio and Marital Status among Negroes." *American Sociological Review* 5 (December): 937-947.

————. 1940b. "Marital Status and Employment of Women: With Special Reference to Negro Women." *Sociology and Social Research* 25: 157-165.

————. 1945a. "Lynching and the Status Quo." *Journal of Negro Education* 14: 576-588.

————. 1945b. "Race and Caste: A Distinction." *American Journal of Sociology* 50 (March): 360-368.

————. 1946. "The Nature of the Anti-Asiatic Movement on Pacific Coast." *Journal of Negro Education* 15 (Fall): 603-614.

————. 1948. *Caste, Class, and Race: A Study in Social Dynamics*. Garden City, New York: Doubleday.

————. 1950a. "Leadership among Negroes in the United States." Pp. 228- 271 in *Studies in Leadership: Leadership and Democratic Action*, edited by A. Gouldner. New York: Harper & Brothers, Publishers.

————. 1950b. "Max Weber on Social Stratification: A Critique." *American Sociological Review* 15 (April): 223-227.

————. 1959. *The Foundations of Capitalism*. New York: Philosophical Library.

————. 1962. *Capitalism and American Leadership*. New York: Philosophical Library.

————. 1964. *Capitalism as a System*. New York: Monthly Review Press.

————. 1965. "Introduction." Pp. 11-22 in *The Black Anglo Saxons*, edited by Nathan Hare. New York: Marzani and Munsell.

————. 1971. "The Question of Pluralism." *Race* 12(4): 385-400.

————. 1974. "Jewish Self-Interest in 'Black Pluralism'." *The Sociological Quarterly* 15 (Spring): 183-198.

————. 1976. *Race Relations: Elements and Social Dynamics*. Detroit: Wayne State University Press.

Darrity, W. 1995. "The Undesirables, America's Underclass in the Managerial Age: Beyond the Myrdal Theory of Racial Inequality." Pp. 112-137 in *An American Dilemma Revisited*, edited by O. Clayton. New York: Russell Sage.

Doyle, B. 1937. *The Etiquette of Race Relations in the South*. Chicago: University of Chicago Press.

Ethridge, J., and B. Kopala (eds.). 1967. *Contemporary Authors*, Vol. 104. Detroit: Gale Research Co.

Fanon, F. 1963. *The Wretched of the Earth*. New York: Grove Press, Inc.

Faris. R.E.L. 1967. *Chicago Sociology: 1920-1932*. California: Chandler Publishing Company.

Frazier, E.F. 1927. "The Pathology of Race Prejudice." *Forum* 77 (June): 856-862.

_____. 1957. *Black Bourgeoisie*. New York: The Free Press.

Ghurye, G.E. 1949. "Caste, Class, and Race: A Study in Social Dynamics," by O.C. Cox, (Book Review). *American Journal of Sociology* 54: 466-469.

Hunter, H.M., and S.Y. Abraham (eds.) 1987. *Race, Class, and the World System*. New York: Monthly Review Press.

Hurst, C.E. 1988. "Race, Class, and the World System," edited by H.M. Hunter and S.Y. Abraham. *Social Forces* 67 (September): 251-252.

Johnson, C.S. 1941. *Growing up in the Black Belt*. Washington, DC: American Council on Education.

Jones, B.A. 1974. "The Tradition of Sociology Teaching in Black Colleges: The Unheralded Professionals." Pp. 121-163 in *Black Sociologists: Historical and Contemporary Perspectives, edited by J.E. Blackwell and M. Janowitz. Chicago: The University of Chicago Press.*

*Miles, R. 1980. "Race and Ethnicity: A Critique of Cox's Theory." Ethnic and Racial Studies* 3 (April): 169-187.

Myrdal, G. 1944. *An American Dilemma*. New York: Harper & Brothers.

Smith, C.U., and L. Killian. 1974. "Black Sociologists and Social Protest." Pp. 191-228 in *Black Sociologists: Historical and Contemporary Perspectives, edited by J.E. Blackwell and M. Janowitz. Chicago: The University of Chicago Press.*

*Spencer, H. 1896. First Principles*. New York: Appleton & Company.

Staples, R. 1972. "The Black Scholar in Academe." *Change Magazine* 4 (November): 42-48.

Weber, M. 1930. *The Protestant Ethic and the Spirit of Capitalism*. Trans. by T. Parsons. London: George Allen & Unqin Ltd.

Wilkinson, D. 1972. "Racism and American Sociology: The Myth of Scientific Objectivity." *Sociological Abstracts* 20: 1888. (Paper read at the annual meeting of the American Sociological Association, New Orleans.)

_____. 1973. "Coming of Age in a Racist Society: The Whitening of America." Pp. 100-118 in *Youth in Contemporary Society*, edited by D. Gottlieb. Beverly Hills, CA: SAGE Publications.

_____. 1990. "Americans of African Identity." *Society* 27 (May/June): 14-18.

_____. 1995. "Gender and Social Inequality: The Prevailing Significance of Race." *Daedalus* 1124: 167-178.

Wilkinson, D., and G. King. 1987. "Conceptual and Methodological Issues in the Use of Race as a Variable: Policy Implications." *The Milbank Quarterly 65* (Supplement 1): 56-71.

Wilson, W. 1973. *Power, Racism, and Privilege: Race Relations in Theoretical and Sociohistorical Perspectives*. New York: The Macmillan Company.

# RETURN TO HIS NATIVE NATION:

## C.L.R. JAMES AND A PEOPLE'S NATIONALISM IN THE CARIBBEAN

Stefano Harney

"I am sick to death that whenever they talk about the West Indian they say he is suffering; he's intelligent but he's looked upon as backward because he came from slavery...I am going to write a book in which I will show that the West Indian had more in him than that" (James 1994).[1] The book C.L.R. James (1963) wrote was *The Black Jacobins*, first published in 1938, an acknowledged classic of revolutionary anti-colonial struggle and of the study of revolutions in general, and for many scholars, the finest book ever written on the Caribbean. But C.L.R. James gives this reason for writing his masterpiece not in the late 1930s, but rather in response to a question from the audience in North London in 1976. The questioner wanted to know why James, and George Padmore, childhood friend and a father of African emancipation, were so much more involved in the anti-colonial struggle and nation-building of Africa, than that of the

Research in Race and Ethnic Relations, Volume 10, pages 43-63
Copyright © 1997 by JAI Press Inc.
All rights of reproduction in any form reserved.
ISBN: 0-7623-0275-5

Caribbean. James holds out *The Black Jacobins* as early evidence of his dedication to the Caribbean struggle and adds that "if they call me back to Trinidad tomorrow, I will go." At first glance, the life and achievements of C.L.R. James might remind the reader of the careers of other great Caribbean men of this century, men like Marcus Garvey, Frantz Fanon, Walter Rodney, and George Padmore, men from the Caribbean whose influence has been felt around the world, but more around the world than in the Caribbean. At a speech in celebration of his Seventieth birthday, however, James tells his audience that the reason that *The Black Jacobins* continued to go into new editions nearly 50 years after it was written is that it "still has a validity today, 1971, because I came originally from the kind of territory which produced Rene Maran, Marcus Garvey, George Padmore, Aime Cesaire, and Frantz Fanon, and we were prepared not only to say what should be done in the Caribbean, but we were trained and developed in such a way that we were able to make tremendous discoveries about Western civilisation itself" (James 1984a, p. 211).

C.L.R. James, like the other men from his territory in the Caribbean, did make tremendous discoveries about Western Civilization, the full scope of which are only now being truly appreciated. The importance of his training and development in the Caribbean can hardly be doubted. His perspectives on Black America, on Africa, and the European metropoles are full of both the wisdom and the distance of his West Indian upbringing.[2] His classic autobiography, *Beyond A Boundary* (1983) is more proof of the importance of Caribbean cultural roots in his tremendous discoveries. Nonetheless, those tremendous discoveries, like those of Marcus Garvey or Frantz Fanon, were made outside of the Caribbean, and sadly, have had least effect in the territory that helped produce them. To consider C.L.R. James as Trinidad does is to consider the loyalty and devotion of a brilliant but often wayward son. When he returned in 1965 to form a Workers' and Farmers' Party and contest a general election, many looked upon him like a star come home, but many more whispered that he had been away too long now to understand Trinidad. Where does the truth lie? Did James take from the Caribbean and give elsewhere, or is his work, as he points out with *The Black Jacobins*, part of half-century project of revolutionary nationalism in Trinidad and in the Caribbean?

It is heartening that the work of C.L.R. James is beginning to receive re-evaluation and to reach a widening audience, stretching for the first time in 50 years into the Leftist political discourse in the United States and Canada. But I want to look in this paper at a still-neglected period in James's work—those essays and public lectures given in the late 1950s and early 1960s upon his return to his native Trinidad around the independence period. I want to argue that he was uniquely ready to think about nationalism in the Caribbean and to navigate the difficult relationship between Lenin's national question and the question of class in his new nation. Just as he had famously lectured Trotsky on the short-comings of Trotsky's analysis of the race question in the United States—arguing that it could not be viewed narrowly as a question of nascent self-determination—he now faced the complexity of external colonial oppression and internal class difference in the Caribbean. He faced that complexity, and the difficulties of creating national consciousness that could not be co-opted by a dominant class, in numerous lectures in union halls and public libraries throughout Trinidad, speaking directly to working people. In fact, I will argue that his nationalist project remains timely today. The Caribbean has no organized, collective analysis of the relationship between neo-colonial rhetoric and internal class oppression, similar to the work in India, for instance, of the Subaltern Studies group.[3] And the Caribbean, rife with corruption, reeling unions, capital and intellectual flight, badly needs such a systematic analysis. James put down the roots of just such a specific Caribbean analysis of nationalism and class. He was peculiarly suited to do so.

C.L.R. James was born at the beginning of the century and lived virtually to the end, dying just before the collapse of the post-war order in Europe, but living to see and think about Polish Solidarity and the U.S. Invasion of Grenada. He came from a town called Tunapuna along the mainline of towns stretching east from Port-of-Spain under the green shadows of the Northern Range in Trinidad. His father was a school teacher and his mother and his aunts were active in the church. His biographer, Paul Buhle, describes his social status well when he notes that the schoolteacher in colonial Trinidad was a position of little financial reward but much social esteem (Buhle 1988, pp. 15-23). James describes much of his upbringing in *Beyond A Boundary* but for now it is worth noting that the advantages of a schoolteacher for a father, and a well-read mother, helped James take the narrow and steep path out of colonial Tunapuna and become a teacher himself at Queen's Royal College in Port of Spain. There James quickly felt the constraints of the colonial (and island) world.

Together with several other young intellectuals and writers he started two journals, *The Beacon*, and then, *Trinidad*. Most of the rest of his circle were from the Port-of-Spain "Coloured" Middle Class, like novelist Ralph De Boissiere, or from the Portuguese entrepreneurial class, like Alfred Mendes and Albert Gomes. Gomes would later become a prominent politician and he would chide James when the latter returned to Trinidad, saying "You know what the difference between all of you and me? You all went away; I stayed." But in retelling the anecdote James adds that "I didn't tell him what I could have told him: you stayed not only because you had money but because your skin was white; there was a chance for you, but for us there wasn't—except to be a civil servant and hand papers, take them from the men downstairs and hand them to a man upstairs" (James 1980, p. 239). (Years later of course, in his mimic-man-like exile in London, Gomes would write of Englishmen approaching him on the street to tell him they had been to his native Pakistan—thus the fluidities and rigidities of the "maze of colour," the title of his somewhat melancholic autobiography.) James left Trinidad and went to England at the invitation of Learie Constantine, the great Trinidadian cricketer, one of the earliest in a line of West Indian cricketers who would make the uneasy economic migration to English county cricket.

In the course of his peripatetic life James would travel the furtive roads of radical politics throughout much of the world; he would help George Padmore and W.E.B. Dubois set up Pan-African conferences that would lead the way to decolonization in Africa; he would be sought out for advice by everyone from Kwame Nkrumah, to Eric Williams, to Stokely Carmichael. And he would move from the most violent anti-colonial atmospheres to the quiet of English county cricket with the naturalness that always belied those roots in a Caribbean territory. He would return to Trinidad in the late 1950s to help Eric Williams and his People's National Movement realize independence and return again in 1964 to form a party to oppose his former pupil and the PNM. But by then he was a world-famous Marxist thinker and Pan-Africanist. On both sojourns he threw himself into the work of making his homeland a better place by lecturing, writing, and stirring up intellectual debate, believing that so much of what he had fought for in the worker's movements of America and Great Britain, and in the decolonization of Africa would be realized in the new Caribbean. As Anna Grimshaw put it, "this is why James seized so readily the chance to be part of Trinidad's movement towards independence, for he conceived of it as much more than the replacement of colonial rule by a Caribbean government" (Grimshaw 1990, p. 22) But James was wrong, or at least, he was overly optimistic. Eric Williams was no Toussaint L'Ouverture, and in post-colonial Trinidad the new boss was the same as the old boss, just darker and able to dig more convincingly into local dialect and culture to rabblerouse. From 1956 onward, Eric Williams and his circle of privileged, educated, and urban Peoples National Movement leaders, developed an anti-colonial rhetoric that as Ivar Oxaal has noted, demonized the European colonizer, implicated the reluctant nationalist Indian Trinidadian leadership, and dis-empowered both the African and Indian trade union leadership, all in a totalizing drive of slave against slaveowner (Oxaal 1982). Trinidad's independence became the simple transfer of power from a British clerk class to a urban, Colored clerk class. The new Trinidad James dreamed about put him under house arrest in 1965, claiming he was a danger to the established order.

But it was also in this period of optimism about Trinidad's future that James would begin to build his intellectual nationalist project, finding its roots in his early work, just as he would find the roots of national independence in the Haitian revolution. His Trinidad never appeared. Too divided by the racial politics first of the colonial office and then of the PNM, and too timid in political nationalism to take on either the old imperialists or the new, Trinidad even rejected non-aligned status. Little changed. As one labor leader remarked, "it has taken an expert on slavery to re-impose slavery on his people" (Ramdin 1982, p. 252). (He was referring to Eric Williams, devoted pupil of James, who wrote the seminal study *Capitalism and Slavery*, and to the same Eric Williams who would betray James and the unions as Prime Minister.) In an immediate political sense, James failed to move Trinidad in the direction his heart hoped. But he also had in mind another kind of nationalism, based on his new thinking about culture, the popular arts, and mass political movement. He sought, in public talks and private memories, to kill off, once and for all what had haunted him since the days of writing *The Black Jacobins*, the idea that the West Indies were without culture and history (and possibility), what Naipaul called the Third World's Third World, where even ideas had to be imported. He was at the height of his intellectual and synthetic powers in the late 1950s and in the 1960s, and it can be argued that his writings on the Caribbean, far from being the record of a famous intellectual returned home in vain, are in fact an unexploded shell of Caribbean history and thought, waiting for the "development of a people" to strike it into a social explosion.

Indeed, C.L.R. James was lecturing to students in Washington D.C. days before the 1970 Revolution in Trinidad, and he predicted just such an explosion. When the explosion occurred, leaders and followers in the movement confirmed that they had found *The Black Jacobins* waiting there for them to uncover its force. The 1970 Revolution combined much that James admired, spontaneous leaderships, public education campaigns, and most important an attempt to balance the privileged discourse of race over class. James wrote in an introduction to a labor history of Trinidad that "Dr. Williams has written in public that one important thing that he has done is to keep the Indian and the African people apart. In reality, it is my belief, and I say it very plainly, that there is no salvation for the people in Trinidad unless those two sections of the population get together and work together" (Ramdin 1982, p. 14). The key to that statement is the dynamic of "working together." The 1970 Revolution featured a march by African Trinidadian students and workers, into the sugar-growing lands of Caroni to demonstrate solidarity with the Indian Trinidadian farm labourer. James's statement might at first bring to mind the dominant discourse on nationalism in Trinidad—peoplehood before justice, and the same race before class rhetoric of Eric Williams. And as we preceded to define the revolutionary nationalism of James it is worth noting Richard Handler's cautionary words in his study on cultural nationalism in Quebec. Handler writes, "nationalist discourse of whatever school shares features with that of other schools and even other places and times. Discourses (to personify for the moment what is only the product of active speakers and interpreters) converse: ideologues and theorists imitate, borrow, and compare among themselves" (Handler 1988, p. 26). It is difficult even for James to speak outside of the discourse on nationalism in the Caribbean. But in the context of the 1970 Revolution, or the works of James, one can immediately see that nationalism for James, like Black Power, is a profoundly revolutionary effort, requiring huge social upheaval and mass political change, much more than mere decolonisation, or the kind of cultural nation-building of some West Indian intellectuals and politicians.

To understand the balance that James achieved between nationalism and revolution, peoplehood and people's power, between race and class, is to understand not only the Jamesian project of revolutionary nationalism in the Caribbean, but also the failure and disunity that has plagued Trinidad and the Caribbean since independence. In fact, as he predicted the bright days of the 1970 Revolution, he also, all too often, predicted the dark days of corrupt leaderships, warring ethnicities, and moral decay that have infested the Caribbean.

At the heart of his project was his conviction that if he gave the people of the Caribbean the intellectual and spiritual inheritance that was theirs, they would do the rest. James spent years in the revolutionary movements of the developed world insisting that all the organizing was finished, that the workers did not require leadership, and that vanguardism led to totalitarianism. He was often rebuffed and misunderstood because of this conviction, even by the most libertarian of Left groups. But his reading of Caribbean history, and Caribbean developments of the recent decades, helped him maintain a deep faith. He would recapture Caribbean history and reconstruct the Caribbean man, and the children of this Caribbean man would meet him "at the rendezvous of victory." He set out to reveal the inevitable Caribbean-ness of every man and woman from that territory, a common history and personality that could never be left behind in travels to London or New York, a common inheritance of power that would produce want he called "an independent current of Western thought" (Philips 1990, p. 15) and would build a revolutionary nationalism "beginning with Cuba and ending with all three Guyanas" (James 1984b, p. 19).

By the time James first heard the call to return to Trinidad in the late 1950s, where he would edit the newspaper of the new People's National Movement, *The Nation*, and advise Eric Williams, he had once again taken up the nationalist project where he left it with the publication of *The Black Jacobins* 20 years before. But even before his brilliant account of Toussaint L'Ouverture and the San Domingo Revolution, he had begun his contribution to Caribbean nationalism with two important works written before he left Trinidad to join the great Trinidadian cricketer Learie Constantine in England. These two works were a novel called *Minty Alley* (1936), and a political tract called *The Life of Captain Cipriani* which was published as *The Case for West Indian Self-Government* (1933). Both reveal the later strategies and directions of his revolutionary nationalism, and both reveal the duplicity and weakness of those who have offered more partial nationalisms. And both forecast the Jamesian nationalist project of rethinking not only the "habitus" of the Trinidadian man and woman, but also epistemological break into revolutionary action.

C.L.R. James has repeatedly defended and championed the Guyanese novelist and critic Wilson Harris and the Trinidadian novelist and essayist, Vidia Naipaul. Both writers are at the front of the Caribbean literary renaissance, but both writers have also needed defending in the Caribbean. Naipaul's notorious comments from his travel essays in the West Indies, *The Middle Passage*, in which he suggested that nothing had ever been created in the West Indies and nothing ever would be, were the beginning of an argument that has lasted to this day. The argument has resurfaced with new poignancy in his recent works again, particularly, as Arnold Rampersad notes, in *A Turn In the South* and *The Enigma of Arrival* (1990). After *The Middle Passage*, many West Indian critics and intellectuals announced that the young Naipaul, who had achieved world-wide acclaim for his novel *A House For Mr. Biswas* and confirmed the literary surge of the Caribbean, denounced him as a Europhilic traitor and stopped reading him. But the change in tone and understanding that Rampersad detects in the recent works would come as no surprise to James, who, champion of the creative Caribbean, always maintained Naipaul was misunderstood. This misunderstanding, according to James, comes from underestimating the Caribbean man, and fearing, unnecessarily therefore, the European side of Caribbean heritage. James explains this point in an essay on the man he considered the greatest social critic of the West Indies, calypsonian, the Mighty Sparrow. Writing of Sparrow and poet Derek Walcott, James concludes that "Behind him, and Mr. Walcott's analysis, there emerges a fact and direction that summarizes the whole West Indian position as I see it, politics, economics, art, everything." James is speaking of Walcott's famous poetic question of African/European heritage, "where shall I turn divided to the bone?" James continues, "We have to master a medium, whatever it is, that had developed in a foreign territory and on the basis seek and find out what is native, and build on that. It is obvious that our present race of politicians are too far gone ever to learn that. But there are signs that this truth is penetrating younger people" (James 1977, p. 201).

Guyanese novelist Wilson Harris recently completed the 1990 Smuts Memorial lecture series in Cambridge, England. He spoke about the dangers of "the progressive realists" in Caribbean fiction. He would know of these dangers. He has been, for decades now, the target of "progressive political" novelists and critics in the Caribbean and elsewhere in the Third World, who view his fantastical and mytho-philosophical texts with suspicion. His texts do not tell realistic stories of colonial exploitation and anti-colonial struggle. He fails to fit the program of nationalists who seek to control the public discourse. His myth-making and Heideggerian liberty look dangerously spontaneous.

And yet James was careful always to include both Harris and Naipaul on any list of great Caribbean writers, always sure to explain that Naipaul's was a personal search, and a personal "area of darkness," not a Jamesonian national allegory. He repeats with great fondness the story of Naipaul writing to James to praise the first half of *Beyond a Boundary*, saying it was the first book that "really explained us." In short, he included Naipaul in his nationalist project, and saw the need for the Caribbean to do for all artist, "what we can do. Let us create the conditions under which the artist can flourish. But to do that, we must have the consciousness that the nation which we are hoping to build, as much as it needs the pooling of resources and industrialisation and a higher productivity of labour, needs also the supreme artist" (James 1977, p. 190). He thought Naipaul's bitter abandonment of (and return to) Trinidad had much to do with ignorance in the middle class, and the lack of conditions of respect and attention for the artist in the Caribbean. Significantly, it is in an introduction to Wilson Harris's work that James reaffirms in 1965 that "the finest study ever produced in the West Indies (or anywhere else I know) of a minority and the herculean obstacles in the way of its achieving a room in the national building—Naipaul's *A House For Mr. Biswas*" (James 1980, p. 172). It is significant both because he reconfirms that his interest in Naipaul is not just aesthetic but nationalistic, and also because he gathers Naipaul together with Lamming of Barbados, Vic Reid of Jamaica, and Harris, to say that "the instinctive feelings and readiness of the West Indian populations for adventurous creation in all fields is proved by the literature these territories produce" (James 1980, p. 171).

James concludes his introduction to Wilson Harris's lecture by saying that he hoped he had made "Harris easier for West Indians to grasp. That is one trouble. Our novelists, as our cricketers, are recognized abroad for what they are, something new, creative and precious in the organizations and traditions of the West. But what they need is what Heidegger recognized in Holderlin—a homecoming" (James 1980, p. 172). He saw Harris and Naipaul, like himself and like Sparrow, as deeply West Indian men, whose achievements abroad should not inspire suspicion but faith that those territories of the Caribbean continued to produce tremendous imaginaries. He later embraces Trinidadian novelists Michael Anthony and Earl Lovelace as truly national writers in the new sense of remaining local, but he never abandons Naipaul and Harris. In the construction of the Caribbean man, or what he calls "The Making of the Caribbean People," every tremendous achievement should be counted. This defence and inclusion should be seen against James's pioneering novel of the 1930s, *Minty Alley*.

*Minty Alley* is not a great novel, and the stiffness of the middle class voyeur in the yards of Port of Spain suggests the stiffness of the schoolteacher's son from Tunapuna walking through the urban slums of Port of Spain for the first time. Alfred Mendes wrote a more interesting novel of black and white Portuguese tension and sexuality in this period, and Ralph de Boissiere probably wrote the most interesting, if uncontrolled, of the novels at the birth of Trinidadian literature.[4] Elsewhere in the Caribbean, Claude McKay had already achieved fame in the United States with his Jamaican novels, and the next twenty years would belong to the French Caribbean, to Aime Cesaire and the Haitian novelists.[5] But that does not diminish the importance of James's novel.

His early novel, together with several short stories, were an important attempt to legitimize the local language and culture, and reject a purely European sensibility. None of the novels written in Trinidad in the Thirties could compare to Aime Cesaire's *Return to My Native Land* (1968) in announcing a powerfully new Caribbean and anti-European imagination, what Wilson Harris calls "the native imagination." But James asserted one thing with his early fiction. He would look at what was native and new in literature as a sign of the readiness of the West Indian people to burst forth in political creativity. Thus Naipaul and Harris, 30 years later, are defended not on facile ideological grounds, but because they are Caribbean men, with Caribbean imaginations, and they stand for the capabilities of the West Indian, past and future. James once remarked that "when

I hear people arguing about Marxism versus the nationalist or racialist struggle, I am very confused" (James 1984a, p. 242). James is being coy in his remark, but he is also making a subtle and advanced point about revolution and the need to guard against new hegemonies springing from old, just as he would repeatedly warn the Caribbean peasant working class not to accept simply a change in the colour of leadership. He saw the trap of a single ideology, any version of Marxism or Black Power, that sought to curtail liberty in the name of revolution. His thoughts on the dangers of either a classless nationalism, or a Europhilic vanguardism anticipated by twenty years the work of another innovative Marxist thinker, Ernesto Laclau. Laclau's and co-author Chantal Mouffe's now oft-cited work insisted that the struggle of the Left must take place in what they termed "plural spaces" that are balanced by "equivalence" on the one hand, and "autonomy" of struggle on the other, and their thoughts have had much recent influence (Laclau and Mouffe 1985, pp. 176-193). James anticipated this search for plural revolutionary spaces, not just in the Caribbean, but also in the United States in the 1940s and early 1950s, when he predicted that students, Blacks, and women would lead a new American revolution.[6] James saw early in the Caribbean context, the danger of excluding potential allies in the struggle, and perhaps something in his past rebelled against the notion of incorrect literature. He certainly understood however, from his early attempts to liberate literature in Trinidad in the 1930's, that the works of Harris and Naipaul served the cause of liberation and pride in the Caribbean, far more than they harmed the unity of approach and narrative. It is a political understanding he might not have had were it not for the creative half of him, and it is an understanding, typically for James, that he reached far ahead of his time.

In a similar fashion, his *Life of Captain Cipriani* helped him connect the modern Caribbean man with his history, and helped him, 40 years later, avoid a false racial consciousness, choosing Caribbean regional liberation instead. "Cipriani was able to take the stand he did because the French Creoles had a long tradition of independent economic life and social differentiation...But there was more to Cipriani...That he was able to discover the tremendous qualities of the Caribbean population...was due to the fact that history had presented him with political opportunities unfolding the capacities of a highly developed people. These soldiers were the descendants of Toussaint's army" (James 1980, p. 188). This theme of the social outsider taking advantage of political upheaval to make tremendous discoveries is a steady one for James, who viewed the Caribbean man, always on the outside and yet often at the centre of historical cleavages, as the prime example of man transcending contemporary understanding to contribute something new. But the importance of his Cipriani work, and his reaffirmation of it decades later, lies more in what it says about his sense of nationalism. Cipriani fought tirelessly for independence after the First World War, and he sought to make the emergent trade unions a vehicle for that nationalism. He had definite advantages—as a French Creole he could say what Afro- or Indo-Caribbean men, and women, could not. But as James notes, he was, despite his skin color, a radical agent of revolution in Trinidad, far more so than the "colored" petit bourgeoisie which would take the nationalist symbol away from him and the other union leaders who followed him. Nonetheless, in the enthusiasm of Black nationalism in Trinidad in the late 1960s, and eventually, inside trade union culture, Cipriani was largely relegated to the position of sympathetic French Creole. A 1989 calypso by Sugar Aloes, called "The Judge," suggested taking down the statue of Cipriani and putting up a statue of Eric Williams instead, and taking down the statue of Lord Harris and putting up one of McCandle Dagger, a leader of the Black Power movement in Trinidad. The calypso was widely popular, and although Sugar Aloes is a well-known sympathizer of Williams's ousted PNM party, the song is telling. In the retelling of the anti-colonial, nationalist struggle, there was little room for a French Creole hero. (Despite the fact that the labour union college in Trinidad is named for him.) Not so, said James, both in the 1930s and in the 1960s. In fact, in a passage partly aimed at his own absence from the struggle, James says pointedly, speaking of Grantley Adams in Barbados and Cipriani in Trinidad that "in those revolutionary days, nowhere else did any member of the black middle class enter into politics. Today a whole lot of them are very noisy politicos, the way is very easy, you get a good salary, you can become a minister, and you can go to England and be entertained by royalty!" And then James adds, "but, Cipriani and Grantley Adams started before World War II. In those days there was nothing but work and danger" (James 1980, p. 189).

From his early works, even before *The Black Jacobins*, the roots of his revolutionary nationalism are already, as Cabral would say, plunged into the hummus of Trinidad. And James had already begun to build what Benedict Anderson would consider a mass nationalism. His embrace of Cipriani and of the vagaries of literary discourse anticipate the rejection of official, state nationalism, as it stretches from Eric Williams to Sugar Aloes. He sought a nationalism that would inspire all the peoples of the Caribbean, not a nationalism that would become simply the tool of Black and Coloured middle class politicos being entertained by English royalty. And ever aware of the need to recapture the creativity and talents suppressed by racism, he nonetheless saw the dangers of a nationalism predicated solely on race, fearing with typical prescience, that racialist nationalism could obscure the aspirations of mass participation and creativity, exchanging White oppressors for Black. But most of all, his early writing predicts his thunderous argument for the tremendous achievements, and consequent potential, of the Caribbean woman and man. By 1966, he could effortlessly end lectures with such operatic climaxes as this one: "Here I shall give a list of names, a list without which it is impossible to write of the history and literature of Western civilization. No account of Western civilization could leave out the names of Toussaint L'Ouverture, Alexander Hamilton, Alexander Dumas (the father), Leconte Delisle, Jose Maria de Heredia, Marcus Garvey, Rene Maran, Saint-John Perse, Aime Cesaire, George Padmore, Frantz Fanon, and allow me to include one contemporary, a Cuban writer, Alejo Carpentier." But James is not finished there, and after mentioning the literary surge of the English-speaking Caribbean he adds: "I end this list by a name acknowledged by critics all over the world as an unprecedented, unimaginable practitioner of his particular art—I refer, of course, to Garfield Sobers" (James 1080, p. 190). Such a remarkable passage was typical of James's talks to audiences in the Caribbean, Britain, Canada, and the United States in the 1960s and 1970s. In the body of those talks we see the perfection of a revolutionary nationalism that defies his political failures in Trinidad, as it challenges the hegemonic discourse both of the class-less nationalism which sought to defeat him and the imperialism that feared him.

A look at his public lectures and essays in the post-independence period reveals that as a creative thinker on nationalism and peoplehood, James has no peer in the Caribbean. His revolutionary excitement is most often expressed through a new kind of literary criticism which takes as its purpose the location of worthy creative achievements not just in individual writers and revolutionaries, but

in Caribbean society as a whole. James insisted, therefore, that
Toussaint L'Ouverture defeated the most sophisticated European
army of its day, not just because he and his brilliance sprung from
the ordinary slave community, but because that brilliance continued
to be reflected in each slave who battled with him. Similarly, the
novels of George Lamming indicate the reinvention of colonialism
not only by a superb modernist novelist, but in the constant telling
and retelling by every Caribbean woman and man. For James each
nationalist and literary figure was sustained not by his exceptional-
ism, but by the very inevitability of his springing from the people.
His lectures can be seen as an evolving set of creative efforts to
imagine a nation and a people. Imagining a people, and not just a
nation, is what gave James his popular nationalism. He believed in
the genius of the people, just as he feared the official nationalism
that sought to manipulate that genius. It was a genius he found not
only in contemporary novelists and cricketers, but also in their
enslaved ancestors, and it is with their history, as told by James, that
an analysis of his revolutionary nationalism should start.

James was adamant about this popular history, and casually stood
Caribbean history on its head to prove it. It was a brave victory for
the Caribbean people, and a bold look at the history of slavery. Since
*The Black Jacobins*, James had been interested in the idea that it
was the African slaves that ended slavery in the New World, through
ceaseless rebellion, revolution (in Haiti), and Civil War (in the United
States). James once claimed that he had given his student, Dr. Eric
Williams, the idea for his seminal book, *Capitalism and Slavery*
(1964, 1970). Williams's book changed the scholarship on slavery
forever, but his contention that slavery was ended not because of new
enlightened attitudes but because it had become economically
unworkable for the imperial powers seems too deterministic for
James. James preferred an explanation of mass genius—from Haiti
to Brazil to Alabama—the slaves themselves threatened slavery.
James goes further in his exploration of slave life and culture in the
plantation economies of the Caribbean. "The Negroes who came
from Africa brought themselves" announced James (James 1980, p.
174). And elsewhere again, "he brought with him the content of his
mind, his memory. He thought in the logic and the language of his
people" (James 1977, p. 243). With words like these James drew his
sword against the common myth that the slave was stripped of all
culture and content by the Middle Passage.[7] Nor, according to James,

was the slave once in the Caribbean, rootless (and this historical point has particular relevance for his modern nationalism.) "A new community was formed; it took its form in the slave quarters of the plantations and the black sections of the cities," James insisted. "It gave them an independent basis for life…and even if they were sold down the river they would find themselves on new plantations. Here, people who shared a common destiny would help them find a life in the new environment" (James 1977, p. 244). James has found the history of community in the Caribbean, challenging the notion of permanent fragmentation and drift caused by the institution of slavery and the colonial economy.

But he has only begun to give back to the people what was theirs. "I want to put it as sharply as possible. The slaves ran the plantations; those tremendous plantations, the great source of wealth of so many English aristocrats and merchants, the merchant princes who cut such a figure in English society (and French too, but we are speaking of English society). Those plantations were run by slaves" (James 1977, p. 181). And for this reason, nationalism after independence means trusting the people who have always run the Caribbean economies with the means of production. "The first point I believe a West Indian political grouping has to take care of in the West Indies is the transfer of the land from the large landowners to a peasant population—a peasant population such as exists in Denmark and Holland, of a highly developed cultural and scientific outlook" (James 1984a, p. 152). James has his eye not only on the historian, both metropolitan and local, but on contemporary politicians who refuse to trust the West Indian peasant. And James goes further, discovering account after account by Europeans of the skills and values of the slave labourers, their absolute mastery and indispensability. He concludes that they made not only the plantation economy, but capitalism, possible in the Caribbean. The skills and know-how of the slaves, their remarkable abilities to adapt to climate, language, and technology, meant that the slaves themselves were the great assets of the plantation economy. In short, James reverses the master-slave relationship, using not literature, but historical fact, or at least historical sources, revealing that the slaves were in fact masters of the economy, and armed with this knowledge, neither the San Domingo Revolution, nor the Grenadian Revolution should be viewed with surprise or scepticism.

This reversal of the master-slave relationship, and this revelation of cultural and technological completeness of the Caribbean masses has dangerous consequences for official nationalism in the Caribbean, as James intended it to have. It is a call for democratic nationalism, not a transfer of power and flags. James has as his target what John Sender and Sheila Smith have identified in post-colonial Africa, noting that "the failure to identify the forces which really exist and are operative, in particular the denial of the existence of a working class, and the absence of an analysis of rural class structures, has resulted in the ideological dominance of a classless nationalism, albeit expressed in the language of socialism" (Sender and Smith 1986, p. 130). James wants no part of this classless nationalism, either in Africa or in the Caribbean. His nationalist project seeks to recognize the technical potential of the working class in the Caribbean, and as early as 1962, in his devastating essay on the West Indian middle class, he already saw the perversion of classless nationalism. "When you try to tell the middle classes of today—why not place responsibility for the economy on the people?—their reply is the same as that of the old slave owners: You will ruin the economy, and further what can you expect from people like these? The ordinary people of the West Indies who have borne the burden for centuries are very tired of it. They do not want to substitute new masters for old" (James 1980, p. 140). James was walking a thin line in these lectures. He wanted to give the Caribbean people the tremendous achievements that were theirs; he wanted them to know the wickedness of colonialism and the genius of their response. But he also worried about this knowledge falling into the wrong hands, being used by a cynical middle class in a toothless nationalist manipulation of the masses.

His revolution strategy therefore tried to bind race and class in a popular nationalism, taking from both what was necessary, but also using each to keep the other in check. Most of his talks, and his autobiographical work from early in this period, *Beyond A Boundary*, maintain a keen awareness of class while insisting on the tremendous achievements of Caribbean individuals, but individuals who have risen from a sea of popular imagination and ability. He challenged, throughout the 1960s and the 1970s, national leaders and intellectual elites who fell back into classless nationalism, whether in Ghana or Trinidad, Chile or Guyana. His commitment to the genius of the descendants of slaves even brought him into conflict with so-called Socialist experiments in the Caribbean, and their intellectual support systems. James admired Michael Manley's conviction in Jamaica, but his belief in the technological and managerial capabilities of the working Caribbean men and women would seem to question the dependency theories of the New World Group of economists who influenced Manley. And his emphasis on local class structures would surely shift some of the blame from multinationals to local elites of all colors (Payne 1984, pp. 2-10). And yet, James had kind words for Manley's effort. He was a product of the Caribbean.

James was particularly careful to guard against an elitist chauvinism or filiopiety in his frequent references to cultural and literary figures in his lectures and papers. Two of his best and earliest available talks, "The Artist in the Caribbean" (1959) and "The Mighty Sparrow" (1961), stressed the vital resource of popular imagination in the careers of great Caribbean men and women. And he placed as much faith in the calypso as in the traditional poem. James has less to say about Carnival. But other intellectual heirs to James have taken up the call to cultural nationalism by privileging the popular arts, including Carnival. Edward Brathwaite, an important founding figure of the Caribbean Artists Movement in London, and then of the influential Carifesta arts celebration in the Caribbean noted that "this kind of cultural awareness/possibility: multi-ethnic, multi-cultural requires a model more flexible than priest or politician, philosopher or the schools can cater for" (Brathwaite n.d., p. 346). More recently, Rex Nettleford has renewed his tireless call for an end to the idea of cultural dependency and inferiority. In his article "The Caribbean: the cultural imperative and the fight against folksy exoticist tastes," Nettleford echoes these independence-era lectures that James gave in the Caribbean. He list the numerous great artist produced throughout the island, and the list has stretched since James first made it. He numbers the popular festivals, dialects, dances, religions, and sports among the strengths of national culture. He also cautions that "the nation-builders—the politicians rather than the elitist planning bureaucrats—have been wise to pay such native "outpourings" from the Caribbean people the attention they have since received in response to the signals from the mass of the population who have always had something to say about their own destiny" (Nettleford 1990, p. 28). James would have been pleased with that "always."

It should be clear by now, to use a Jamesian rhetorical phrase, that James used history to level nationalism. (In a similar vein, one is aware of James's lifelong struggle to reclaim Lenin as great leveller and true egalitarian facing both the administrative hierarchies of Trotsky and the productive hierarchies of Stalin.) Highlighting the ordinary genius of the slave, and linking great Caribbean figures to the social and cultural ferment from which they sprang, he gave back that interior, egalitarian history, that history from the bottom up missing from Caribbean state nationalism. His cricket writing is a fitting place not only to end this look at his nationalist project. For James the entire Caribbean, has already, in tact, a people and a history. He would not agree with the position put forward by Brackette Williams in the article "A Class Act: Anthropology and the Race to Nation Across Ethnic Terrain." Williams states the classic case of a plural society held in check by an ethnically distinct minority elite when he writes that "to clarify both the material and ideological impact of the race/class/nation conflation on political relations among members of the same objective class we must recognize that for those outside this conflation its construction results in a national process aimed at homogenizing heterogeneity fashioned around assimilating elements of heterogeneity through appropriations that devalue and deny their link to marginalized others' contributions to the patrimony (be these immigrant groups or home-grown minorities), thereby establishing what Gramsci refers to as a transformist hegemony" (Williams 1989, p. 435). James can perhaps add a note of optimistic defiance of this determinist analysis. He would say there is a fully imagined nation, beneath the putative nation Brackette Williams is studying, made of more than residual cultures in Raymond Williams phrase, or informal organizations to use Abner Cohen's phrase. His cricket writing indicates that this imagined nation exists in the habitus of the Caribbean people, but also in the creativity that makes and remakes habitable texts of identity, that breaks and rebuilds that habitus.

"What I want to challenge" starts James, as he would often start a lecture on history to a trade union, "is the belief invariably expressed about his innings that (Learie) Constantine brought to this Test the carefree and impudent manner in which he played Saturday afternoon league cricket...There was no air of gaiety or impudence in the innings that he played or in thousands that he scored. There were times when he would amaze spectators by the audacity, even the daring of his strokes but it was all very seriously and systematically done" (James 1980, p. 254). What James is challenging is a crypto-racist description of Trinidad's greatest cricketer as a carefree colonial. But it is what he substitutes, or more importantly, quotes Constantine substituting for this misreading of the interior history of the Caribbean man, that crystallizes the Jamesian nationalist project and rejects the static models of plural competition (the academic equivalent of official nationalism in post-colonial politics) in the nation-space. James notes that Constantine wrote frequently and eloquently on the game, among other topics, and quotes, "Conditions are such in the West Indies that we shall never be able to play cricket in the style that it is played by so many Englishmen and not a few Australians, and it is my firm belief that we can learn the atmosphere of Test cricket, get together as a side in order to pull our full weight and yet as a side preserve that naturalness and ease which distinguish our game" (James 1980, p. 254). Here is Constantine, attributing his genius to a common cultural style of his people, recognizing and naming that style for himself, proving again the Jamesian nationalist project.

## NOTES

1.    An earlier version of this article was published jointly by Zed Books and University of the West Indies Press in Harney (1996). I would like to thank Zed and UWI for permission to publish this version here.

2.    There has been a flowering of James scholarship since his death in 1989. The most important has been Anna Grimshaw's *The C.L.R. James Reader*, (1992). The C.L.R. James Society produces a journal dedicated to making unpublished material available and providing critical comment. New articles and biographies continue to appear almost monthly as James is uneasily claimed by anti-Marxist cultural studies cadres of American academia and simultaneously by factional Marxist cadres. But this struggle for his legacy, in both Britain and the United States is the subject of another article.

3.    For a kind of manifesto of the work of the Subaltern Studies group, see Guha (1982).

4.    An excellent reference and bibliographical source about early Trinidadian writing, is Sander (1988). However, the tension of ethnicization and creolization among the Portuguese Trinidadians, is more evident in books like Charles Reis's amateur history of the Portuguese clubs of Port-of-Spain (1945). The minutes of the meeting are often dominated by tension between true Madeirans of the older generation together with newly arrived relatives, versus creolized Portuguese who "mixed with Creole women" and want to use the club to through fetes.

5.    The best single study of Caribbean fiction and society is Dash (1981), but see also Case (1985).

6. See two Jamesian scholars Anna Grimshaw and Keith Hart, writing on this prescience in an article, "Clairvoyance from stateside" in the *Times Higher Education Supplement*, March 24, 1989, p. 17, which accompanied an unpublished excerpt from a C.L.R. James manuscript on the United States.

7. It is worth noting, at the risk of repetition, that James's contention that the African slave did have a world view and a culture despite the hardships of enslavement, predates the important work on slave culture in the United States by scholars like Eugene Genovese and Leon Litwack. See, for instance, Genovese (1974), and Litwack (1979).

# REFERENCES

Brathwaite, E. 1986. "Doing It Our Way." *New Community* 3(4).

Buhle, P. 1988. *C.L.R. James: The Artist as Revolutionary*. London: Verso.

Case, F. 1985. *The Crisis of Identity: Studies in the Guadeloupean and Martiniquan Novel*. Sherbrooke, Quebec: Naaman.

Cesaire, A. 1968. *Return to My Native Land*. Paris: Presence Africaine.

Dash, J.M. 1981. *Literature and Ideology in Haiti, 1915-1961*. New Brunswick, NJ: Barnes and Noble.

Genovese, E. 1974. *Roll, Jordan, Roll: The World the Slaves Made*. New York: Pantheon Books.

Grimshaw, A. 1990. "Popular Democracy and the Creative Imagination: The Writings of C.L.R. James, 1950-1963." *Third Text* 10 (Spring).

_____. 1992. *The C.L.R. James Reader*. Oxford: Blackwell.

Guha, R. 1982. "On Some Aspects of the Historiography of Colonial India." Pp. 1-7 in *Subaltern Studies I*. Oxford: Oxford University Press.

Handler, R. 1988. *Nationalism and the Politics of Culture in Quebec*. Madison, WI: University of Wisconsin Press.

Harney, S. 1996. *Nationalism and Identity: Culture and the Imagination in a Caribbean Diaspora*. London and Kingston: Zed Books and University of the West Indies Press.

James, C.L.R. 1936. *Minty Alley*. London: New Beacon Books, 1971.

_____. 1933. *The Case for West Indian Self-Government*. London: Hogarth.

_____. 1963. *The Black Jacobins*. New York: Vantage Books.

_____. 1977. *The Future in the Present*. London: Alison & Busby.

_____. 1980. *Spheres of Existence*. London: Alison and Busby.

_____. 1983. *Beyond a Boundary*. New York: Pantheon.

_____. 1984a. "George Padmore: Black Marxist Revolutionary—A Memoir." P. 263 in *At The Rendezvous of Victory*. London: Alison and Busby.

_____. 1984b. *80th Birthday Lectures*. London: Race Today Publications.

Laclau, E., and Mouffe, C. *Hegemony and Socialist Strategy*. London: Verso.

Litwack, L. 1979. *Been in the Storm So Long: The Aftermath of Slavery*. New York: Knopf.

Nettleford, R. 1990. "The Caribbean: The Cultural Imperative and the Fight Against Folksy Exoticist Tastes." *Caribbean Affairs* 2(2).

Oxaal, I. 1982. *Black Intellectuals and the Dilemmas of Race and Class in Trinidad.* Cambridge, MA: Schenkman.

Payne, A. 1984. "Dependency Theory and the Commonwealth Caribbean." Pp. 2-10 in *Dependency Under Challenge*, edited by A. Payne and P. Sutton. Manchester: Manchester University Press.

Philips, M. 1990. "The Caribbean Mind" (interview). *Time Out* 11-17 (July).

Ramdin, R. 1982. *Chattel Slave to Wage Earner: A History Of Trade Unionism in Trinidad and Tobago.* London: Martin Brian and O'Keefe.

Rampersad, A. 1990. "V.S. Naipaul." *Raritan* 10 (1).

Reis, C. 1945. *Associacao Portugueza Primeiro de Dezembro.* Port-of-Spain, Trinidad.

Sander, R. 1988. *The Trinidad Awakening.* New York: Greenwood Press.

Sender, J., and Smith, S. 1986. *The Development of Capitalism in Africa.* London: Methuen.

Williams, B.F. 1989. "A Class Act: Anthropology and the Race to Nation Across Ethnic Terrain." *Annual Review of Anthropology* 18.

Williams, E. 1964. *Capitalism and Slavery.* London: Deutsch.

_____. 1970. *From Columbus to Castro.* London: Deutsch.

# PART III

CULTURAL POLITICS

# PRAGMATISM AND RADICALISM IN THE SOCIAL THOUGHT OF CORNEL WEST

Earnest N. Bracey

Cornel West remains the premier social commentator about race in America. Indeed, a compelling figure for many blacks in the academia, West has become in the words of Henry Louis Gates, Jr., chairman of the famous African-American Studies Department at Harvard (West's alma mater), "the preeminent African-American intellectual of our generation"; (Mills 1993, p. 16; Monroe 1996, p. 42) or it's been touted that West is "the most important black intellectual of the 1990" (Stanley 1994, p. 1). West, a top-notch academic has also been described by the *Washington Post Magazine* as a "radical, preacher, intellectual heavy and brother from around the way" (Mills 1993, p. 14; Stanley 1994, p. D4). According to the *New Yorker,* he is an "unusual mixture of intellectual seriousness, dandyish elegance and laid-back street sensibility" (Stanley 1994, p. D4).

Research in Race and Ethnic Relations, Volume 10, pages 67-86
Copyright © 1997 by JAI Press Inc.
All rights of reproduction in any form reserved.
ISBN: 0-7623-0275-5

No problem of our time has preoccupied the revolutionary or radical West more than race and the demise of modern black intellectuals. For instance, West has stated that "most black intellectuals are still in academic cocoons and have very little sense of out-reach to the larger public spheres in the black community and to the larger society...." [He goes on to note]: "They have not been highly influential in the mainstream of Black America, but they've been exemplary critics of American capitalist civilization" (West 1990, pp. 50, 52).

Conservative black intellectuals, of course, know no bounds when it comes to using government policies to protect their turf and advance their political agenda, such as abolishing programs that might benefit minorities and women. Some black conservatives, like economist Walter Williams of George Mason University, have even claimed that "liberals have done more harm to blacks than the Ku Klux Klan" (Conti and Stetson 1993, p. 7). This rhetorical nonsense and absurdity, of course, must be challenged head-on, and West, as well as other new black intellectuals will (and must) continue to tackle such important issues in the coming years.

On the other hand, one can well imagine how the intellectually recalcitrant West might prove profoundly disappointing to conservative black and white American intellectuals and dissenters, not because he is not honest and careful in his efforts, or lacks credibility, and authenticity in his arguments about culture, class and religion, but because his substantive work is generally classified as "contemporary liberalism" (Puddington 1993, p. 63). Although West's points of view and work bears many traces of brilliance and complexity, there are those who vehemently attack his brand of scholarship or legitimacy, as did the disgruntled Leon Wieseltier, the *New Republic* magazine's literary editor, who critically wrote: "West's work is noisy, tedious, slippery, sectarian, humorless, pedantic and self-endeared. His judgement of ideas eccentric" (Wieseltier 1995, p. 31).

One, of course, might be delusionary if he or she thinks that West's "eclectic disquisitions on race and politics" (Applebome 1996, p. 27) will be embraced wholly by all scholars; but it is obvious he does not care about that, and places more weight on how "to tell the truth about America" (Monroe 1996, p. 47). More importantly, one must understand, as West emphatically states: "White academics who have attacked Black intellectuals as too "parochial" because they seem concerned only with race, are in deep denial about the historical role of race in American society" (Mills 1996, p. 45).

One thing is also for certain, West is not necessarily the defender or champion of the so-called black race, because he proves to be interested in a variety of intellectual and dynamic public issues, such as democratic socialism, the greed of corporate elites, trade unionism, sexism and Black homophobia; African philosophical history, Marxist thought, and racial rapprochement. Moreover, West does not come across as being an angry black man or hostile to whites, as "he refuses to blame all the troubles of the inner city on white racism, and he is critical of black appeals to racial solidarity" (Puddington 1993, p. 62). According to West, "we have Black liberals who remain so preoccupied with race—and race is very important— that the issues of environment, gender, class, and empire tend to be overlooked" (Hooks and West 1991, p. 43).

Nonetheless, before we can evaluate or criticize West for his scholastic acumen, intellectual prowess, or academicism, we must try to understand our notion of what this black intellectual represents. Obviously West's entire illustrious career and brilliant stint as an academician has been a very rich, complex, and productive period in his life. Enjoying several intellectual and academic positions, for instance, West was Assistant Professor of Philosophy of Religion in 1977 at Union Theological Seminary in New York City, (West 1991, pp. XXIV-XXX) and he has taught at the Yale Divinity School (West 1991, pp. XXIV-XXX). He also held the coveted position of director of Afro-American Studies at Princeton while also teaching in the renown religion department (West 1991, pp. XXIV-XXX). But wooed away by the charismatic Henry Louis (Skip) Gates, to help form one of the nation's power houses in Black Studies, West has been professor of Afro-American studies and the philosophy of religion at Harvard since the fall of 1994.

West has also published over twelve books, including *Prophetic Thought in Postmodern Times,* which won the American Book Award in 1993, and the recent bestsellers, *Jews and Blacks: A Dialogue on Race, Religion, and Culture in America,* co-authored with Michael Lerner (Lerner and West 1996); and the insightful and prophetic, *The Future of the Race,* with MacArthur Genius Award winner, Henry Louis Gates, Jr. (Gates and West 1996). One can certainly admire the sheer volume of West's work.

And besides the many honorary doctorates and accolades received by West, perhaps he is especially proud—being a theologian himself—of receiving the honorary Doctor of Humane Letters from the Virginia Theological Seminary in 1995 (Brochure 1995-1996, p. 85). About religion, which is germane to our overall discussion, West has written:

> American religious life is losing its prophetic fervor. There is an undeniable decline in the clarity of vision, complexity of understanding, and quality of moral action among religious Americans. The rich prophetic legacies of Sojourner Truth, Walter Rauschenbusch, Dorothy Day, Abraham Heschel, and Martin Luther King, Jr., now lay nearly dormant—often forgotten—and the possession of a marginal few. Political and culture conservatism seems to have silenced most of the prophetic religious voices and famed the vast majority of churches, temples, synagogues, and mosques. Prophetic religion indeed is at the crossroads in present day America (West 1988, p. IX).

Furthermore, with the premier of *Race Matters*, a collection or compendium of eight essays published by Beacon Press in 1993, West has become an academic superstar. Indeed, he skyrocketed to success in the academy, achieving overwhelming criticism and praise. The best-selling *Race Matters*, undoubtedly, his most accessible and popular work is a useful and important addition to the black cultural and intellectual genre. *Race Matters* makes a strong initial impression, even on casual readers who may simply be struck by the breath of West's knowledge about so many contemporary issues. Prolific writer and political commentator, Nat Hentoff wrote in his review of West's book that:

> *Race Matters*, brief as it is, should have resonance for years to come. It ought to be required reading in college and university courses and in high school curricula as well. It is bound to provoke instructive debates in courses in sociology, politics, and black studies (Hentoff 1993, p. 96).

West's *Race Matters* does offer a crucial way and key in many respects to understand one of our most important and intractable problems in American—race. It certainly gives us an understanding of a black academician who, through his books, lectures and articles, always come across as a pragmatist. Although West prefers to call himself a "radical democrat" or a progressive," (Mills 1996, p. 25) we know exactly where he is coming from. Which is to say, as Hentoff tells us, West "is an unflinching realist with a remarkable ability to plumb the dynamics of the nihilism...that is so crushing a weight on those blacks without hope and therefore without any coherent sense of a future" (Hentoff 1993, p. 96). Indeed, the whole idea of West's prolific and prodigious output and intellectual work, by definition, rejects the expedient and practical means and ideas of bland and esoteric theories to explain our economic woes and political affairs, which in itself is a study in pragmatism. "American pragmatism," West writes:

> emerges with profound insights and myopic blindness, enabling strengths and debilitating weakness, all resulting from distinctive features of American civilization: its revolutionary beginning combined with a slave-based economy; its elastic liberal rule of law combined with an entrenched business-dominated status quo; its hybrid culture in combination with a collective self-definition as homogeneously Anglo-American; its obsession with mobility, contingency, and pecuniary liquidity combined with a deep moralistic impulse; and its impatience with theories and philosophies alongside ingenious technological innovation, political strategies of compromise, and personal devices for comfort and convenience (West 1989, p. 5).

What exactly does all this mean? Or better yet, what does pragmatism mean for black Americans? West writes that "pragmatism's primary aim is to discern, delineate, and defend particular norms through highlighting desirable possibilities present in the practices of a specific community or society (West 1982, p. 21). So West in this sense tries to interpret and give meaning to the destructive course America has taken (and is taking) in terms of culture, diversity and race relations. Towards this end, he often predicts or prophesize about the tragic and deadly consequences of our actions. For example, in an editorial in the *Democratic Left* magazine, shortly after the L.A. Riots, West wrote:

> When the Rodney King verdict was put forth, the chicken came home to roost. It came home to roost because so much of the effects and consequences in that post-industrial city, shot through with post-modern culture and politics, have created a feeling of powerlessness. People could not put up any longer with this sense of powerlessness, and hence, an expression of outrage. The combination of politics, meaninglessness, frustration, alienation, all of these things interwoven created the tragic lives of each and every person dead from the riots. And yet these lives are now shaking the foundations of the nation such that even President Bush coming to L.A. at least has to say a word about race. I'm sure he hadn't planned to two weeks before. He got motivated. That's very important, because Bush, is part of a larger political discourse, since 1968, in which allusions

to race have been central to the conservative domination of politics (West 1992, p. 17).

West, of course, doesn't criticize for the sake of criticizing, and he often presents ways and ideas for more people to participate in the democratic process, but he is also disillusioned, frustrated, and deeply "disturbed by the transformation of highly intelligent liberal intellectuals into tendentious neoconservatives owing to crude ethnic identity—based allegiances and vulgar neonationalist sentiments" (West 1989, p. 7). West's outrage of discontent is mirrored by professor Michael Dyson's remarks:

> The problem and possibilities of black public intellectuals are huge. We've got a chance to make a difference in the world—something a lot of folk can't say, a chance a lot of scholars can't get. We shouldn't allow pettiness or jealousy to stop us. If black intellectuals keep bickering, bellyaching, and bitterly attacking one another, we'll blow it. And we shouldn't allow the forces and resources of the marketplace to set us against one another. We should be using our minds to shine a light on the real foes of black folk and democracy: poverty, capital flight, right-wing extremists, religious fundamentalists, and the politics of conservatives and neoliberals that hurt the working class and the working poor. Of course, we shouldn't mute our criticisms of black figures, as long as they are just (Dyson 1996, p. 75).

This all says that West has little use for neoconservatives and their protracted and sometimes fascist agenda. This group includes a new breed of black conservative intellectuals and politicians that have acquiesced or accommodated to the ruling elites or mainstream conservative American (Puddington 1993, p. 63), without so much regard to the lost generations of poor minorities. It is in this vein that West does not hesitate to discuss the hypocrisy of the conservatives. Again West writes about the short-comings of black intellectuals, which can apply as well to black conservatives, black scholars, and black politicians, or black leaders in his classic book, *Keeping Faith: Philosophy and Race in America:*

> The predicament of the black intellectual need not be grim and dismal. Despite the pervasive racism of American society and anti-intellectualism of the black community, critical space and insurgent activity can be expanded. This expansion will occur more readily when black intellectuals take a more candid look at themselves, the historical and social forces that shape them, and the limited though significant resources of the community from whence they come (West 1993, pp. 84-85).

Such ruminations can serve a specialized function: to help us better consider West's personal character and development, and understand the forces that shaped him. But no matter how careful and thoughtful a scholar and writer he can be, there will be those careless critics, like Leon Wieseltier, who will attack West's academicism and intellectual capabilities. For instance, Wieseltier wrote that West "is not a philosopher, he is a cobbler of philosophies; and so he reports the pragmatist and historicist tidings and proceeds to the manufacture of what he needs" (Wieseltier 1995, p. 34). So what is wrong with this interdisciplinary, holistic and amalgam approach to scholarship? Nothing. Critics, also discontent with West's ideas, often label his scholarly work as the "scholarship of advocacy." But as West has explicitly stated:

> I do not consider the terrain of philosophy to be either a professional arena in which playfully to solve technical problems of little human consequence or a privileged platform from which to oversee the claims of other disciplines. Rather, I understand philosophy to be a social activity of intellectual pursuit always already infused with cultural concerns and political choices often unbeknown to its participants. As an active Afro-American participant in the philosophical enterprise, I merely try to make my cultural concerns and political choices crystal clear (West 1982, p. 12).

All that West is saying here is that he doesn't set out to write any consciously philosophical work, but if philosophy can explain things, (it should be used), he will use it. A fuller image about the man, moreover, shines through everything that he writes, especially what he brings to light—(or to the academic table)—about Affirmative Action, black-Jewish relations, black "rage," and the demyslification of black sexuality. Indeed, according to journalist Sylvester Monroe, West has "staked out race and class as the intellectual arena in which he [can] have the most impact in everyday lives" (Monroe 1996, pp. 45-46). One is struck moreover, by West's ability to accurately portray and analyze certain controversial issues of recent years, such as repressive economic policies and his view that "American capitalism is evil" (Puddington 1993, p. 63). When in 1995, West gave an address describing how white racism and white supremacy has undermined our democracy, he noted that "American business has enormous wealth and power that it can use either to advance the cause of multiracial democracy—or to hinder it. To date, the business world has not lived up to its promise. Economic growth has not led to higher

wages and greater employer-employee loyalty for most Americans"
(Ettirre and McNerney 1995, p. 13). In the same vein, West stated,
as a guest lecturer at Virginia Commonwealth University in 1994,
that "current debates on Eurocentrism and multi-culturalism avoid
focusing on issues such as white supremacy, racism, elitism and
poverty....It says nothing about the decline of the economy, the
distribution of wealth in this country, or the rise of executive salaries
when plants are closing and workers are being laid off. It says nothing
about the down-sizing of the American middle class" (Stanley 1994,
p. B3). West also interestingly points out that America has "never
had a public debate in this country about 1 percent of the population
owning 37 percent of the wealth....or 10 percent owning 86. That
debate's never taken place" (Mills 1996, p. 25). My assessment and
understanding of West's ultimate solution to our race and class
problems is: There must be a redistribution of the wealth in this
country, where *everyone* can benefit, own property and have an equal
opportunity to live a decent and middle-class lifestyle, as well as
participate in the political life of the American community.

As one follows West's marvelous career, one feels an almost affinity
to the man, as he is the genuine article. About his scholarship and
intellectual insight, West has stated: "My writings constitute a
perennial struggle between my African and American identities, my
democratic socialist convictions, and my Christian sense of the
profound tragedy and possible triumph in life and history. I am a
prophetic Christian freedom fighter principally because of distinctive
Christian conceptions of what it is to be human, how we should act
toward one another, and what we should hope for" (West 1991, p.
XXVIII).

About his arguably charmed life, West has written: "I was nurtured
in the bosom of a living black Christian family and church (Shiloh
Baptist Church in Sacramento, California) and I remain committed
to the prophetic Christian gospel. I am the product of an Ivy League
education which reinforced my unfathomable interest in and
unquenchable curiosity about the Western philosophical tradition,
American culture, and Afro-American history—and I have an
affinity to a philosophical version of American pragmatism" (West
1982, pp. 11-12).

Critically reflecting on the difficulties and hardships of raising his
son, Clifton, and the miracle of fatherhood, West has commented:
"The most important things for black fathers to try to do is to give

of themselves, to try to exemplify in their own behavior what they want to see in their sons and daughters, and, most important, to spend time with and give attention to their children. This is a big challenge, yet it is critical as we move into the twenty-first century. The most difficult task of my life was to give the eulogy for my father. Everything else pales in the face of this challenge. Hence what Dad means to me....constitutes who and what I am and will be" (Willis 1996, pp. 47-48).

Such modesty, honesty and selflessness, undoubtedly shows the moral character of the man. West also gets personable with others, as he can (and does) converse with the average person with aplomb and with-out missing a beat in the language of the mean streets, which is the central core of his true being: He is totally down to earth intellectually in that he has an uncanny ability to always think on his feet.

West is also the most widely read black academician and public intellectual in the United States today, with the possible exception of his contemporary, the hip-hop intellectual, Michael Eric Dyson, who is Professor of Communications Studies at the University of North Carolina, Chapel Hill; or Henry Louis Gates, as West deals with divisive social and racial issues that no one wants to fully address. And West is a paradox of sorts, for he has stated:

> I represent a strand of the black freedom struggle that, these days, is very much cutting against the grain. You talk about an analysis that highlights class and gender as well as race, and sexual orientation *and* ecology. To try to be synthetic and synoptic in that way is very much cutting against the grain (Mills 1996, p. 17).

The evolution of such a brilliant mind and intellectual did not start in a vacuum. West was born in Tulsa, Oklahoma and "raised in a segregated, working-class neighborhood of Sacramento, California, the son of a school-teacher and a civil servant" (Mills 1996, p. 19). According to journalist, David Mills, West's "grandfather was a Baptist minister for 40 years in Oklahoma, so the black church was 'fundamental' to his growing up" (Mills 1996, p. 19).

It cannot be said of West, moreover, as with many public black intellectuals—in which the likes of conservative economist, Thomas Sowell often criticizes—that he is not a truly gifted and rigorous scholar or lacks intellectual responsibility, as his ambitious work in

*Keeping Faith* should dispel such doubts and convince everyone that he is a brilliant intellectual of the first magnitude. More importantly, if one suspects that West thrives on controversy, and exposure to the public limelight in discussing black contemporary nihilism "that increasingly pervades black communities" which he writes about so well in *Race Matter*, perhaps he does. As a corollary to West's thesis of nihilism, he writes in *Race Matters* that: "Nihilism is to be understood here not as a philosophic doctrine that there are not rational grounds for legitimate standards or authority; it is, far more, the lived experience of coping with a life of horrifying meaninglessness, hopelessness, and (most important) lovelessness. The frightening result is a numbing detachment from others and a self-destructive disposition toward the world. Life without meaning, hope, and love breeds a coldhearted, mean-spirited outlook that destroys both the individual and others" (West 1993, pp. 14-15).

West, like the late and great Horatio Alger, has very vigorously and righteously made himself—that is, he is an intellectual self-styled or self-made man. Even as a brilliant undergraduate at Harvard, he refused to ignore or compromise his "blackness," race, or forget his black cultural roots. Often West invokes the ideas of "Black consciousness." About his experience at Harvard, for instance, West has been quoted as saying:

> The important thing to keep in mind is that in 1970, I was coming out of a town, Sacramento, that was deeply affected by social movements....the Civil Rights Movement, the Black Power Movement, [and] the Black Panther Party had a major impact on me. So, in a fundamental sense, I was convinced that I was, to the best of my ability, going to be myself within the Harvard context (Monroe 1996, p. 43).

If one interprets his words accurately, there should not be any doubt where West stands or what he believes in as an individual; nor should his ability be underestimated or misconstrued. He is proud of being a black man. Take also for example, this important passage, written by West in 1986, and taken from the *Socialist Review*:

> The black community does not possess the necessary wealth and power—nor will it possess them in the future—to alleviate the deplorable plight of the black working poor and underclass. Indeed, black America can do much better with its economic and cultural resources than it presently is doing. But the notion that the destiny of black America can be set right by means of

black economic development (as argued by black liberals) can only lead black people into a political cul-de-sac. As the great Martin Luther King, Jr., repeatedly noted, the destiny of black America is inextricably bound with that of America. In fact, to reject this claim is to reinforce the very aims of the right: to enshrine the operations of private business, to racially polarize the political process, and to black trans-racial strategic alliances that challenge the prevailing business assault (West 1986, p. 45)

As one can perhaps ascertain, West's concern for all members of society, especially the disadvantaged, the poor and down-trodden speaks volumes, as he also rightly believes our corporate world has not lived up to its potential to advance the notion of a multiracial democracy. Indeed, for West the theory of racism and socialism are inextricably intertwined: hence, his life long interest in Marxism and other socialist ideas and concepts. West has stated for instance that:

Today we are still struggling with the same question raised by King, namely: Can America be a genuine multiracial democracy? Can our nation spread freedom, opportunity and democracy out to all of its citizens, or will the blessings of liberty continue to be enjoyed only by a privileged few? Several obstacles stand in the way of developing a genuinely multiracial democracy in America, not the least of which is its history. Two hundred forty-four years of slavery, white supremacy and other "institutionalized evils" cannot be washed away by 30 years of multiracial experimentation (Ettorre and McNerney 1995, p. 13).

The source of West's conviction about entrenched racism in America, moreover, is to be found in his own life experiences. Knowing that blacks have always been the political and social underdogs in America, West often tries to help poor minorities, as he did in Boston while at Harvard, as an undergraduate, attending "on a partial academic scholarship, [and] studying philosophy, literature and Near Eastern languages," (Mills 1996, p. 24) by helping, "run the Black Panthers local prison outreach and breakfast program" (Mills 1996, p. 24).

In the final analysis, West's early years, and experiences as a youth with the Black Panthers, are intrinsic things that has shaped him as a brilliant scholar and new-wave black intellectual, as well as practical theoretician on modern day prejudices, hatred and discrimination in our society.

On this point, an early and poignant essay that West wrote about Marxism, entitled, *Toward a Socialist Theory of Racism* gives one a sense of his personal commitment about such matters:

It also should be evident that past Marxist conceptions of racism have often prevented U.S. socialist movements from engaging in antiracist activity in a serious and consistent manner. In addition, black suspicion of white-dominated political movements (no matter how progressive) as well as the distance between these movements and the daily experiences of peoples of color have made it even more difficult to fight racism effectively....

The only effective way the contemporary democratic socialist movement can break out of this circle (and it is possible because the bulk of democratic socialists are among the least racist of Americans) is to be sensitized to the critical importance of antiracist struggles....

We must frankly acknowledge that a democratic socialist society will not necessarily eradicate racism. Yet a democratic socialist society is the best hope for alleviating and minimizing racism, particularly institutional forms of racism (West 1996, p. 7).

West's statements have the grace and eloquence of a man possessed by a keen desire to point out and exorcise indefatigable racism, as well as bear witness to the historical past of prejudice and discrimination that has always plagued our nation. As West succinctly puts it:

blacks, after coming to the New World in chains as slaves, have yet to escape their past as have European immigrants. Europeans came to America and discovered they're White. When Irish brothers and sisters arrive, no matter how much they hate the British, they discover they have something in common by hating black Americans....

Black bodies have been subject to all kinds of psychic fear....Having the "wrong lips, skin color, hair, texture and skin pigmentation" and being considered less intellectual than whites have led to intangible but real issues of identity. The loss of identity is manifested in the violence now sweeping American (Stanley 1994, p. B4).

We can see from these passages that West does indeed have a strong grasp of the intellectual and historical traditions of Africa and blacks in the diaspora in particular. In West's speeches and written work to date, the academic and public discourse about the phenomenon presented, especially on the history of African-Americans is in good hands with West. And what he writes is significant in and of itself, despite those dissenters and naysayers who would try to, perhaps, silence him. For instance, Wieseltier has gone so far as to say that: "West's published work is an endless exercise in misplaced Marxism" (Wieseltier 1995, p. 34). But in that same paragraph, Wieseltier writes that West "seeks to devise a Marxist ground for American

Grievances, and in this alas, he succeeds brilliantly" (Wieseltier 1995, p. 35).

Of course, this far in his thinking, West is quite at one with Marxist denunciations of a bourgeois society, such as the United States, for its unfair wages for the working poor, alienation and continued segregation of the classes, and races, incomprehensible verbal dialogue such as advanced by the Right, as well as racism, war rationalization, unabashed consumerism, and police use of force to neutralize petty criminals. Furthermore, as Puddington, in his discussion of West's attack of black conservative leadership, has written: West on a number of issues "plays loose with the facts: While black conservatives may have written critically of the tendency among black intellectuals to sympathize with authoritarian regimes of the left, mostly they focus on domestic controversies like affirmative action, busing, and welfare" (Puddington 1993, p. 63). But in fairness to West, we must look at what he has said regarding this particular issue—about wrong-minded "conservatives, who say race is not as important as the liberals think; that instead what is important is individual responsibility" (West 1990, p. 60). Individual responsibility is an important catch phrase, or are great buzz words, but they have never created jobs for the poor-working classes and those who would like to pull themselves up from their bootstraps, without boots.

Also, it certainly bears pointing out that America was founded on racism and built and maintained on the ideology of racism, which continues today, as it seems we are racing backward in human relations. Writes West in *Prophesy Deliverance*:

> The notion that black people are human beings is a relatively new discovery in the modern West. The idea of black equality in beauty, culture, and intellectual capacity remains problematic and controversial within prestigious halls of learning and sophisticated intellectual circles. The Afro-American encounter with the modern world has been shaped first and foremost by the doctrine of white supremacy, which is embodied in institutional practices and enacted in everyday folkways under varying circumstances and evolving conditions (West 1982, p. 60).

In an interesting interview with feminist writer, bell hooks in *Emerge* magazine, for instance, West bluntly noted:

> What we have is one set of narrow figures criticized by another set of narrow perspectives. What the left presents is a way of fusing the struggle against

racism, with a concern about class, gender, environment that makes black
people a part of the world but doesn't lose them within the context of our
homes, of black communities (West 1990, p. 60).

One could compare West with the griots of ancient Africa who
told the history of their tribes through the oral traditions. He not
only speaks to vast and multiracial audiences, in the oral tradition
about ethics, religious philosophy, and many of the public and moral
issues of our time, but he also writes about blacks and many of these
issues as well. For example, in a remark that is indicative of his
insights about politics—or post-modern politics—and the
predominance of conservatives in the field, West writes:

Our country produces political leaders that lack any kind of broad moral or
social vision, that are mediocre leaders. Post-modern politics are a politics
of image and are characterized by the break down of the accountability
mechanism between politicians and their constituency. Politicians spend their
time running for the next election, waiting for a response from demoralized
and demobilized citizens—more and more Americans reject politics as a
meaningful vehicle for change, hence the erosion of the public trust in those
institutions of government (West 1992, p. 17).

West's scholarly work is unusually broad, and he knows what he's
writing about; however, his written words does not display a
consistent linear-thinking or single vision about what we can expect
about the future of our democracy and how blacks can solve all of
the socio-economic exigencies facing us. Still the logic of all of West's
arguments are built on facts, as well as the strength of his passion.
In the recently published book, entitled, *The Future of the Race*, West
offers black Americans this novel solution to our dilemma:

On the crucial existential level relating to black invisibility and namelessness,
the first difficult challenge and demanding discipline is to ward off madness
and discredit suicide as a desirable option. A central preoccupation of black
culture is that of confronting candidly the ontological wounds, psychic scars,
and existential bruises of black people while funding off insanity and self-
annihilation. Black culture consists of black modes of being-in-the-world
obsessed with black sadness and sorrow, black agony and anguish, black
heartache and heartbreak without fully succumbing to the numbing effects
of such misery—to never allow such misery to have the last word (West 1996,
p. 81).

This particularly provocative work also records West's ideas and thoughts about the legendary and foremost black intellectual of our time, W.E.B. Dubois. West wrote: "My fundamental problem with Du Bois is his inadequate grasp of the tragicomic sense of life—a refusal candidly to confront the sheer absurdity of the human condition. This tragicomic sense—tragicomic rather than simply "tragic, because even ultimate purpose and objective order are called into question—propels us toward suicide or madness unless we are buffered by ritual, cushioned by community, or sustained by art. Du Bois's inability to immerse himself in black everyday life precluded his access to the distinctive black tragicomic sense and black encounter with the absurd" (West 1996, pp. 57-58).

Within a broad humanistic perspective, West's analysis of Du Bois is not a rejection of his remarkable scholarship, but I believe he's telling us that Du Bois did not relate to the cultural victimization of blacks, nor mainstream black leadership. Moreover, in West's view, perhaps Du Bois refused "to remain, in some visible way, organically linked with African-American cultural life" (Berube 1995, p. 73). When West categorizes the works by Du Bois he does not seem to realize that some may say that his writing is superficial or intellectual over simplification. What ever the drawbacks of West's doleful criticisms and prophetic work, it effectively underscores his popular influence and mass appeal or the popularity of what he has to say. Rooted literally in the tradition of the black church, also, West's thoughts are more cogent in that he conveys a highly developed sense of specific African-American social and historical situations. West never ceases to believe that we cannot solve our problems "over which American is now agonizing" (Puddington 1993, p. 64). Moreover, West believes as Frederick Douglass, the great black-American abolitionist did: that we must continue to agitate until every American can "participate as fully as possible in the debates that shape his or her society and culture," (Berube 1995, p. 79) without losing oneself or being dehumanized. West made the significance of blacks being themselves plain: "we have got to come up with mature forms of black self-love, black self-respect in which whiteness is not a point of reference, either negative or positive....Why would anybody even question that we have to prove ourselves to white persons? Thank God my family tradition never, ever incorporated the notion that I had to prove my humanity to anybody. They accepted me on my terms, with all the ugliness and the positiveness that makes me my mama's child" (West 1993, p. 28).

In an interesting passage discussing this same point, Michael Eric Dyson in *Race Rules: Navigating the Color Line* writes:

West is right to grapple with issues of morality and behavior, matters that are largely taboo for the left. He's also right to zoom in on the market forces and market moralities that besiege black culture. Still, as an explanation for what ails us, nihilism has severe problems. First, nihilism is seem as a cause, not a consequence, of black suffering. The collapse of hope, the spiritual despair that floods black America, the clinical depression we suffer are all the pernicious result of something more basic than black nihilism: White racism. I don't mean here just the nasty things many white folk believe about black folk. I'm referring to the systematic destruction of black life, the pervasive attack on the black sense of well-being, the subversion of black self-determination, and the erasure of crucial narratives of black self-esteem that are foundational to American versions of democracy. Nihilism is certainly self-destructive. That's because black folk were taught—and have had it reinforced across time, geography and ideology—that our black selves weren't worth loving or preserving. Nihilism is the outgrowth, not the origin, of such harsh lessons. Without the destruction of white supremacy, black nihilism will continue to grow (Dyson, 1996, pp. 136-137).

West's best work or analysis about black-Jewish relations is in *Jews and Blacks: A Dialogue on Race, Religion, and Culture in America* which essentially is the recorded conversations between Cornel West and, perhaps, America's most preeminent liberal Jewish intellectual, Michael Lerner, where they explore deep thoughts and exchange ideas and opinions about race, the struggle for social justice, and the disintegration of the Jewish-Black alliance that once existed in America. Writes West in the introduction to *Jews and Blacks:*

Both Jews and Blacks are a pariah people—a people who had to make and remake themselves as outsiders on the margins of American society and culture. Both groups assumed that the status quo was unjust and therefore found strategies to survive and thrive against the odds. Both groups defined themselves as a people deeply shaped by America but never *fully* a part of America. Both groups appealed to biblical texts and relied on communal bonds to sustain themselves—texts that put a premium on justice, mercy, and solidarity with down-trodden, and bonds shot through with a deep distrust, suspicion, even paranoia, toward the powerful and privileged. Both groups have been hated and despised peoples who find it difficult, if not impossible, to fully overcome group insecurity and anxiety as well as truly be and love themselves as individuals and as a people. Wearing the masks, enduring petty put-downs, and coping with subtle insults remains an everyday challenge for most Blacks and some Jews in America (Lerner and West 1996, pp. 2-3).

In the above passages, one can detect West's most personal thoughts about the tenuous relationship between two formerly oppressed racial and allied groups. Nowhere else has West revealed himself so accomplished a master of the Black-Jewish situation. In fact, the above passages stand behind West's entire work about blacks and Jews. In trying to make this black-Jewish tie or controversial alliance clear, and to reach the largest possible public, West earlier discussed the relations and root cause for the division between blacks and Jews in *Race Matters*. However, Puddington has written: "West's observations on blacks and Jews conform to a clear pattern: he attributes a perspective to all blacks or many blacks or some blacks which in fact represents little more than his own opinion or an opinion limited to the relatively small fraternity of like-minded black leftists" (Puddington 1993, p. 64). Puddington's criticism is disingenuous at best and he is wrong, of course, because often black intellectuals of the Right defer to West because his opinions are often right, and for me, they are cathartic, especially when speaking about Jews, and especially their avowed hatred for some black leaders today, such as Nation of Islam's black leader, Minister Louis Farrakhan.

West's work thus far contains some astute observations about where we are headed in this country, especially the historical significance and modern-day conflict between blacks and Jews. Nor does his work lack discussions of pragmatism and the historical insights necessary to accurately analyze African-American critical thought, which is "an interpretation of Afro-American history, especially its cultural heritage and political struggles, which provides norms for responding to challenges presently confronting black Americans" (West 1982, p. 22). West also writes that "Despite its limitations, pragmatism provides an American context for Afro-American thought, a context that imparts to it both a shape and a heritage of philosophical legitimacy" (West 1982, p. 21).

Others, or opponents, whose sense of displeasure with West, given by the volumous criticism and numerous death threats (Monroe 1996, p. 47) proves that he is getting his message across to the American public. Being a celebrated Harvard Professor, and receiving acclaim for his standing-room-only speaking engagements doesn't hurt him either.

When West was a young man, he overcame many mental and physical obstacles, including the illness of asthma; [and] later he played football with a fierceness, even for his small size, extolling in the joys of the game, just as he rejoices today in the fact of being a political activist throughout the years. As West recalled:

> My first noteworthy political action—besides marching with my family in a civil rights demonstration in Sacramento—was the coordination of a city-wide strike of students demanding courses in black studies. At the time there were four black student body presidents in Sacramento high schools (including myself). My good friend Glenn Jordan and I decided to launch this effort during the 1969-1970 school year, and we had good results (West 1991, p. XVII).

All of these things sets West apart from other modern day public intellectuals. But he has also paid his dues. West is an admirable scholar, a man of flashy brilliance, and sustained efforts. Future generations of blacks will admire the originality of West's work and ideas, as they contain much important information. He can never be a Du Bois, but he is in the thick of things as an academic and deep thinker, and perhaps one-day he will be heir to W.E.B. Du Bois' legacy. Like Tom Wolf of the *Right Stuff* fame, West is an exemplary figure, an intellectual dandy, or dapper, who often supports gold-watch chains and wears expensive three-piece suits, debonaire-style, because he can (Mills 1996, p. 19). West can, of course, relate and interact with the best and less of individuals in our society, and no matter how unpopular his positions are on certain issues. He is also apt to play a political role at best in the future of America.

Meanwhile, West has continued to criticize and sting the Right with his characteristical attack on those conservatives who think they are right. For example, West has stated:

> We have to have markets, we have to have material incentives....But we also know markets generate levels of inequality, especially in relation to basic social goods like food, shelter, health care, jobs, so forth. Which means that we can't rely solely on markets for that. And if you do, you're going to end up with a society so polarized that levels of disorder and anarchy and chaos result there from. So you have to have some non-market concerns—welfare state (Mills 1993, p. 25).

The conclusions that I infer from West's remarkable work and philosophy are valid for the rest of the United States—or the world—for that matter. What he shows essentially is that he has a vision of how things ought to be. West reigns in black intellectual circles and reminds us all of our shortcomings as scholars; although "he hasn't won the hearts and minds of African-American students" (Mills 1993, p. 17) West's sense of personal fulfillment is most clearly revealed in the insightful pages he wrote in 1991 in *The Ethical Dimensions of Marxist Thought:*

> My passionate interest in philosophy....remains....primarily motivated by the radical historical *conditionedness* of human existence and the ways in which possibilities and potentialities are created, seized, and missed by individuals and communities within this ever changing condition, including our inescapable death, illness, and disappointment. This attention to the historical character of all thought and action has led me to be suspicious of intellectual quests for truth unwilling to be truthful about themselves, including my own. So though I find delight in the life of the mind-inseparable from, yet not identical with, struggles for freedom—I do not put primary value on intelligence or book knowledge (West 1991, p. XVII).

West, indeed, is a public figure, a part of the new black intellectual vanguard—or black liberal academics—whose scholarship and intellectualism cannot be denied or summarily dismissed. Over the course of time, he will proved to be like W.E.B. Du Bois, one of America's most memorable and towering figures in higher education and the academe, or academy community. Now he is on the cutting edge of classic black American scholarship, and should remain on that perch for some time, or until someone else can quietly take his place. He is saying things that are far-reaching, but must be said, and we must listen if we are to survive as a nation.

## REFERENCES

Applebome, P. 1996. "Can Harvard's Powerhouse Alter the Course of Black Studies?" *The New York Times* (November 3), 4A.

Berube, M. 1995. "Public Academy." *The New Yorker* (May).

Conti, J.G., and B. Stetson. 1993. *Challenging the Civil Rights Establishment: Profiles of a New Black Vanguard*. Westport, CT: Praeger.

Dyson, M.E. 1996. *Race Rules: Navigating the Color Line*. New York: Addison-Wesley Publishing Company, Inc.

Ettorre, B., and D.J. McNerney. 1995. "Changes and Challenges For Managing Human Capital, Human Resources Conference and Exposition Report." *HR Focus* (June).

Gates, Jr., H.L., and C. West. 1996. *The Future of the Race*. New York: Alfred A. Knopf.

Hentoff, N. 1993. "Preaching in the Streets and in the Academy." *The Journal of Blacks in Higher Education* 1 (Autumn).

hooks, b., and C. West. 1991. *Breaking Bread: Insurgent Black Intellectual Life.* Boston, MA: South End Press.

Lerner, M., and C. West. *Jews and Blacks: A Dialogue on Race, Religion, and Culture in America.* New York: A Plume Book.

Mills, D. 1993. "The West Alternative." *The Washington Post Magazine* (August 8).

Monroe, S. 1996. "Cornel Matters." *Emerge* 7(10, September).

Puddington, A. 1993. "Immoderate Moderate;" Review of *Race Matter*, by Cornel West. *Commentary* 96(2, August).

Newman Stanley, B. 1994a. "Racism Cuts to 'Heart of Democracy,' Scholar Emphasizes." *Richmond Times-Dispatch* (January 21).

————. 1994b. "West Quest: Street-Smart Intellectual Cornel West Deals with the Praise, the Criticism." *Richmond Times - Dispatch* (February 8).

Virginia Theological Seminary, Catalogue. 1995-1996.

West, C. "A Response to L.A." *Democratic Left* (May/June).

————. 1982. *Prophesy Deliverance: An Afro-American Revolutionary Christianity.* Philadelphia: The Westminster Press.

————. 1986. "Left Strategies: A View From Afro-America." *Socialist Review.* 16 (2, March/April).

————. 1988. *Prophetic Fragments.* Trenton, NJ: Africa World Press, Inc.

————. 1989. *The American Evasion of Philosophy: A Genealogy of Pragmatism.* Madison, WI: The University of Wisconsin Press.

————. 1990. "With The People in Mind." *Emerge* 2 (1, October).

————. 1991. *The Ethical Dimensions of Marxist Thought.* New York: Monthly Review Press.

————. 1993a. *Race Matters.* Boston: Beacon Press.

————. 1993b. *Keeping Faith: Philosophy and Race in America.* New York: Routlege.

————. 1994. "Breaking Bread: A Multiracial Dialogue." *Democratic Left* (May/June).

————. 1996. "Toward a Socialist Theory of Racism." *DSA Home Page*, http://ccme-mac4.bsd.uchicage.edu/DSA Race/West (January 1).

Wieseltier, L. 1995. "The Unreal World of Cornel West: All and Nothing At All." *The New Republic* (March 6).

Willis, A.C. (ed.). 1996. *Faith of Our Fathers: African-American Men Reflect on Fatherhood.* New York: A Dutton Book.

# JAMES BALDWIN:

## THE FIRE NEXT TIME AND BLACK INTELLECTUALS

Rodney D. Coates and Sandra Lee Browning

*What it comes to, finally, is that the nation has spent a large part of its time and energy looking away from one of the principal facts of its life. This failure to look reality in the face diminishes a nation as it diminishes a person, and it can only be described as unmanly....Human freedom is a complex difficult-and private-thing. If we can liken life, for a moment, to a furnace, then freedom is the fire which burns away illusion. Any honest examination of the national life proves how far we are from the standard of human freedom...for the greatest achievements must begin somewhere, and they always begin with the person. If we are not capable of this examination, we may yet become one of the most distinguished and monumental failures in the history of nations [Baldwin 1959a].*

James Baldwin, viewed by many to be the heart and soul of the 1960s civil rights movement, captivated readers the world over with his ability to personalize and articulate racial strife in America. Baldwin,

Research in Race and Ethnic Relations, Volume 10, pages 87-114
Copyright © 1997 by JAI Press Inc.
All rights of reproduction in any form reserved.
ISBN: 0-7623-0275-5

whose writing career started in 1944, was a product of American Apartheid. Growing up in Harlem, he learned about America from literally the "bottom of the well." Baldwin's works brilliantly articulated black hopes and dreams, disappointments and frustrations, coping strategies and plans. Few American writers, black or white, have known the fame or the infamy, the adulation or the condemnation, the respect or the contempt of James Baldwin. Variously described as being both prophet and heretic, poet and scoundrel, pacifist and activist, equivocal and ambivalent, Baldwin remains one of those paradoxical figures that defies categorization. Even now, after death, his spirit through more than 40 years of essays, novels, plays, and critiques refuses to be silent. Baldwin was the water that soothed a troubled black psyche; he was also the raging fire that rose from the centuries of racial duplicity and hatred. The purpose of this paper is to examine Baldwin's intellectual contribution to this nation and his people. As such it will also explore the process of self-actualization and proactitivity so evident in his writing.

## COMING OF AGE

Born in Harlem, on August 2, 1924, James Arthur Baldwin died on November 20, 1987. The eldest of nine children, he anticipated, chronicled and outlived the civil rights activism of the 1950s and 1960s. His stepfather, a store front preacher, demanded extreme religious rigor from his nine children. Although Baldwin would initially follow the path of his stepfather into the ministry and even serve for a brief time as teen preacher at the Fireside Pentecostal Church in Harlem. Baldwin never fully embraced either his stepfather or the apocalyptic religion which was central to that ministry. (Baldwin 1955) The tension produced by these ambivalent relationships, between his stepfather and religion, ultimately would be played out in the best of Baldwin's writing.

Baldwin, graduating from high school in 1942, left the church and his community to settle in Greenwich Village. Forced, by the death of his stepfather, to help support his brothers and sisters, Baldwin obtained a job in the defense industry in Belle Meade, New Jersey. It was here that the writer would come into contact with the full extent of America's racism, discrimination, and have to endure the stigma of segregation. Reflexively, Baldwin reports, whites responded to his color. Baldwin, always somewhat arrogant, by white standards, soon became a marked man and soon thereafter was out of work.

After a series of odd jobs, from waiter to messenger, his luck began to change. He met Richard Wright in 1944 who would, in 1945, help him obtain the Eugene F. Saxton fellowship. Ostensibly the fellowship was to aid the young writer to finish his first novel. Even though this would make him financially independent, he nevertheless could not complete the novel he had begun. Increasingly he felt stifled even as his essays and short stories were being published in such periodicals as the *Nation*, *New Leader* and *Commentary*. Eventually, Baldwin moved to the south of France in 1948, in search of freedom. During this period he would meet and becomes friends with Jean-Paul Sartre, Saul Bellow, Norman Mailer, Josephine Baker and Marlon Brando. Slowly through essays and book reviews, James Baldwin climbed the literary ladder of success. Living in isolated Swiss mountain retreats such as the American writers colonies at MacDowell and Yaddo, over the next three years Baldwin would produce his first three novels.

These novels had one consistent theme, individual responsibility. To a great extent they reflect Baldwin's search for his own identity.

I left America because I doubted my ability to survive the fury of the color problem (t)here....I wanted to prevent myself from becoming merely a Negro; or, even, merely a Negro writer. I wanted to find out in what way the specialness of my experience could be made to connect me with other people instead of dividing me from them (Baldwin 1959b).

Although Baldwin's search lead him to discover Africa and the Third World. This discovery rather than leading him to embrace a sort of of Pan-Africanism, in fact served to reaffirm his American identity. This must have seemed a strange farce to the young writer, having escaped America just to rediscover it, in himself, in a strange land. The farce, however cruel, served to radicalize and inspire this black intellectual.

Nowhere is this best seen then his first novel *Go Tell It on the Mountain* published in 1953. This novel, part autobiographical and part fictional, examined the crises of identity and becoming for the black individual and community. *Go Tell It on the Mountain*, and those that would follow, provided the reader an intimate portrait of black existence which combined Henry James' stream-of-consciousness with Hemingway's penchant for understatement (Powers 1984). The novel ends prophetically by calling blacks, through the central character, to leave behind the shackles of their racial past and venture into a new world determined by their own efforts. His call, a theme which runs throughout his works, was for proactive responses rather than knee-jerk reactivity. For Baldwin, this proactive black was the key to self-actualization and realization which ultimately would open the doors to freedom and being.

## THE BLACK INTELLECTUAL CONFRONTING REALITY

The black intellectual is at once both visionary and radical. The crucible which produces this complex mixture is structured by centuries of denial, ignorance and the constancy of racial bigotry. Baldwin understood this crucible and understood that only freedom could break the chains which it produced. In *Go Tell It On the Mountain* we observe this basic theme. In many ways the book, while allowing Baldwin to analyze his relationship with his stepfather, proved to be more than a trip down memory lane. As observed by Allen (1975) "The central action of the novel is John's initiation into manhood—a ritual symbolization of the psychological step from dependence to a sense of self." Foster asserts that John's conversion allows him to accept his blackness and with this acceptance he gains a newfound freedom. John "finds grace not in rejecting blackness but in seeking it the only way it is available to him—as a black man" (1971).

The difficulties facing blacks in general and the black intellectual in particular continued to be the central theme through such early works as *Notes of a Native Son* (1955), *Nobody Knows My Name* (1961), *Another Country* (1962), *The Fire Next Time* (1963a), and *The Amen Corner* (1968). In these volumes Baldwin provided a clear and unique view of the problems faced by black Americans. The urgency of his message in these text prophetically warned America of the consequences of ignoring the increasing black rage he observed in urban centers. America, either black or white, with its history of innuendo and complacency was not yet ready for the literary realism provided by Baldwin.

From Baldwin's first essays this literary realism provided one of the first, if not last, truly critical appraisal of America, its major black and white institutions, and its political and intellectual leaders of his day. Oddly enough, while his brutal honesty in these essays would open the doors of the white literary establishment—as witnessed not only by publications but also by such prestigious awards as the Eugene F. Saxton fellowship in 1945, the Rosenwald fellowship in 1948, the Guggenheim fellowship in 1954, and in 1956 he received a fellowship from the Partisan Review, a grant from literature from the National Institute of the Arts and Letters and the National Institute of Arts and Letters Award—it would be castigated by many in the black civil rights community. As observed by Gates:

> If Baldwin had once served as a shadow delegate for black America in the congress of culture, his term had expired. Soldiers, not delegates, were what was wanted these days. "Pulling rank," Eldridge Cleaver wrote in his essay on Baldwin, "is a very dangerous business, especially when the troops have mutinied and the basis of one's authority, or rank, is devoid of that interdictive power and has become suspect." he found in Baldwin's work "the most grueling, agonizing, total hatred of the blacks, particularly of himself, and the most shameful, fanatical, fawning, sycophantic love of the whites that one can find in any black American writer of note in our time." According to Amiri Baraka, the new star of the Black Arts Movement, Baldwin was Joan of Arc of the cocktail party. "His spavined whine and plea" was—"sickening beyond belief." In the eyes of the young Ismael Reed, he was "a hustler who comes on like job" (Gates 1992).

Was Baldwin essentially a "hustler" who earned a living by pimping blacks and loving whites, or is this the price that one pays for intellectual realism and honest critique? Why would he be so loved by those who he constantly criticized and so hated by those whom he spent a lifetime loving? Perhaps answers can be found in his essays.

Baldwin began writing essays as a means of survival. They literally paid the rent and put food on his table, and ultimately opened the door to the literary world. He was paid from 10 to 20 dollars for each essay, at first mostly book reviews by the *New Leader*. During this early period, while identifying himself as a socialist, he became incensed with the paternalism found in many of the books and novels dealing with people of color. These book, characterizing the black as victim, Baldwin would argue, would merely serve to guarantee the status quo. What was needed were insightful critiques of the black situation which pointed out not only the problems but also the sources, both internal and external, of these problems in the black community. West, echoing Baldwin came to remarkably similar conclusions, argued:

> Like all Americans, African-Americans are influenced greatly by the images of comfort, convenience, machismo, femininity, violence, and sexual stimulation that bombard consumers. These seductive images contribute to the predominance of the market-inspired way of life over all others and thereby edge out nonmarket values-love, care, service to others-handed down by preceding generations (West 1994).

Most damaged by these negative influences are those living in extreme conditions of poverty who have "limited capacity to ward off self-contempt and self-hatred." The net result is the production of what West refers to as pockets of 'collective clinical depression' particular seen in poorer black communities (West 1994).

When the church and other social institutions no longer function as buffers to these negative images and values, explains West, we observe the development of nihilistic threats to self and community identity. Baldwin, writing at what had to be the beginning of this process, cogently discusses the debilitating effects upon the black community.

These themes lay at the heart of Baldwin's early essays. For example, one of the first essays Baldwin would see published was his 1948 article entitled "The Harlem Ghetto" which appeared in *Commentary*. Through his words the reader senses a sort of realism as they are at once transported to this place and time.

> All of Harlem is pervaded by a sense of congestion, rather like the insistent, maddening, claustrophobic pounding in the skull that comes from trying to breathe in a very small room with all the windows shut (Baldwin 1948).

This essay, highly critical of black politicians, the black press, and the black community in general certainly made no friends within that or the larger black community of America. Baldwin does more then provide description, he also reveals the underlying causes of these surface conditions. Thus, "The Harlem Ghetto" could be viewed as a sociological analysis of the Harlem community.

The Harlem ghetto was a contrived community controlled and manipulated by a "social(ly) hostile" municipal power structure. Baldwin argues that the black rage which produced the violence of the mid 1930s and 1940s was only met by band-aid solutions and window dressings.

If an outbreak of more than usual violence occurs, as in 1935 or in 1943, it is met with sorrow and surprise and rage; the social hostility of the rest of the city feeds on this as proof that they were right all along, and the hostility increases; speeches are made, committees are set up, investigations ensue. Steps are taken to right the wrong, without, however, expanding or demolishing the ghetto. The idea is to make it less of a social liability, a process about as helpful as make-up to a leper. Thus, we have the Boys' Club on West 134th Street, the playground at West 131st and Fifth Avenue; and...a housing project called Riveton in the center of Harlem... (Baldwin 1948).

Neither the black press or political leaders were particularly effective in the eyes of Baldwin. Both, "perpetually embattled," were at worst inept, co-opted, or self serving, or at best basically powerless pawns in a game where the rules were in constant flux and determined by external players.

That is, Negro leaders have been created by the American scene, which thereafter works against them at every point; and the best that they can hope for is ultimately to work themselves out of their jobs, to nag contemporary American leaders and the members of their own group until a bad situation becomes so complicated and so bad that it cannot be endured any longer...(S)ome Negro leaders and politicians are far more concerned with their careers than with the welfare of Negroes, and their dramatic and publicized battles are battles with the wind. Again, this phenomenon cannot be changed without a change in the American scene (Baldwin 1948).

His comments regarding the Black press were even less flattering. The Black press, according to Baldwin, had little to do with actual news and more to do with sensationalism devoting most of its columns to "murders, rapes, raids on love-nests, interracial wars, any item-however meaningless-concerning prominent Negroes, and whatever racial gains can be reported for the week-all in just about that order" (Baldwin 1948). While this policy did result in a tremendous readership it did little to either raise substantive issues or provide solutions to critical problems. It should be understood, that while critical of the Black press, Baldwin nevertheless concluded that it was merely a product of this particular social-historical moment and as such mirrored the major print media of the day.

It is not the Negro press that is at fault; whatever contradictions, inanities, and political infantilism can be charged to it can be charged equally to the American press at large. It is a black man's newspaper straining for recognition

and a foothold in the white man's world. Matters are not helped in the least
by the fact that the white man's world, intellectually, morally, and spiritually,
has the meaningless ring of a hollow drum and the odor of slow death (Baldwin
1948).

No sociological analysis of a community would be complete
without consideration of the its religious institutions and values. Here
Baldwin demonstrates considerable keenness as he debunks the
conventual wisdom of the day by declaring that the black church
provides more than just "childlike emotional release." He argues that
the principal purpose of religion within the ghetto functions as a
"complete and exquisite fantasy revenge." The church, rather than
being the opiate keeping the people happy and complacent as
suggested by Marx, was a very real and concrete way of analyzing
and coping with everything from black rage, racial injustice, war, and
the insanity of western existence.

It does not require a spectacular degree of perception to realize that bitterness
is here neither dead nor sleeping, and that the white man, believing what he
wishes to believe, has misread the symbols...quite often the Negro preacher
descends to levels less abstract and leaves no doubt as to what is on his mind;
the pressure of life in Harlem, the conduct of the Italian-Ethiopian war, racial
injustice during the recent war, and the terrible possibility of yet another very
soon. All these topics provide excellent springboards for sermons thinly coated
with spirituality but designed mainly to illustrate the injustice of the white
American and anticipate his certain and long overdue punishment (Baldwin
1948).

Baldwin increasingly became more and more critical of religion
and doctrinal representations of God. While, many would come to
view this critical appraisal of religion as a rejection of religion, others
saw it as a strong endorsement of the basic tenets and beliefs of
Christianity. Such simplification, as observed by Lynch (1993)
ignores not only the complexity but also the subtlety of Baldwin's
writing. Baldwin, objecting to the image of an unforgiving God of
hate, revenge, and destruction, sought to reveal how such beliefs
could be extremely damaging to people, especially those who already
suffer from low self-worth and self love. "People," he asserted. "ought
to love the Lord because they loved Him, and not because they were
afraid of going to Hell" (Baldwin 1962). Baldwin also objected to
the pervasive sense of doom and punishment that further served to

promote fear, spitefulness, and the inability to forgive oneself. Such a God preyed on the weak, subjected them to continuous feeling of insecurity and guilt. From such a God a people could never achieve victory for their fate was already sealed and predetermined. The image that such a God evokes, Baldwin suggests is one where:

> There was no love in the church. It was a mask for hatred and self-despair. When we were told to love everybody, I had thought that meant everybody. But no. It applied only to those who believed as we did, and it did not apply to white people at all (Baldwin 1963).

Envisioning the infinite possibilities of another God, one of love and forgiveness, Baldwin argued that many who claimed to be Christians were indeed betraying the first principles of Christianity.

> I understand...that all men are the sons of God and that all men are free in the eyes of God..."We shall overcome," and meaning it and believing it, doing day by day and hour by hour precisely what the Christian Church is supposed to do, to walk from door to door, to feed the hungry, to speak to those who are oppressed, to try to open the gates of prison for all those who are imprisoned (Baldwin 1968).

As a consequence, America's and the church's inability to practice what it preached—equality and justice for all or basic love—lied at the root of most of the problems of both. Baldwin equated the black ghetto with America's lack of morality. Thus, the ghetto was like a litmus test for America in general. It was essentially the ontological and phenomenological consequences of racism, bigotry and evidence of moral decline of the Nation. As explained by Lynch (1993) throughout Baldwin's novels, the pathologies evidenced in most of his characters derived from an imperfect conceptualization of a basically Old Testament God who threatened, punished, condemned and intimidated. The psychological trauma produced by this is seen in terms of anger, fear, disgust, and guilt in these characters.

Baldwin would repeatedly revisit this theme as he attempted to discover and define what may be termed a contemporary God. This contemporary God was one of freedom not subjugation, one of joy and not sadness and one of love not hate.

> To be with God is really to be involved with some enormous, overwhelming desire, and joy, and power which you cannot control, which controls you.

I conceive of my own life as a journey toward something I do not understand,
which in the going towards, makes me better. I conceive of God, in fact, as
a means of liberation and not a means to control others (Baldwin 1960).

## RADICAL RELIGION, CIVIL RIGHTS, AND PROACTIVE LEADERS

Balwin's preeminence as an intellectual was assured when the New
Yorker serialized the *Fire Next Time* (1963). Baldwin believed that
only by critically analyzing and understanding the dynamics of race
and racism as moral problems could America assure equality and
freedom for all of its peoples. Here the reader will also find his
musings regarding the inadequacy of American race relations and
personal reflections as to how these forces effected his own
development as a Harlem youth. Through these writings Baldwin
continues his journey into discovery, not only of his people and
country but also himself. And through this journey he found sanity
in an insane world. This collection of essays held back nothing as
it critically appraised white America and racism, the Black Muslim
movement and its founder Elijah Mohammed, and predicted the
black rage which would soon engulf the country if calls for social
justice went unheard from the nation's dispossessed.

In examining the Nation of Islam and the teachings of Elijah
Mohammed, Baldwin looked for promise but only saw pipe-dreams,
looked for love but only saw hate, and looked for redemption but
only saw condemnation. He had hoped that such a movement would
help a demoralized people realize their own self-worth, their own self-
destiny, and their own identity. Unfortunately, he saw a movement
built on racial hatred, fueled by lies, and propagated by a theology
of despair and victim hood. Baldwin writes extensively of a meeting
he had with Elijah Mohammed in which the founder of the Nation
of Islam lays out the basic premises of his movement:

> Elijah's mission is to return "the so-called Negro" to Islam, to separate the
> chosen of Allah from this doomed nation. Furthermore, the white man
> knows...himself to be a devil, and knows that his time is running out, and
> all his technology, psychology, science, and "tricknology" are being expended
> in the effort to prevent black men from hearing the truth. The truth is (that
> the) Blackmen ruled the earth and the black man was perfect....They want
> black men to believe that they, like white men, once lived in caves and swung
> from trees and ate their meet raw...Allah allowed the Devil, through his

scientists, to carry on infernal experiments, which resulted, even more disastrously, in the creation of the white woman (Baldwin 1962).

Baldwin reasoned that this formulation represented nothing new within the rhetoric of the oppressed save "explicitness of its symbols and the candor of its hatred." Accordingly, throughout American history, whites were cast as the chief cause black suffering and consequently the chief agent of evil. In a society in which blacks and people of color have historically been discriminated against, segregated, abused and hated it is difficult to distinguish paranoia from real dangers. When one ceases, as argued by Baldwin, to make the distinction between paranoia and real threats all are evil and all are seen as enemies. It then becomes very easy by those oppressed to adopt the same type of lies that have been used to oppress them but this time reserving all good to ones own group and vest all evil into the other. Is not this the very same lie which was used by white racist to justify oppression of blacks? Blacks are not to be loved by mere virtue of their being black, but because they were human. If there were problems which need to be addressed within the black and other oppressed communities, they need to be addressed not because they are black problems but because they are problems of humanity.

This country was, however, not ready for such realism especially from a black intellectual. To be a black intellectual in America, Baldwin argued, requires constant apology as one is continuously being challenged to demonstrate their authenticity. America with its overtly anti-intellectual bias, was especially critical of black intellectuals. In many ways this bias is based on the irrational fear of presumed subversive intents of the intellectual. For the black intellectual, as observed by Baldwin and countless others, this results in the tendency to label and in the process ghettoize nonwhite scholars. We therefore have the classics and then black or women classics, we have great works of art and then we have black or Hispanic art, we have sociology and then there is black or feminist sociology. This places a tremendous burden on the ability of such scholars to develop the full potential of their creative capacity. Unfortunately, when such an Herculean effort is achieved, these great artists, thinkers or scholars are explained away as merely exceptions (Baldwin 1959b).

The history of America is the history of not only these exceptions but of these people who have been defined, castigated, subjugated and relegated to the margins of our national psyche or is its psychosis.

> The (Black) in America, gloomily referred to as that shadow which lies athwart our national life, is far more than that. He is a series of shadows, self-created, intertwining, which now we helplessly battle....He is a social and not a personal or a human problem; to think of him is to think of statistics, slums, rapes, injustice, remote violence; it is to be confronted with an endless cataloguing of losses, gains, skirmishes; it is to feel virtuous, outraged, helpless, as though his continuing status among us were somehow analogous to a disease...which must be checked, even though it cannot be cured (Baldwin 1951).

Ultimately Baldwin would argue that any insult borne by blacks for being blacks were insults attacking the national identity as well, any loss of freedom (regardless of how small) results in a collective loss by us all, and the dehumanization of blacks resulted in the dehumanization of America. Rawls philosophically argued that these principles constitute the basis of social justice. He asserted that the level of freedom and justice present within a society should be measured by how it treats it lowest citizens (Rawls 1971).

Although one could identify countless examples of this process of dehumanization, Baldwin argued that "...nowhere is this more apparent than in our literature on the subject—'problem' literature when written by whites, 'protest' literature when written by Negroes." (Baldwin 1951). While these two traditions represent almost extremes where in the former Blacks are castigated as being simple, vile, and disreputable, in the latter Blacks as victims are excused for such. They have been equally praised by critics for essentially the same reasons. Herein lies their problem as explained by Baldwin, they both suggest, at their core, that to be born black is the worst thing that can happen to an individual. Both traditions imply that blacks have no agency or free will, that they are either naturally or by virtue of their circumstances forced to succumb, subvert, and destroy.

It was this line of thinking which led Baldwin to ultimately cast both Harriet Beecher Stowe and her *Uncle Tom's Cabin* and his former mentor Richard Wright and his *Native Son* into the same category of protest or victim literature. In both there is an attempt to assert the victim status of the oppressed and by so doing help them gain greater freedom. What they lack in literary style, historical accuracy, or realism, Baldwin chided, they gain in missionary zeal.

> Thus the African, exile, pagan, hurried off he auction block and into the fields, fell on his knees before that God in Whom he must now believe; who had

made him, but not in His own image. This tableau, this impossibility, is the heritage of the Negro in America: "Wash me," cried the slave to his Maker, "and I shall be whiter, whiter than snow!" For black is the color of evil; only the robes of the saved are white (Baldwin 1949).

Such an attitude, reflected in so-called classics, merely added wires to the cage which encapsulated blacks. Life and its struggles for were reduced to tragedy that even in death there was no salvation. He is denied in one fell action his ancestry and his reality, she is bereft of purpose or control, they are the brutal creations of myth and fantasy. Baldwin rejected this myth and argued that humanity cannot be created or bestowed but must be realized. And ultimately accepted.

The failure of the protest novel lies in its rejection of life, the human being, the denial of (their beauty, dread, power, in its insistence that it is his categorization alone which is real and which cannot be transcended (Baldwin 1949).

Mellowed by time, Baldwin did reevaluate Richard Wright's *Native Sun* and consequently to recast his criticism of the book. An argument had been made that Baldwin had misread and thus unduly criticized Wright's work. Wright, it was argued, was using the character Bigger Thomas to represent the symbolic creation of black by a white-racist America. Baldwin countered, that if this indeed was the case then Bigger Thomas might represent the new black full of rage that through his actions frees himself violently from the chains of his oppression. But this would be really stretching the story. Even if this were the case, Baldwin argue, then the case was still weak. If, Bigger Thomas reflected this new black, then he also reflected both the guilt and fear of blacks represented in American society. Such a black however asserted Baldwin represented nothing either to be feared or given validity. The representation merely confirms the judgment that he should be condemned to die.

To present Bigger as a warning is simply to reinforce the American guilt and fear concerning him, it is most forcefully to limit him to that previously mentioned social arena in which he has no human validity, it is simply to condemn him to death. For he has always been a warning, he represents the evil, the sin and suffering which we are compelled to reject (Baldwin 1951).

Consequently, we through Wright's *Native Son* do not discover anything new, we are once again confronted by a creation of white racist myths, stereotypes and of course guilt. It would have been genius if Wright could have developed these themes, they however exists through speculation. Wright ignores or rather evades these implications and thus provides nothing new to the discourse. Baldwin observed that violence was the chief medium of expression for all too many black writers, including Wright. Such violence, appearing gratuitous and compulsive, never actually gets analyzed or consequently understood. Baldwin argued that at the core of this violence was rage produced by the social castration of the American black.

> Thus, when in Wright's pages a Negro male is found hacking a white woman to death, the very gusto with which this is done, and the great attention paid to the details of physical destruction reveal a terrible attempt to break out of the cage in which the American imagination has imprisoned him for so long (Baldwin 1961a).

Baldwin wanted to remove the veil of intellectual complacency and complicity in this myth. He wanted intellectual realism to dominate writing about the American black, a realism which would destroy the distortions and debasement associated with this identity and show the real, the humane that is manifested in the daily lives of blacks everywhere.

The journey into discovery always begins with the person in the mirror. Baldwin discovered that by embracing his own blackness, he embraced himself. For all too long, it seems, he would repeatedly argue, to be black meant either constant denial or rejection. Through denial the black is cut adrift, isolated and subsequently ignored, while rejection only produces frustration, anxiety and ultimately paranoia. Either way oppression serves "to destroy (blacks) sense of reality."

> In the case of the American Negro, from the moment you are born every stick and stone, every face, is white. Since you have not yet seen a mirror, you suppose you are too. It comes as a great shock around the age of five, six, or seven to discover that the flag to which you have pledged allegiance, along with everybody else, has not pledged allegiance to you. It comes as a great shock to see Gary cooper killing off the Indians, and, although you are rooting for Gary Cooper, that the Indians are you (Baldwin 1965).

While biologists and anthropologists, educational and social statisticians, psychologists and criminologists would spend decades attempting to explain, extol and or identify the essence of blackness, Baldwin would argue that such an essence could only be found in the political. Racism stripped of its horror, ignoring the countless rapes and murders, lynchings and destructions, was and is about blatantly obtaining, manipulating and perpetuating power. This power constructed a diabolical systems of slavery, Jim Crow and segregation which built railroads and highways, picked cotton and planted tobacco, and laid the foundation for the American economy and Southern oligarchy. Internationally, western racism took the form of colonial imperialism, and perpetrated the same madness throughout Asia and Africa. Race, he came to understand, was neither a human or a personal reality, it was a political reality. For political reasons, such racial myths were constructed and utilized to oppress not only blacks but also unwitting poor whites.

> It is, of course, in the very nature of a myth that those who are its victims, and at the same time, its perpetrators, should...be rendered unable to examine the myth, or even to suspect, much less recognize, that it is a myth which controls and blasts their lives...The poor white was enslaved almost from the instant he arrived on these shores, and he is still enslaved by a brutal and cynical oligarchy. The utility of the poor white was to make slavery both profitable and save and, therefore, the germ of white supremacy...was made hideously to flourish in the American air. Two world wars and a worldwide depression have failed to reveal to this poor man that he has far more in common with the ex-slaves whom he fears than he has with the masters who oppress them both for profit (Baldwin 1964).

As the Civil Rights Movement took central stage in America, Baldwin became more and more aggressive in his writing and for a time his popularity soared. During this period three of his works, *Nobody Knows My Name, Another Country,* and *the Fire Next Time* had all been listed for several months on the New York Times bestseller list and had been translated in over a dozen different languages. Baldwin also had the distinct honor of seeing more than one of his plays produced on Broadway. *Blues for Mister Charlie* (1964), a dramatization of the events surrounding the cruel murder of Emmit Till, and *The Amen Corner* (1968), another exposition of Pentecostal religion, were Broadway successes which saw many revivals. In these plays, as with much of his other literary works, Baldwin deals with a number of themes which ranged from the historical and contemporary significance of black-white relations, personal and group identity as expressed in both sexual and social-psychological complexities and crises, the relationship between love and power in the structure of human existence, America's materialist foundations and how they tharwted moral development, and the responsibility of the intellectual to promote realism and truth in their work (Collier 1972).

Baldwin further argued that the black intellectual should help blacks change their relationship to material society. No longer was the black in America to be perceived as an object, controlled by the externalities of either fate or oppression. This does not mean that Baldwin dismissed the object, quite the contrary, he recognized that the process of objectification had underlying significance to the American psyche. By making this important discovery, Baldwin was able to shed light upon our ability to effectively deal with the race problem.

> But I have always been struck, in America, by an emotional poverty so bottomless, and a terror of human life, of human touch, so deep, that virtually no American appears able to achieve any viable, organic connection between his public stance and his private life…This failure of the private life has always had the most devastating effect on American public conduct, and on black-white relations (Baldwin 1971).

Because of this tremendous fear of their private selves, Baldwin argued that Americans invented "the Negro Problem" to serve not only as a scapegoat but also in order to guarantee their own purity. Sociologically, if you will, the function of Blacks in America was to provide an ultimate negative by which whites could gauge not only their humanity but also their civility. Thus, Blacks became the embodiment of evil, immorality, corruption, and indecency. Blacks, thereby constituting the bottom rung on the ladder of humanity, afforded whites a means for self justification and emulation. Baldwin demonstrated that white guilt and self-hatred were projected upon blacks making them simultaneously scapegoats and sacrificial lambs.

> That the scapegoat pays for the sins of others is well known, but this is only legend, and a revealing one at that. In fact, however the scapegoat may be made to suffer, his suffering cannot purify the sinner; it merely incriminates him the more, and it seals his damnation….The suffering of the scapegoat has resulted in seas of blood, and yet not one sinner has been saved, or changed, by this despairing ritual. Sin has merely been added to sin, and guilt piled upon guilt (Baldwin 1971).

Frantz Fanon three years later would come to remarkably similar conclusions. He argued that irrational levels of fear and loathing associated with both anti-Semitism and racism could be traced to a type of substitutive neurosis. This particular form of neurosis is where the fears of inferiority, impotence, inadequacy becomes substituted or mirrored in the other. Fanon, using Freudian psychology, goes one step further in arguing that these ethnic and racial phobias may indeed be unresolved sexual frustrations or fantasies which are proscribed by social conventions. Hence, race represents such a personal bias by which racists attempt to construct some sort of defense against their own perversions. Fanon argues:

> Granted that unconscious tendencies toward incest exists, why should these tendencies emerge more particularly with respect to the Negro? In what way, taken as an absolute, does a black son-in-law differ from a white son-in law? Is there not a reaction of unconscious tendencies in both cases? Why not, for instance, conclude that the father revolts because in his opinion the Negro will introduce his daughter into a sexual universe for which the father does not have the key, the weapons, or the attributes (Fanon 1967).

Blacks viewed thusly represent the terrible unknown monster which lurks in our individual and collective consciousness. Embodied in this monster are all the fears, anxieties and evils that civilization requires us to repress. But total repression is not accomplished for they are conveniently projected upon Blacks and others deemed "untouchable" by dominant society.

> The civilized white man retains an irrational longing for unusual eras of sexual license, of orgiastic scenes, of unpunished rapes, of unrepressed incest. In one way these fantasies respond to Freud's life instinct. Projecting his own desires onto the Negro, the white man behaves "as if" the Negro really had them. When it is a question of the Jew, the problem is clear: He is suspect because he wants to own the wealth or take over the positions of power. But the Negro is fixated at the genital; or at any rate he has been fixated there (Fanon 1967).

Baldwin became convinced that this genital fixation lay at the root of the Atlanta child murders. His interests was so strong in this case that he returned from his self-imposed exile to try to understand what, outside of the obvious race, factors connected the 23 murders. Baldwin saw more than coincidence in the fact that these assaults took place in Atlanta. For as observed by Baldwin, many Georgian blacks took pride in identifying as reflected in the statement "I'm not from Georgia. I'm from Atlanta" (Baldwin 1985). Atlanta, as explained by Patricia Turner, was centrally important to southern blacks because it was:

> The city that Sherman burned during the Civil War, in which Booker T. Washington delivered his racially self-effacing compromise speech of 1895, and that witnessed several of the most bitter civil rights confrontations in the 1960s, had by 1979 emerged as a particularly comfortable environment for blacks (Turner 1993).

Atlanta was the truly new south for blacks, the place where the new black could be successful. Desegregation of the city had allowed a sizable black middle class community not only to come into being but also to thrive. It was the center of black intellectual developments that boasted not only W. E. B. Du Bois but also Martin Luther King. It especially represented the spiritual center of the civil rights movement and the brightest gem of on the civil rights crown. Atlanta demonstrated what blacks could do if racism was removed. Although the subsequent indictment and conviction of Waine Williams would prove Baldwin wrong in this connection, the promises behind his reasoning are still quite telling as they suggest an important causal link to understanding America's preoccupation with race (Turner 1993).

Intellectuals throughout the ages, whether they were called prophets or poets, activists or artists, have characteristically been castigated by their peers. They exists, as Baldwin explained, in a state of aloneness where like lepers even their best friends often shun their presence. This aloneness "is much more like the aloneness of birth or death. It is like the fearful aloneness that one sees in the eyes of someone who is suffering, whom we cannot help" (Baldwin 1962b). This aloneness is brought about for the sheer fact that the intellectual chooses or is forced to see past the illusions that make our lives so comfortable. We want our artists and intellectuals to, explained Du Bois, uplift the race by highlighting only that which is good and lie to us about that which is bad.

> We want everything that is said about us to tell of the best and highest and noblest in us. We insist that our Art and Propaganda be one. We fear that evil in us will be called racial while in others it is viewed as individual. We fear that our shortcomings are not merely human but foreshadowing and threatenings of disaster and failure (Du Bois 1946).

We, as social animals, tend to perpetuate all manor of myths, stereotypes, and convenient distortions of the past in order not to deal with the reality of our existence, our past or the uncertainties of the future. Hence, every child in America knows of how George Washington cut down the mythical cherry tree, or how Abe Lincoln could not tell a lie, or how Daniel Boone hunted down bear with his buoy knife. We teach our kids of the savage "injuns" and how in search of freedom the "Puritans" and others chose to settle in the America first "discovered" by Christopher Columbus. These myths protect a certain image, provide a certain level of comfort and help us avoid the chaos that many suppose would come with truth.

> It is for this reasons that all societies have battled with that incorrigible disturber of the peace-the artists. I doubt that future societies will get on with him any better. The entire purpose of society is to create a bulwark against the inner and the outer chaos, in order to make life bearable and to keep the human race alive (Baldwin 1962b).

Ellison would argue that the tremendous amount of energy it takes to deal with this chaos prohibited many blacks from developing either their artistic or intellectual capabilities. Blacks, he argued, "not quite citizens and yet Americans, full of the tensions of modern man, but regarded as primitives" were in a desperate search for identity. An identity which must be bolstered by "slum-shocked" institutions (Ellison 1964).

Faced with family disintegration, church splintering, decreasing reliance upon folk wisdom or customs the only image held out to blacks by white racists was that of Uncle Tom. The Uncle Tom myth was such a reliable friend to southern racists because he was essentially a sexless saint with the power to absolve racist of their duplicity.

> In a way, if the Negro were not here, we might be forced to deal within ourselves and our own personalities, with all those vices, all those conundrums, and all these mysteries with which we have invested the Negro race. Uncle Tom is, for example, if he is called uncle, a kind of saint. He is there, he endures, he will forgive us, and this is a key to that image. But if he is not uncle, if he is merely Tom, he is a danger to everybody. He will wreak havoc on the countryside. When he is Uncle Tom he has no sex-when he is Tom, he does-and this obviously says much more about he people who invented this myth than it does about the people who are the object of it. (Baldwin 1960).

An empowered Black represented something new in America and something greatly feared by racists. A black who no longer felt guilt about their blackness, or subservient because of their blackness, or shamed by their blackness represented Baldwin's new black. Critical in the development of this new black were the teachers charged with molding young minds. As explained by Baldwin, the chief goal of education was to prepare a new generation to assume the roles assigned to it by society. This however represents a paradox. On the one hand, the role of education is to prepare an individual to become consciously aware and a critical appraiser of information. But society insists that the chief role of education is to produce persons capable of performing specific tasks and occupy specified roles. But such programming goes against the first principle. If the educational institutions are successful in producing a person who views existence for themselves, asks questions of their existence, and able to live with both the questions and the answers, then there is a great likelihood that they will also question and identify problems within society.

> The purpose of education...is to create a person the ability to look at the world for himself, to make his own decisions...(and in this) way achieves his own identity. But no society is really anxious to have that kind of person anxious to have that kind of person around. What societies really, ideally, want is a citizenry which will simply obey the rules of society (Baldwin 1963b).

Those blacks, traditionally educated in America, cannot help but be not only mis-educated as asserted by Woodson, but argues Baldwin, also schizophrenic. On the one hand, such a child is brought up believing in the American dream of freedom and justice, while on the other, they are assured that not only have they never made any contribution but that they will never make a contribution to civilization. While he learns to dream of the promise, he is constantly bombarded with the reality of his experience. Children, impressionable creatures that they are, soon learn that their place has been assigned not among the stars and crystal palaces but on the streets and in ghettos. Baldwin urged educators and schools to break this chain, to take on the challenge in the creation of a new black identity. The development of this new black represented, as argued by Baldwin a new era for blacks and America. This new development:

> [Represented]...the end of the Negro situation in this country, as we have so far known it. Any effort, from here on out, to keep the Negro in his "place"

can only have the most extreme and unlucky repercussions. This being so, it would seem to me that the most intelligent effort we can now make is to give up this doomed endeavor and study how we can most quickly end this division in our house...If we are not able, and quickly, to face and begin to eliminate the sources of this discontent in our own country, we will never be able to do it on the stage of the world (Baldwin 1961b).

For Baldwin the only real answer to this dilemma rested in teachers willing to teach the historical truth which would allow blacks to achieve dignity, self-love and self-awareness.

Now if I were a teacher...I would try to teach them...that those streets, those houses, those dangers, those agonies by which they are surrounded, are criminal. I would try to make each child know that these things are the results of a criminal conspiracy to destroy him. I would teach him that if he intends to get to be a man, he must at once decide that he is stronger than this conspiracy and that he must never make his peace with it. And that one of his weapons for refusing to make his peace with it and for destroying it depends on what he decides he is worth (Baldwin 1963b).

Any type of social action aimed at ameliorating the problems created for Blacks in America requires knowledge. Unfortunately, merely knowing is not enough, one must be willing to act upon such knowledge. A commitment to act, as argued by Baldwin, automatically targets the individual both within but external to the specific community (Baldwin 1962c). Consequently, both teachers and students, could not achieve this monumental task alone, they would have to be aided by courageous leaders able to get past traditional ways of doing, acting and being. Only through such a process of collaboration and transcendence, Baldwin would argue, could we hope to overcome the barriers of ignorance, complacency, and despair.

The paradox—and a fearful paradox it is—is that the American (Black) can have no future anywhere, on any continent, as long as he is unwilling to accept his past. To accept one's past—one's history—is not the same thing as drowning in it; it is learning how to use it. An invented past can never be used; it cracks and crumbles under the pressures of life like clay in a season of drought. How can the American (Black's) past be used? The unprecedented price demanded—and at this embattled hour of the world's history—is the transcendence of the realities of color, of nations, and of altars (Baldwin 1962a).

It would be more than 30 years before another black intellectual would call for the such a transcendence. Cornel West, much like Baldwin, argued that race based or race effacing leaders and intellectuals represented a problematic that actually stood in the way of resolving problems of racism and oppression. What is needed, asserts West, are leaders capable of advancing a position because of its moral or humane qualities. As West argued:

> Gone are the days when black political leaders jockey for label "president of black America," or when black intellectuals pose as the "writers of black America," The days of brokering for the black turf...are over. To be a serious black leader is to be a race-transcending prophet who critiques the powers that be (including the black component of the Establishment) and who puts forward a vision of fundamental change for all who suffer from socially induced misery (West 1994).

Baldwin in his search for such leaders identified both Malcolm X and Martin Luther King, Jr. These two leaders, coming from opposite ends of the political and religious spectrum, not only captivated the Nation but Baldwin as well. By the time Baldwin met Malcolm X, Baldwin was being cast as an integrationists and Malcolm a racist. Such simplicity, needed by a media dependent upon sensationalization and 60 second sound-bites, did either justice. For Baldwin, Malcolm was a man determined to empower his people and bitter at their treatment in America. Accordingly, Baldwin stated that:

> Malcolm considered himself to be the spiritual property of the people who produced him. He did not consider himself to be their savior, he was far to modest for that...but he considered himself to be their servant...Malcolm was not a racist...His intelligence was more complex than that; furthermore, if he had been a racist...He would have sounded familiar and even comforting, his familiar rage confirming the reality of white power... (Baldwin 1972).

The power that Malcolm X held, Baldwin explained, was not his hatred for whites but his tremendous love for blacks and his willingness to put his life on the line because of such. Malcolm was a threat because he intelligently perceived the that only revolutionary transformations of the American society could lead to the freeing of blacks. Recognizing that such a revolution would not take place, Malcolm did not believe that integration would work. How could he trust the intentions of a country that had a history of broken promises, halfhearted attempts at reconciliation, and racism. But Malcolm, believing that America was a house on fire argued who would want to be integrated into a "burning house." Malcolm called for a type of black nationalism which would counter the Americanism which had made victims of 22 million blacks. Rather than the American dream he spoke of the American nightmare. Repeatedly he emphasized the process by which racism had not served to cripple but also brainwash blacks. He urged blacks to radically change their thinking, to develop a new identity based upon black pride, African identity, and self-reliance and control of their own destinies. Malcolm's dominant themes, more and more socialistic, spoke directly to the needs of the majority of blacks who existed in poverty. Malcolm articulated the rage and the frustration for an increasingly hostile contingent of blacks. His rhetoric, extremely hostile against whites and America, uncompromisingly assaulted the complacency that had existed for so long. Whites, for the first time, were forced to hear and read of this brutally frank ambassador from the Nation of Islam. In Baldwin's *The Fire Next Time*, whites were essentially being asked to choose between Malcolm and Martin, between rage or compromise. But a choice, however painful, that America could no longer put off.

> The Muslims do not expect anything at all from the white people of this country. They do not believe that the American professions of democracy or equality have ever been even remotely sincere. They insist on the total separation of the races. This is to be achieved by the acquisition of land from the United States-land which is owed the Negroes as "back wages" for the labor wrested from them when they were slaves, and for their unrecognized and unhonored contributions to the wealth and power of this country (Baldwin 1961c).

While Baldwin admired Malcolm's intellect, courage and determination he nevertheless did not believe that such a solution was politically viable. America, he reasoned, would never give up its land to anyone much less to blacks. He also had doubts if such a strategy, separation, was economically feasible. Where would the trade, investment, and development partners come—Baldwin would ask. Certainly if history provides any indications, the only land America may be forced to give up would be certain to be void of any political, natural, or economic resources necessary to sustain a peoples autonomy. Further, as with the case of Cuba, America would ensure that no sustainable investment or development capital would be available. Consequently, Baldwin reasoned that the only way to avoid open race war and realizable solutions to the problems of black liberation lay in the nonviolent policies advocated by Martin Luther King.

Martin Luther King, Jr. gained national attention as the leader of the Montgomery bus boycott. King's exhortations and demonstrated leadership skills helped move the civil rights movement from the courtroom to the streets. Out of the Montgomery boycott came a coalition of black southern clergymen who organized the Southern Christian Leadership Conference (SCLC). King, as the first elected leader of the SCLC, successfully changed the center of gravity from within the civil rights movement. Before the founding of the SCLC, the center of gravity and the struggle for civil rights had been mostly dominated by Northern civil rights organizations. Now a group of black churches became the dominant spokespersons and resistance against white oppression. More than anything else the simultaneity of King and these events would launch the 1960s civil rights movement.

While King would proclaim that segregation was dead, Baldwin would ask "just how long, how violent, and how expensive the funeral" was going to be (Baldwin 1961c). It was in King that Baldwin saw a reflection of his own intellectual and personal strivings. Baldwin was captivated not only by King's public persona but also his private humility. He saw none of the trappings of ego, self-indulgence, or pettiness so often seen in others who had risen to such heights.

> At that time in Montgomery, King was almost surely the most beloved man there....there was a feeling in this church which transcended anything I have ever felt in a church before. Here it was, totally familiar and yet completely new...When King rose to speak-to preach-I began to understand how the atmosphere of this church differed from that of all the other churches I have known. At first I though that the great emotional power and authority of the Negro church was put to a new use, but this was not exactly the case. The Negro church was playing the same role which it has always played in Negro life, but it had acquired a new power (Baldwin 1961c).

Baldwin concluded that this new power, adding to the Black church's traditional role of protest and condemnation, but through King the struggle had become personalized. He not only understood their struggle but also became the symbol of that struggle. The power of King lied in his intimate knowledge of his people while insisting that they do not accept a victim mentality. Unlike the Nation of Islam, King while identifying the problems caused by whites and racism, also pointed out the problems caused by blacks themselves—such as the failure to take personal responsibility for their savings, families, crime in their own communities, drug and alcohol addiction, and insisted upon a strong work ethic. In terms of the racist being hated, King argued that they should be pitied and forgiven. Baldwin overheard King say:

> ...that bigotry was a disease and that the greatest victim of this disease was not the bigot's object, but the bigot himself. And these people could only be saved by love. In liberating oneself, one was also liberating them... (Baldwin 1961c).

As explained by Baldwin, King's role was a double one, not only was he concerned with eliminating all barriers which prevented full participation of Blacks in America life, but also to prepare blacks for such participation.

So moved, Baldwin joined a string of black celebrities (to include Lena Horne, Harry Bellefonte, Sidney Poitier, Jim Brown, Aretha Franklin, and James Earl Jones) who lent their talents to the civil rights movement. On the lecture circuit or through his essays, from pulpit to auditorium, from sit-ins to marches—Baldwin and other celebrities could be seen speaking up, sitting down and being arrested for "the cause." Baldwin, determining that such a role would be presumptuous, never really thought of himself as a spokesperson. His art and protest merged, as like never before he utilized his talents to sway a people and a nation from their racist past.

Baldwin painfully recounts how star, after bright black star, were cut down in their prime. First Malcolm, then Martin and finally Medgar—all shot, all dead, and with them a major portion of Baldwin's soul died with them.

> I did not want to weep for Martin; tears seemed futile. But I may also have been afraid, and I could not have been the only one, that if I began to weep, I would not be able to stop. There was more than enough to weep for, if one was to weep-so many of us, cut down, so soon. Medgar, Malcolm, Martin: and their widows, and their children (Baldwin 1972).

Baldwin had prophesied the wrath that would come earlier in *the Fire Next Time*. Few heeded his call. After the murders of Medgar, Malcolm and Martin a sea of fire engulfed urban America from the East to the West coast. From Oakland and Watts to Harlem and Chicago, from Atlanta to East L.A. the smoke could be seen as black rage was ignited over and over again. The long hot summers of 1965 and 1966 produced more than a 20 separate riots as racial unrest threatened to consume America in fire and rage. Urban blacks rampaged violently declaring that their demands were just and the time had come to end the duplicity and racial injustice. National Guard troops, called out to secure the peace, patrolled Chicago, Cleveland, Dayton, Milwaukee, San Francisco, Cincinnati, New Haven, Providence, Wilmington, Cambridge, Maryland, Boston, Buffalo, and Milwaukee. The National Advisory Commission on Civil Unrest reported to President Johnson that close to 150 violent outbreaks of racial unrest ravaged the country in 1967 alone. While sociologists and politicians would hide behind their surprise and claim that no one could have predicted such an outpouring of rage, others merely pointed to the quiet poet whose writings had foretold of the fire next time.

Some have argued that Baldwin changed his writing to attempt to recapture the spotlight now held by such black radicals as Huey Newton, Bobby Seale or Angela Davis (Gates 1992). We would argue that it was a direct response to the deep sense of loss as Baldwin lived through these catastrophes. One notes a kind of bitterness, a strange emptiness that pervades Baldwin's writing from this point onward. Granted, still there is the brilliant use of language, the wit and the candor, but missing is the hope. A hope which, however veiled, gave all of his earlier writing a freshness, a life. In his later writings one only finds endless questions raised through a sea of despair.

> Questions louder than drums begin beating in the mind, and one realizes that…To be an Afro-American, or an American black, is to be in the situation, intolerably exaggerated, of all those who have ever found themselves part of a civilization which they could in no wise honorably defend-which they were compelled, indeed, endlessly to attack and condemn-and who yet spoke out of the most passionate love, hoping to make the kingdom new, to make it honorable and worthy of life….And there is a level on which the mockery of the people even their hatred, is moving because it is so blind: it is terrible to watch people cling to their captivity and insist on their own destruction…the shape of the wrath to come (Baldwin 1972).

If the measure of true genius and intellectual greatness is measured by the staying power of ones work, then Baldwin most assuredly must be ranked among the brightest stars that this nation has produced. Through 10 novels, 17 separate collections of essays, and six plays the voice of Baldwin informs yet another generation of life and love, promise and hope, racial hate and religious bigotry, self and identity. Through these pages, Baldwin can be heard in both whispers and shouts, articulating the rage and despair, hatred and complacency, and the warning if we choose to ignore the racist cancer eating at the heart of America. Will we, take the path of love and peace, or will we be consumed by the fire next time?

## REFERENCES

Allen, S.S. 1975. "Religious Symbolism and Psychic Reality in Baldwin's Go Tell it on the Mountain." *CLA Journal* 19 (December): 173-174.

Baldwin, J. 1948. (1985). "The Harlem Ghetto." *Commentary*, February. *In Price of the Ticket*. New York: St. Martin's/Marek.

_____. 1949. (1985). "Everybody's Protest Novel." *Partisan Review*, June. *In Price of the Ticket*. New York: St. Martin's/Marek.

_____. 1951. (1985). "Many Thousands Gone." *Partisan Review*, November/ December. *In Price of the Ticket*. New York: St. Martin's/Marek.

_____. 1955. (1985). "Notes of a Native Son." *Harper's Magazine*, November. *In Price of the Ticket*. New York: St. Martin's/Marek.

_____. 1959a. (1985). "Nobody Knows My Name." *Partisan Review*, winter. *In Price of the Ticket*. New York: St. Martin's/Marek.

_____. 1959b. (1985). "The Discovery of What It Means to Be an American." *The New York Times Book Review*, January 25. *In Price of the Ticket*. New York: St. Martin's/Marek.

_____. 1960. (1985). "In Search of a Majority." Address at Kalamazoo College. *In Price of the Ticket*. New York: St. Martin's/Marek.

_____. 1961a. (1985). "Alas, Poor Richard." *In Price of the Ticket*. New York: St. Martin's/Marek.

_____. 1961b. (1985). "A Negro Assays the Negro Mood." *In Price of the Ticket*. New York: St. Martin's/Marek.

_____. 1961c. (1985). "The Dangerous Road Before Martin Luther King." *In Price of the Ticket*. New York: St. Martin's/Marek.

_____. 1962a. (1985). "Down At The Cross." *The New Yorker*, November. *In Price of the Ticket*. New York: St. Martin's/Marek.

_____. 1962b. (1985). "The Creative Process." Excerpted from Creative America: Ridge Press. *In Price of the Ticket*. New York: St. Martin's/Marek.

_____. 1962c. (1985). "A Letter to My Nephew." *The Progressives* (December) appears as "The Fire Next Time." *In Price of the Ticket*. New York: St. Martin's/Marek.

_____. 1963a. *The Fire Next Time*. New York: The Dial Press.

_____. 1963b. (1985). "The Negro Child-His Self-Image"; originally published in *The Saturday Review* (December). *In Price of the Ticket*. New York: St. Martin's/Marek.

_____. 1964. (1985). "Nothing Personal," written with Richard Avedon. *Atheneum. In Price of the Ticket*. New York: St. Martin's/Marek.

_____. 1965. (1985). "The American Dream and The American Negro." Address at the Cambridge Union Society of Cambridge University, February 1965. Originally published in *The New York Times Magazine*, March. *In Price of the Ticket*. New York: St. Martin's/Marek.

_____. 1968. (1985). "White Racism or World Community?" *Ecumenical Review*, October. *In Price of the Ticket*. New York: St. Martin's/Marek.

_____. 1971. (1985). *No Name in the Street*, originally published by Dial Press. *In Price of the Ticket*. New York: St. Martin's/Marek.

_____. 1985b. *The Evidence of Things Not Seen*. New York: Henry Holt.

Collier, E. 1972. "Thematic Patterns in Baldwin's Essays: A Study in Chaos." *Black World* 21(8): 28-34.

Du Bois, W.E.B. 1946. (1985). "Memorandum to the Secretary for the NAACP Staff Conference." In *Against Racism: Unpublished Essays, Papers, Addresses, 1887-1961*, edited by H. Aptheker. Amherst: The University of Massachusetts Press.

Ellison, R. 1964. "Harlem is Nowhere." Originally published in Harper's Magazine, reprinted in *Voices in Black and White*, edited by K. Whittemore and G. Marzorati. New York: Franklin Square Press.

Fanon, F. 1967. *Black Skin: White Masks*. New York: Grove Press.

Foster, D.E. 1971. "'Cause my house fell down': The Theme of the Fall in Baldwin's Novels." *Critique* 13: 55.

Gates, H.L. 1992. "The Fire Last Time: What James Baldwin Can and Can't Teach America." *The New Republic* 206(22): 37-42.

Lynch, M.F. 1993. "The Everlasting Father: Mythic Quest and Rebellion in Baldwin's Go Tell it on the Mountain." *CLA Journal* 37 (December): 156-175.

Powers, L.H. 1984. "Henry James and James Baldwin: The Complex Figure." *Modern Fiction Studies* 30 (Winter): 651-667.

Turner, P.A. 1993. *I Heard it Through the Grapevine: Rumor in African-American Culture*. Berkeley and Los Angeles: University of California Press.

Rawls, J. 1971. *A Theory of Justice*. Cambridge, MA: Harvard University Press.

West, C. 1994. *Race Matters*. New York: Vintage Books.

# PART IV

## PUBLIC INTELLECTUALS

# POLITICAL ENGAGEMENT AND AFRICAN AMERICAN SCHOLARS IN THE AGE OF THE AFRICAN AMERICAN INTELLECTUAL CELEBRITY

Alford A. Young, Jr.

An obvious feature of the over 100 year history of African American scholarship, irrespective of its disciplinary grounding or specific empirical considerations, has been its concern with the ways for and means of social progress for black Americans. Undoubtedly, in the last decade the impetus for much of this scholarship has remained. What has been different about the past decade, however, is the emergence of the African American public intellectual as a prominent social type that is not only highly visible to a non-black audience, but also endorsed by it (as well as a wider black audience). The appearance of this group of scholars in the academic landscape has far-reaching potential implications for the changing status within and relations of African American scholars in the academy. The degree

Research in Race and Ethnic Relations, Volume 10, pages 117-146
Copyright © 1997 by JAI Press Inc.
All rights of reproduction in any form reserved.
ISBN: 0-7623-0275-5

of public visibility that these scholars have secured has allowed them to function as direct participants in elite discourses on race relations. Moreover, African American public intellectuals have now been recognized by other African Americans and many non-African Americans as crucial participants in the struggle for the social advancement of black Americans. Their opinions and ideas help to define the contemporary political terrain for black Americans; both in terms of the issues to be addressed and the argumentative approach taken with respect to those issues.

The emergence of contemporary African American public intellectuals in the public sphere has re-fueled a long-standing debate about the capacity for intellectuals to function as political agents (Anderson 1994; Berube 1995; Boynton 1995; Phillip 1995; Rivers 1992, 1993). This debate has involved inquiry into the exact roles that such figures can, should, or should not perform in the political sphere, as well as how they relate to those portions of the public that remain beyond the institutional domains that encapsulate the intellectual life (the university being the prime example of such a domain). Some of the effects of that debate comprise the basis for this inquiry. More specifically, this inquiry concerns the contrasting conceptions of political engagement as articulated by some African American public intellectuals and by some "less public" contemporary African American scholars.

The task for this paper is to explore the concept of political engagement as it has been articulated by some public African American intellectuals and other critical commentators, and compare these views with those of some contemporary African American sociologists who function in a less public capacity. For the present purposes, political engagement will be defined as intentional involvement in initiatives for social change. The most explicit form of this engagement is direct and consistent involvement in specific organizational or social initiatives for change. Specifically, in considering the case of African American public intellectuals, this paper first will explore the following:

1. The emergence of the category of black public intellectual in the past decade,
2. The social roles that they have constructed and that have been constructed for them,
3. The contradictions and difficulties that are embedded in the pursuit of their socio-political agenda.

Secondly, this paper will discuss a variation of political engagement by investigating three cases of three less publicly visible African American sociologists. These scholars have been and continue to be involved in pragmatic social activities that pertain in some direct way to the political arena (advocacy, policy-formation, etc.). The perspectives of these scholars were collected by open-ended interviews. These interviews are a part of a larger project on the life histories and contemporary worldviews of African American scholars who pursue research on some aspect of the African American experience. The political activities of these scholars typify modes of engagement that involve an array of obstacles and possibilities. However, the life experience of scholars such as these (especially the tribulations involved in their efforts) are not adequately recognized and/or critically evaluated in academic research. Much of this consequence is a result of the public preoccupation with the political engagement paradigms that have been articulated by and about African American public intellectuals.

A principal assertion in this work is that the models of engagement by less public intellectuals can inform about, as well as contextualize, the potential consequences of the types of engagements pursued by both African American public intellectuals, and intellectuals more generally. Hence, positioning the debate about the public intellectuals next to a discussion of the ordeals of the less public scholars creates a means for an expanded notion of intellectual engagement in the political sphere. The effort to expand this notion will be made complete by the final part of this inquiry, which involves some comparisons between the nouveau public intellectuals and those who function in less public domains. To begin the analysis we turn to the emergence of the African American public intellectual.

## THE EMERGENCE OF THE CONTEMPORARY AFRICAN AMERICAN PUBLIC INTELLECTUAL

Although figures such as Frederick Douglas, W.E.B. DuBois, Alain Locke, Carter G. Woodson, and others have been placed deservedly into the category of intellectual, historically that status resonated almost entirely within the African American public imagination. Quite often, these figures have been and continue to be regarded by non-black Americans (to the extent that they are regarded at all) as individuals whose ideas and ideologies were significant for African Americans, but marginal for the broader American social context. The particularity of the present moment, however, is that those African American scholars who have achieved the stature of a public intellectual have done so by virtue of being recognized as such by both white and black Americans. Most significantly, both communities share much of the same premises for their acceptance of these figures as public intellectuals. These scholars are viewed as people of letters who have chosen to speak publicly about race-specific affairs that the public has determined to be among its most critical concerns (Boynton 1995, p. 53).

In the most general sense, the contemporary African American public intellectual has been described as a scholarly figure who is not wedded to a single disciplinary context for social inquiry, nor to the academic community as its sole, or even its primary, audience. As one writer offered, the contemporary African American scholar is informed by a strong moral impulse to address a general, educated audience in accessible language about the important issues of the day (Boynton 1995, p. 53). Some of the individuals who have been regarded in this category include literary critics Henry Louis Gates, Houston Baker, Shelby Steele, and bell hooks; social scientists William Julius Wilson, Orlando Patterson, Glen Loury, and Walter Williams; humanists such as Cornel West and Michael Eric Dyson, and legal scholars such as Derrick Bell and Randall Kennedy.

The difficulty about creating a rigid definition for this category of scholars is that African American public intellectuals who have emerged from the academy are not usually defined according to some qualitative or quantitative measure of their scholarly productivity, but in large part by the level of public notoriety that they generate, and the personal associations that they maintain with each other and other public figures. Therefore, this coterie of individuals lacks any precise demarcations for their identity as public intellectuals. In fact, the only common feature that these scholars share may be the depths of their public visibility and the public consumption of their publications. However, the lack of a cohesive categorization scheme does not deter from a comparative analysis of how political engagement is pursued by some of the scholars who are regularly invoked in delineations of African American public intellectuals. Therefore, for the present purposes the emphasis will remain exclusively on individuals who hold academic positions. Additionally, and for the sake of a more focused analysis, this work will focus on those scholars who maintain left-of-center political perspectives. These scholars function in a somewhat different social milieu than do conservative African American thinkers, and it is the left-of-center constituency that appears to has reaped the largest portion of the recent public preoccupation with the new category of African American public intellectual.[1]

Much of the public attention that has been generated around the emergence of the African American public intellectual is a result of four circumstances (Berube 1995, p. 75; Boynton 1995, p. 56; Phillip 1995, p. 1). The first is the rapidly increased access to print media and to electronic media such as talk shows. This has provided the American public with consistent exposure to these individuals. Second, there has been an increase in the presence of African American tenured faculty in prestigious university positions. This occurrence has provided these scholars with an institutional context for creating and maintaining a broader social visibility in the intellectual milieu for their research, ideas, and opinions. Third, pervasive public attention to matters pertaining to race has also fueled the increased interest in the contributions of these scholars. This increased public attention on matters pertaining to race in the United States has emerged in both conservative and liberal constituencies. Regardless of the politico-ideological orientations these debates, they have buttressed the visibility of these scholars both in intellectual and more public venues as the scholars have been called to participate in, or observe and critically evaluate some of these discussions. Fourth and finally are the consequences of the increased rates of publication of the non-traditional academic commentary generated by these scholars. This work maintains a central focus on race, usually addressing contentious public issues and is written precisely for broader public consumption.

Taken together, these four circumstances exhibit how purposive action on the part of these scholars, as well as social factors that they could not directly manipulate, have produced their current prominent status. That prominence has major implications for the type of social roles that these scholars perform, and the political consequences of that activity.

## THE POLITICAL SIGNIFICANCE OF THE SOCIAL ROLES OF AFRICAN AMERICAN PUBLIC INTELLECTUALS

The are two general frames for locating the means by which contemporary African American public intellectuals conduct what they view as politically relevant activity. The more recent of the two is a culturalist orientation. The African American public intellectuals who are associated with this frame regard their involvement in cultural criticism and social commentary as the central features of their political engagement. More specifically, many of these scholars attempt to explicate the social and political significance of varied forms of African American cultural practice. Research and public commentary on rap music and the specific behaviors and expressive modalities of African American urban youth (e.g., clothing and oral communicative styles) have served as the empirical points of emphasis for some of this cultural inquiry (Dyson 1993). Not surprisingly, it is often the case that humanist scholars—and literary critics more specifically—concentrate on this brand of socio-political engagement.

One of the most prominent examples of this form of engagement was the appearance and testimony of Harvard University-based literary critic Henry Louis Gates at a Florida trial for the members of the rap group, Two Live Crew. A second example is Houston Baker's publication of *Race, Rap and the Academy* (1993). This work is a commentary on rap music by a well-regarded "establishment" figure in the American intellectual scene. The arguments in the work are put forth by employing a combination of formal academic lexicon and the expressive terminology employed by African American youth. Other examples of this genre of political engagement comes from the litany of work produced by bell hooks, who commonly writes about public culture and cultural artifacts within the context of cinematic critique, quite often focusing on the work of film-maker Spike Lee, among other public figures, as points of focus for her arguments (hooks 1984, 1990, 1992).

In essence, much of this mode of inquiry and public commentary aims at validating various forms of African American cultural expression, although this approach also includes attempts to maintain a critical perspective on certain aspects of those expressions (e.g, sexist or hetero-sexist revelations in rap music or film). The effort to validate some of these cultural practices is in part an effort to counteract what others have termed the profligate and unsophisticated responses of a wayward black urban constituency to the conditions that effect their lives (for instances, see Baker 1993; Dyson 1993; Rose 1994). The activities pursued by African American public intellectuals who are committed to the culturalist perspective have generated significant public attention because that perspective incorporates and interprets as aspects of the African American urban life experience that are distant and often incomprehensible to those who have little intimate exposure to the low-income African American urban context.

A second brand of engagement concerns the attempt of African American public intellectuals to function as commentators on the "public affairs" circumscribing African American life. Most often, this effort is construed by these scholars as an attempt to affirm the complexity of, and pose critical questions about, the socio-political status of contemporary black American urban life. One such example of this approach is Cornel West (1993).[2] The collection of essays that he published in the volume entitled *Race Matters* is a typification of this effort. Works such as that attempt to transmit general existential and moral interpretations of African American life in a manner that employs some of the lexicon of academia while remaining accessible to a broader public (Anderson 1994, pp. 43-44; White 1993, p. 62). In combining these approaches an attempt is made to speak on the behalf of black Americans to the larger public while maintaining some critical perspective about them. Such work usually is devoid of the explication or testing of formal hypotheses. It also does not contain elaborate theoretical construction. Instead, these works offer exegeses that allow insight into the intricacies of African American life that are not often consciously considered by many African Americans as well as non-African Americans.

Although not identical to the type of objectives evident in the work of Cornel West, a classic example of this mode of functioning is William Julius Wilson, a scholar who has dedicated his academic career to attempting to connect academic research with the public via the national policy arena (Wilson 1987, 1991, 1996). Wilson and others like him have not been as focused on promoting exegetical commentary as they have been on formal policy formation. However, it is clear that Wilson very much remains a public figure for a number of interrelated circumstances. First, the policy arena constitutes a crucial portion of the public arena, thus providing him with a natural connection to the public. Second, his focus is on national policy, which garners greater visibility than would a more localized focus. Third, his focus on national policy involves intimate and consistent interaction with national policy makers, who are some of the most publicly visible social actors in American society. The case of William Julius Wilson contains greater complexity, however, given that although he attempts to speak for a broader policy agenda in the public consciousness he is often still regarded as a "race-man" in the way that West and others may be. This is the consequence of an African American scholar speaking about public policy issues that, although of pertinence to the whole of American society, are usually regarded as particular to the situation of African Americans.

In contrast to the culturalist approach, the latter approach is more directly focused on objectives that concern enhancing the social, economic, and political status of African Americans. The uniqueness of the latter approach is that the African American public intellectuals who pursue it are more preoccupied with politics in the traditional understanding of the term. However, many of these scholars also attempt to frame their arguments in terminology that is not exclusive to academic audiences (or to those non-academics who consume such material). It is important to note that the cultural perspective clearly involves political consequences as well. For example, the effort to reconstitute certain aspects of African American life as cultural practice with complex implications (and doing so *not* in terms of a culture of pathology perspective) allows for the potential for black Americans to acquire a more substantive regard for their humanity in the minds of non-blacks. This status is a critical prerequisite for any progressive discussion of black American social progress along traditionally defined social, political, and economic parameters. Indeed, the uniqueness of the approach of scholars who promote this frame is that they make explicit the political significance of their arguments about African American cultural expression.

As this overview has elucidated, regardless of the nature of their empirical points of reference or the structure of their arguments, African American public intellectuals do converge in some way on the political arena—and more specifically on the quest for progressive political change that can enhance African American life—as an objective for their efforts.

## THE CRISIS OF THE AFRICAN AMERICAN
## PUBLIC INTELLECTUAL

The emergence of the African American public intellectual prompted an initial period of excitement and intrigue both within and beyond the academy. Their emergence reflected what many observers believed to be a broadening of the scope of the academic community. The African American public intellectual was viewed as the proponent of a new, previously suppressed voice that had finally emerged in the formal academy. However, the social functioning of the African American public intellectual was a matter of critical consideration soon thereafter. Undoubtedly, some of the critical consideration might have been due to envy that was precipitated by the escalation in status of this community of African American scholars. Alternatively, some of it has also predicated upon a critical reaction to the often superficial flavor of the milieu that circumscribes high profile individuals. Additionally, this attitude was heightened by the often stark contrast in both style and content between formal academic debate and discussion and the type of social commentary produced within the media, the latter of which can sometimes appear to be banal treatments of scholarly matter. At least one of the questions at hand for these critical observers concerns the emergence of a relevant practical politics from what often seems to be media-driven publicity quests. An underlying facet of the earnest criticism that has been levied against African American public intellectuals concerns alternative notions of what should constitute appropriate political engagement for African American scholars. Therefore, the issue is not simply a matter of negative reactions to intensified status differentials in the African American scholarly community, but of approaches toward political engagement and definitions of appropriate political terrain.

The debate over political terrain that has resulted in severe criticism being levied upon African American public intellectuals for what some consider to be a vacuous relationship between them and tangible socio-political arenas. In one argument, the literary critique Michael Berube offers that African American public intellectuals claim that their work maintains a pragmatic political relevance, but the case remains that many of them do not facilitate meaningful structural change in public institutional life, especially given that their notion of what is political tends to be in the less-pragmatic arena of culture and cultural criticism (Berube 1995, p. 79). Berube argues that the right wing intelligentsia has been efficacious in creating a legitimated ideology about the functioning and management of public sphere institutions and systems (e.g., public schools, higher education, etc.). In his view the right-wing project has eclipsed any collective effort by left-wing public intellectuals to promote alternative political visions in the public sphere that facilitate any actual contestation within and about these institutions and systems. An elaboration of his view follows:

> The black public intellectual has created a niche at the time when the other traditional elements of the public, public schools, public welfare, public education, are taking a beating, so that they must be more tangible in claiming what is their relationship to the public other than their image (Berube 1995, p. 79).

The case of Cornel West, one of the most visible of the African American public intellectuals, has been made particularly relevant to this criticism. At least one writer has offered that West can appear hopelessly utopian in his proscriptions for society (White 1993, p. 62). In part the utopian portrayal emerges from his discursive style, which often involves an elaborate manipulation of language in the course of conveying his arguments (and one which appears especially appealing when transmitted by visual or print media), but remains difficult to transfer into practical socio-political strategies or policies. At its most extreme, Cornel West and others who occupy the category of African American public intellectual appear to their critics to have successfully commodified talk and packaged it as little more than entertainment for a public that believes at least in part that consumption of such talk in and of itself comprises politically significant activity.[3]

A harsh criticism is offered by Adolph Reed in his discussion of contemporary black public intellectuals:

> [They] pose to claim authority both as certified, world class elite academics and as links to an extra-academic blackness, thus splitting the difference between being insiders and outsiders. In the process, they are able to skirt the practical requirements of either role—to avoid rigorous, careful intellectual work and protracted, committed political action (Reed 1995, p. 35).

In addition, Reed argues that in the arena of the African American public intellectual "the prominence of the author counts more than the weight of the utterance" (Reed 1995, p. 35).

Indeed, the criticism of African American public intellectuals in large part focuses on the role of the media in positing a political relevance for these scholars simply because they are the focus of significant media attention. It remains that the quest for even the most committed and sincere of the black public intellectuals will be to confront the remarks of the writer, Robert Boynton, who argues the following:

> The quandary of the contemporary black intellectual is how to be both an insider and an outsider at the same time, how to balance the requirements of truly independent thinking with the inherently co-opting demands of mass public culture (Boynton 1995, pp. 68-70).

Boynton concluded his query with a series of critical questions that must be explored in any serious consideration of the situation of the African American public intellectual:

1. Will their impact be enduring or is it a part of the commercialization of the day?
2. Will enough substantial work be left behind after the op-ed pieces and editorials are written?
3. Will they become better thinkers over time or only better known thinkers over time (Boynton 1995, pp. 68-70)?

The questions posed by Robert Boynton set the context for an evaluation of the myriad effects of the age of the African American intellectual celebrity. Of course, more time is needed to determine what the answers are for the issues that Boynton raised. However, what can be done at present is to consider the African American public intellectual in comparative context to more traditional African American scholars. To be clear, this is only one of a list of constituencies that African American public intellectuals can be compared to in an effort to ascertain what enduring effects the public scholars may offer.[4] The importance of the particular comparison pursued in this paper is that both kinds of scholars have formal status in the academy. Therefore, they both elucidate possibilities for configuring how a politics can and does emerge for scholars who desire such engagement. Both also elucidate certain forms of contradiction and inadequacy concerning practical political engagement. The major difference is that African American public intellectuals, by the nature of their stature, are immersed within a more public discussion about their situation with respect to the political sphere. On the other hand, the situation of the less public scholars involves less critical attention to the circumstances. Hence, the decision to assess one group against representations of the other not only helps to better contextualize the issues and types of impact of each group, but to also shed light on the under-regarded figures who maintain a meaningful, if much less known, political relevance.

## UNPUBLICIZED POLITICS—THE CASE OF THREE "LESS PUBLIC" AFRICAN AMERICAN SOCIOLOGISTS

The importance of drawing a comparison between the public figures discussed earlier and those who are less public are twofold. First, the less public figures in many ways are more embedded in the life and culture of higher education in that they are more directly accessible to students, and can sustain unmediated day-to-day interaction with them, than can many African American public intellectuals who are housed in the academy. The less public scholars are more actively immersed into the micro-politics and/or social dynamics of their institutions largely because they have more time for such activity, or at least are not as involved in more public engagements such that they cannot respond to more local, institutionally specific, matters. Secondly, the less public scholars are more advantageously situated in local politics and the local polity, which maintains a particular significance for the everyday life of black Americans as distinct from that of national-level discourse. The cases chosen for this paper reflect each of these conditions, as well as a set of circumstances that are particular to each specific case.

The rest of this paper consists of an exploration of three African American sociologists who exemplify a general pattern of political engagement, but who each maintain their own nuanced way of explaining and enacting that approach in their lives. The form of political engagement involves direct and consistent dialogue with local-level practitioners, professionals, and policymakers. In addition to other forms of engagement, each of these scholars has served on municipal or community boards, planning committees, research councils that address social issues, or institutions that pertain to the lives of African Americans (and not necessarily exclusively to them). As they informed me in the course of our discussions, each scholar made the choice to pursue these activities as a part of their realizations of roles and purposes for academic research to enhance the lives of black Americans. Additionally, these activities helped these scholars at the time in which they determined to pursue academic careers to create viable approaches toward meeting the needs of black Americans. Through local involvement they were able to bridge the academic life with the affairs of African Americans, many of whom have no direct relationship to the academic community. While unique and distinct in various ways, the three cases explored here are meant to illustrate the experiences of the larger social category of "less public" African American scholars. Consequently, following a consideration of all of the cases will be a comment on the general issues and concerns relevant to that social category.

The exploration of the three "less-public" African American scholars comes from a long-standing research initiative on African American social scientist and humanist scholars that I have been pursuing. The project involves both open-ended structured interviewing and archival research on Afro-American scholars who study the black American experience. The larger objective of this research is to explore the interconnections between the personal, political, professional, and intellectual dimensions of the lives of Afro-American scholars who pursue research on the black American experience. This project also involves an exploration of whether these dimensions have changed for black American scholars over the twentieth century, and if so, then how they have changed. Finally, this project ventures into how intrapersonal factors have affected and are effected by such changes. The following analyses provide further information as to how these less-public scholars have chosen to pursue their careers and how they define and talk about political engagement as a part of their lives.

## CASE I—THE TRADITIONALIST

The first scholar to be considered here exemplifies a common pattern of localized political engagement. In addition to the tasks mentioned earlier, this scholar also maintains traditional roles such as a mentor to African American students and advisor to student-run organization. This individual is a senior scholar who determined to pursue a professional career in sociology after a number of years of study in graduate school that left him with no clear sense of what he wanted to do with his life. Upon the advice of his faculty advisors he continued to pursue graduate studies in sociology, and soon thereafter decided to make a professional career out of scholarship and teaching in that area of study. He was born and reared during the depression in the central part of the United States. As a young child his family exposed him to literature and was very attentive to exposing him to the best educational opportunities avail to him at that time. This took place even thought he wavered in his commitment to academic excellence throughout his childhood. It was early in his undergraduate years when a sociology professor commented to him that he was capable of doing better academic work. This motivated him to work harder in school, as well as to explore more substantively the field of sociology. He eventually determined to become a professor, and his career interests and pursuits evolved as his career matured. Over time he also acquired a more enriched sense of the challenges and concerns facing African Americans.

This scholar has been on the faculty of Historically Black Colleges and Universities (HBCUs) as well as at predominantly white institutions. During that time he has been and continues to bring academic research into local policy arenas, especially in the area of race and urban education. He has been involved as a formal and informal advisor and consultant to public sector educational institutions and organizations. He has also been a formal and informal counselor and advisor to undergraduate and graduate students (many of them students of color) throughout his career in academia. In discussing his principal commitments as a scholar and teacher he offered the following:

> I felt that one of the most important things I could do was serve as a role model and a facilitator for students, to help increase the number and percent and quality of Black professors in the world. I thought that was very important...I was never much of an organization man...You know, running for office and being on committees and all that kind of thing. And I'm not mocking it at all, it's just that there's nothing in that that interest me...the main things that I was interested in (was) publishing and helping students

A significant effort in this scholar's career was to create an informal network of scholars and policymakers who studied under his guidance and who went on to maintain variant levels of involvement with organizations and institutions that comprise the social policy arena. By operating within this micro-political context, this scholar has been pivotal in creating and expanding a critical mass of individuals who attempt to further agendas on race-specific social change. Unlike many of the public intellectuals who speak directly to a larger public, this scholar typifies the model of the institution builder through his networks of former students.

While the efforts of this scholar may not achieve the visibility of the public intellectuals, it does contribute to the formation of a viable constituency of individuals who occupy specific positions and affect specific outcomes in policy-relevant activities. It is unfortunate that for this scholar visibility and recognition is often limited to those who have studied under him or have had direct interaction with him (although it must be pointed out that this scholar also has enriched his visibility as a consequence of his academic research and publishing). However, the structural apparatus that this scholar has formed, and the role that he has performed in his direct interaction with a succeeding generation of scholars and advocates creates the potential for significant social impact. Before discussing further the actual and potential implications of such an impact it is important to assess other dimensions of this scholar's life as they relate to the topic at hand.

The choices that this scholar made concerning his conduct in the academy calls for specific investigation into how he located scholarship into his pattern of social engagement. Although he did assert a political motive for his scholarly endeavors, this did not obstruct his commitment to a code of scholarly standards for his work. A part of his vision of the political significance for his scholarship had to do with whom he identified as the relevant audiences for his work. He offered the following comment on this matter:

> There are several audiences....I suppose one audience is the general sociology, social psychology-education community. But I suppose my primary audience is Black scholars in sociology, psychology and education....I'd like to have other kinds of impact, but that's the audience that I target my work to. In other words, I don't try to write for AJS or ASR. I try to write for what

I consider more accessible audiences. The *Journal of Negro Education, Urban Education*, or you know, those journals that are not considered the top, most prestigious journals in the field, but that reach a practitioner kind of audience.

One of the immediate themes emerging from his comments is that they portray an ideal type depiction of African American scholarly and social engagement prior to the age of the African American intellectual celebrity. This scholar maintains clear commitments to the constituencies within and outside of the academy that have been traditional foci in the history of African American intellectual life— black students in the first case, and in the second, an institutional apparatus that greatly affects black Americans; public education.[5] Hence, this scholar functions as a traditionalist in multiple ways.

Thus far not much has been said about difficulties or disappointments concerning the efforts of this scholar. There are a set of personal predicaments, however, that come with his particular orientation toward the academic life. In responding to a question about possible unfulfilled objectives in his career, this scholar stated:

Well, if I could have made more of a mark intellectually, I wish I could have done that....Going back to that old myth, the belief that that stuff really matters in the field, to your academic reputation. And I don't think mine is as bright and shining as I'd like it to be....Well, you know, if I could ideally do what I wanted to do I'd write a great book. I guess I still deep down have that desire to leave a mark on the academic world, which I don't feel that I've left. So if I could do anything I wanted to do, be anything I wanted to be, I guess I'd go out in a blaze of glory with a great book.

Indeed, some of this predicament may be a consequence of this scholar's having to function in the age of the African American intellectual celebrity, coupled with the demands and constraints that have confronted black scholars throughout their existence in academia. The requests and expectations made by African American students for guidance and support in navigating their experiences in higher education have been more acute for African American scholars (Moore and Wagstaff 1974). Clearly, this prevents those scholars who are most committed to providing that kind of support from having the time to pursue strict scholarly interests. African American scholars who choose to accept this additional role are faced with a restricted capacity to reach their scholarly potential. Whether this scholar could have created the type of publication that would have allowed him to "go out in a blaze of glory" remains an open question. Above and beyond all else, the fact that he chose certain endeavors over more scholarly-specific ones certainly limited his potential to do that.

In a comment that offers a fitting summary to the views of this scholar on the particularities of his life in academia he said:

> ....I said earlier that I consider myself to be an advocate for the black community. Most of my colleagues would say that advocacy is alien to the academic life, that you can't really be a scholar and an advocate. So I see myself and most African-American and minority and women scholars being more on the advocate side than is typical of the white male, old boy type of scholar.

It is clear from the preceding commentary that while issues of invisibility and non-recognition may be the case for this scholar with respect to his status in the age of the public African American intellectual, the dawning of that age does not necessarily disrupt his capacity to function. Whatever tensions and anxieties that he endures stem in large part from a combination of the traditional expectations of black students concerning the role performance of African American scholars in institutions of higher learning and the conscious choices and decisions made by him. However, what is important about asserting a connection between the life and work of this scholar with the age of the African American intellectual celebrity is that an unrecognized—or less than deservedly recognized—arena for political engagement lingers. This lack of recognition is a matter not solely of insufficient public acknowledgement of service-minded scholars (although some may view that argument as an in and of itself justification for the greater recognition of these figures). More critically, the absence of recognition means an under-consideration of the progressive political possibilities that emerge out of such activity of the part of these scholars. A greater recognition may lead to a delimiting of political possibilities for black Americans (and other oppressed people) by evaluating the trials and tribulations that come with the involvement of scholars in the local scene. In considering the next two cases, the possibilities as well as the problems with engaging in this arena on behalf of black Americans will be elucidated further.

# CASE II—THE COMMUNITY-LEVEL
## ORGANIC INTELLECTUAL[7]

This sociologist virtually stumbled into the discipline after an undergraduate experience that he found intellectually rewarding primarily because of the sociologists that he encountered while in the course of his studies. He decided to pursue a career in sociology and determined more specific career objectives as his career matured.

This scholar was reared in the rural southwest where he was exposed to the codes of pre and post civil rights era racial conduct and interaction. As he stated during our discussion, his being reared in a low-income, small town environment also factored in his inclusion of class-based issues such as stratification and inter-class relations in his evolving research agenda. Eventually, this scholar chose to focus much of his research on issues pertaining to race and class relations, especially African American intra-race relations.

In talking about the issues and concerns that comprise his long-term political project, he explained to me that his objective was to inject a publicly accessible "social philosophy" on race and racial issues into community-level dialogue. For him this meant, quite literally, the inclusion of his research and ideas into the planning and implementation efforts of neighborhood organizations and institutions in African American communities. His current location in a large metropolitan area allowed him access to such community groups, and he regularly speaks and participates in community forums and planning groups in ways that allow him to introduce his research and opinions into community-level collective, deliberative processes.

In connecting this effort to questions of an audience for his scholarly work this sociologist said:

> It depends on what kind of research I'm doing. Typically, if it's to go into the trusty Sociology Journal Number One, then it's fellow sociologists or fellow social scientists, and a very small segment even of that group...Increasingly though, my research is geared not just toward sociologists but towards a broader audience of informed laypeople, I would call them, for policy makers and people like that. And so, I can take, or at least I tell myself that I can take some of my scholarly work, translate it into simpler terms or things that are more useful for people in their daily lives and discuss those kinds of issues in terms that they will understand and do that. And I've increasingly started doing that. And I've increasingly started

talking about issues, you know, in public forums in that way....I realized that there is an audience for what we call social science but other people call social philosophy. There is an audience for many of the issues that sociologists discuss. So why not discuss these issues with people who want to know about it, especially if people give me credibility. They say, we value your opinions, we value what you thoughts are on this issue. Well, fine, I'll share that with you.

This scholar was involved in planning associations and professional organizations that created a formal setting for him to promote his ideas. Thus, he was able to secure consistent and direct access to the public in order to disseminate academic material to non-academic entities. In a literal sense, he regarded himself as an ideologist who informed local community initiatives of important considerations as they went about their work.

In discussing some of the ramifications of intimate communication with civic organizations this scholar said:

Well, I'm sure that it probably raises some questions in the minds of some people about how value free my research is. That's okay. I don't see myself as being totally value free, but I'm sure that some people would hope to dismiss my research by saying, well, you know, this guy has a vested interest in a certain set of outcomes or a certain set of findings or something like that. That doesn't bother me.

In discussing the often arduous task of formulating and/or translating academic work into a digestible form for the non-academic public he stated:

I think that far too many of them [scholarly paradigms that are applied to the case of African Americans] are driven by implicit models of pathology, implicit models that use whites as the normative yardstick by which everybody else is to be measured. And so anything that is a deviation away from the way that whites do things is considered inappropriate or wrong, bad or pathological or something like that. And I think that, you know, again, sometimes the Black scholar who wants to be successful in the academic realm has to buy into some of that language, some of those perspectives, some of those approaches to even engage in a dialogue about these issues. The problem becomes once you adopt those models, that language, it's very difficult to see how what you're doing is any different from what a white scholar is doing. So, that's what I would say about that. It's tricky. But much of it is driven by these wrong-headed notions. Much of the research is just driven by assumption that are faulty and wrong to begin with. But you have to adopt

some of those assumptions, or some of those ways of talking about issues
even to get involved in the conversation.

The previous comment depicts some of the tensions that emerge
from working within academic discourse in order to make an impact
in the public. In many ways this comment provides a more
provocative understanding of such tensions than do the expressions
of African American public intellectuals. First, this scholar refers to
the relevance, implications, and consequences of disseminating
research into public debate. These matters are not often emphasized
in the generic public commentary of African American public
intellectuals. In their activities the public figures are unencumbered
by the constraints of working within and against research paradigms
or prior expositions on a topic. As the case of the less-public scholar
conveys argues, when compelled to respond to specific findings and
assertions in formal academic discourse, the academic dialogue
becomes more restrictive for facilitating public debate. Additionally,
this compounds any suspicion or confusion in the public about the
potential virtues of academic research for improving their lives. For
this scholar there continues to be a struggle to remain immersed in
debate and discussion in the academic community, but to make sense
to black Americans and to avoid negating any aspect of their
humanity by formally participating in academic discourse.

Another implication that results from the previous comment
concerns the different social statuses that public and less public
African American scholars occupy in modern American life. A large
part of the success of the public figures is their apparent ability to
transmit complex ideas to a public in comprehensible forms. What
is evident in the present case is that a difficulty exists in trying to
make such connections with a public that has consistent and direct
access with a member of the scholarly community, and therefore can
interchange with that scholar. This is in opposition to the public
simply functioning as a recipient body to the commentary of scholars
through mechanisms that lack an intimate interactive capacity (e.g,
the media, academic publications, etc.). This particular case
elucidates the difficulties of attempting to function as an organic
intellectual. The final scholar considered here portrays more vividly
the practical difficulties in trying to locate oneself in the everyday
life of those not in the academic community while also trying to
maintain adherence to the mores of academia.

## CASE III—AN ALTERNATIVE COMMUNITY-LEVEL ORGANIC INTELLECTUAL

The final case to be considered here is one of a scholar who gradually moved into sociology while attempting to focus his interests during his years of undergraduate study. His commitment to sociology was crystallized in the 1960s during his experience as a teacher in a program to train inner-city educators. This program heightened his awareness of the relationship of inequality to social opportunity, and he decided to pursue the academic life in order to investigate more substantively those and other questions.

As with the previous case, this scholar was reared in the rural environment (in this case in the central region of the country). He was also exposed to the pre-civil rights era codes of racial conduct and interaction, and witnessed a gradual change during the late 1950s and 1960s. In a situation similar to that of the previous scholar, this scholar's being reared in a condition of economic deprivation resulted in his desire to inter-connection of race and class perspectives in his research efforts. His eventual area of research interest became deviance and its relation to the urban condition.

This scholar is quite similar to the preceding case in how he conducts his involvement with public constituents and organizations. The critical difference, however, is in the latter scholar's attitude toward the status of academic knowledge in facilitating pragmatic social change. In fact, this scholar maintained the viewpoint that research and scholarship had a limited utility in changing the attitudes on race, power, and subordination in society at-large, especially with respect to those who were in hegemonic positions.

After years of teaching and research, and securing senior status in a large urban higher educational institution, this scholar came to the following position about the social utility of academic contributions:

> I think I'm beginning to think more, more like the writings of Derrick Bell, and, and what Toni Morrison and others have written, that racism is so embedded in the society that no amount of critical discourse, no amount of critical theory, is going to seriously make a dent in racism in this country in our lifetime. And I, I've really reached that conclusion. But it is not a conclusion that's completely as fatalistic as it might be. I mean, 'cause I think that that realization is an important realization that Black scholars have to get to. If they're being honest about particular societies. I mean, if they're living in sort of, some utopian world, fantasy world, about their particular

society, they might not reach that point. But I think if you're really critiquing a society and looking at it very carefully, as, as I think sociologists should, social analysts should, you have to, I mean, look at your own personal, you're looking through your own personal lenses, but you also have to look at the world out there, so to speak, too.

Later on in the discussion this sociologist stated the following:

Even through using rules of logic and evidence and all the other kinds of things that are supposed to be a part of the academic enterprise, if you can't use that to dislodge some of the racist perceptions on the part of academic sociology, how are you going to change people in Arkansas? You know, the historically embedded racism on the part of people in places like Arkansas?

Although this sense of disappointment with the possibilities for scholarship persisted, this sociologists still committed his work and efforts toward the formation of tangible social policies that could lead to the enrichment of the lives of lower-income black Americans. He explained this disposition as simply being what he was trained to do, thereby motivating him to pursue it in order to optimize whatever minimal positive outcomes he could generate. In order to find some means of tacit progressive impact with his work this scholar attempted to incorporate in his approach a confrontation with other policy-relevant scholarship that he viewed as racist and oppressive. On this matter he had this to say:

I think research on Black Americans has, I would say, been problematic to some extent. But I find it more problematic now, the direction that it seems to be going, than I think I might have said ten, fifteen years ago. I think in some ways that the research on Black Americans is shifting towards a kind of a neo-Social Darwinism…In a whole bunch of arenas. In the area of crime and violence, for example, I see from my viewpoint plentiful evidence of that. I think in the area of looking at family structure, there's a lot of movement in that direction. In the area of trying to explain why it is that Blacks are relatively underprivileged in comparison to white Americans and some other ethnic, non-white ethnics in the United States. There's a movement in that direction. And I, that's one of the things I think we need to struggle against in, in research. Even I think we're contributing to that. As a group of scholars we're contributing to that to a great extent. And that's what I'm often reacting to now in, in my own work, is the extent to which I find that trend so pervasive that your own individual research efforts can't sort of go against the tide, in a way. That your research has been re-interpreted or interpreted in that direction even when you don't want it to be interpreted in that direction.

This comment was a precursor to later remarks about how this scholar positioned academic knowledge within his own perspective as a political agent. He went on to say that for him the most useful application of academic research was first and foremost as a means of informing himself with requisite information for the choices that he made concerning political engagement. He consciously tried to avoid a traditional approach of viewing scholarship itself as a means of motivating directly the public beyond the academic milieu. Therefore, he viewed himself as an "expert" who provided specific points of information on crime and criminal justice issues, and racial issues more generally, to other politically motivated actors, but saw no real value in attempting to function as an ideologist on the behalf of black Americans. His choice to do this had much to do with his disdain for regarding elaborate academic arguments as tools for political struggle. In a final comment on the status of academic research in pragmatic political engagement this scholar said:

> [If] you really take academic arguments too seriously, you lose the perception that, that to some extent academic arguments don't count, among a large portion of the public, you know, that the academic arguments are purely to be used politically in a way that, I guess that's the point I was making at the presentation [a talk that he gave earlier in the month of the interview that was attended by this researcher]...I think that some academics, and even myself at times when I've allowed myself to drift a little bit too much into the logic of academia, is that you become a little bit unrealistic about the politics of the real world. And you see the politics of the real world sometimes, even when you think you're seeing those politics clearly, you're really looking at them in too much of a kind of a rational way, too much of a kind of a logical, science way, when politics are not like that at all. They're completely without regard to those kinds of rules...the basic politics of those kinds of arguments [concerning black Americans and social issues] have nothing to do with that data and with the logic and testing that social sciences calls into it. I think that's one reason why I don't like academic, purely academic settings, you know, more like the ASA [American Sociological Association] because I think that very often the ASA is given as an example of kind of an organization that's really insular and caught up into that kind of protecting themselves from the real world....So I really go to conferences where people are meeting with politicians, you know, like the conference I went to where you were arguing your academic arguing in the midst of the same context the politician's arguing, and that people from the community argue.....(T)hey respect what you're saying, they respect that you can support your argument, but you also have to respect what they're saying, you know, quite apart from

the logic of science or anything like that. And you also have to realize that they have power in what they're saying, quite apart from any kind of scientific research.

This final case is intriguing for what it offers about perceived limits for the place of scholarship in public discussion. It is important to note, however, that this scholar displayed no frustration or anxiety about the limits that he has identified (although the design of this study precludes a more in-depth exploration of the possibility that such feelings were maintained at a deeper level of consciousness). More importantly, and withstanding any counter-claims about his remarks on the status of scholarship in the public domain, his particular awareness meant for him an ability to create what he felt is a viable approach to the political arena. He did this by making scholarship a tool for his personal enrichment as a political agent, and not as a resource for political change in and of itself.

As with the previous case, the approach taken by this scholar toward political engagement offers a model that is not highly recognized for its unique perspective on the tribulations of scholarly involvement in local public affairs. The reverence that intellectuality has acquired in the age of the African American intellectual celebrity overshadows a necessary and critical understanding of how the intellectual life connects with other spheres of everyday life. The lack of attention to the latter concerns means that a vital context for linking intellectual life with pragmatic social change remains under-developed. The consequences of this under-development will be addressed in the following sections's discussion of what less-public political engagement for African American scholars means in the age of the African American intellectual celebrity.

## CONCLUSION—DIVERGENT PERSPECTIVES ON THE POSSIBILITIES FOR POLITICAL ENGAGEMENT

Examined within the context of the age of the African American intellectual celebrity, the cases discussed here offer an entirely different dimension of the political significance of scholarly involvement in the pursuit of beneficial social change for black Americans. In large measure the overriding predicament for the less-public African American intellectuals concerns the issue of recognition. While individuals like the scholars discussed here are providing a tangible service to African Americans (as well as other subjugated people) they do not receive the wide-spread attention that the more public African American scholars do. Therefore, public attention is focused on the celebrities due to their public appeal while those that are tangibly bound to projects and initiatives that can benefit black Americans suffer minimal public regard for their efforts. Most importantly, the existence of the African American intellectual celebrity may be taken by the public as a significant socio-political achievement at the expense of recognizing that pragmatic activity which may actually enhance the lives of African Americans in ways that the more public figures could not. Taken in this light, the emergence of the African American public intellectual may be less a potential causal force for social change in American society than an unfortunate statement of how political engagement is preempted by a misguided preoccupation of the public with media-generated visibility and stature as fundamental signs of social progress. This circumstance points to the larger and more complex issue of what African Americans (or any people, for that matter) regard as relevant politics, and relevant political terrain, in the contemporary period. Of course, the examples provided in the second part of the work depict that at least some degree of practical engagement is expected, and therefore has some importance, for African Americans.

If African Americans outside of the academy are not encouraged to acknowledge the significance of the less public figures then the potential for that constituency to understand the connection of academic life to socio-political concerns will be shortsighted. This is so because the local context often effects one's personal life in a more immediate fashion. As recent research on class consciousness has shown, the local scene is that terrain wherein actors often consider and realize an importance for larger scale circumstances and events.[6] Consequently, the efforts of the less public scholars with respect to this terrain can have direct relevance on how the larger context affects, and is effected by, ordinary citizens. More importantly, a recognition of the status of scholarly engagement in the local context may create the space for a more expansive discussion on the tensions and anxieties involved in the efforts of the less-public scholars to engage in public affairs. In this way, the community outside of academia can be brought closer to the world of the scholars, instead of the usually asserted (but still no less important) emphasis on bringing scholars closer to the non-academic constituency.

It is by no means a simple task to construct a greater public recognition of the efforts of scholars such at those discussed in the second half of this work. Indeed one such step toward that direction would be for "less-public" scholars to utilize professional organizations as platform and forums for discussing their pragmatic efforts in communities beyond academia. Moreover, informal networks or new organizations could be created that support, inform of, and devise efforts for scholars to engage in local initiatives and discuss their tribulations over involvement in the public. Of course, it would be of critical importance that individuals who are not scholars be brought into these encounters so they are not is restricted to the academic community.

Certainly, there are professional scholarly organizations that already attempt to do some of this work. For example, a review of the program agendas of the Association for Black Sociologists, Association of Black Psychologists, and the Association for Black Political Scientists indicated the efforts made by these organizations to create such an expansive dialogue. However, endeavors such as these should also raise questions not only about the possibilities, but the shortcomings and difficulties that concern scholarly engagement in the public. This would allow views such as those expressed by the sociologists in this work to be confronted and interrogated both by other scholars as well as non-scholars. The consequences of these developments, it they were to occur, might be the cultivation of a more politically sophisticated African American constituency that has a better grasp on the ways that the involvement of scholars in local affairs might potentially enrich the lives of black Americans. However, before any of this can occur, it is essential that a critical account of the present situation with respect to public and less-public African American intellectuals be taken into consideration so that the public vision of scholarly engagement in public affairs is not construed too narrowly.

The attention given here to the importance of more local engagement should not be taken as a complete refutation of any constructive outcomes that may emanate from the age of the African American intellectual celebrity. There are some positive benefits in the emergence of a public African American intellectual stratum. The very fact that these scholars have achieved public visibility means that issues of race maintain a significant status in public attention. Moreover, these figures may initiate responses by others to pursue specific actions (e.g., demonstrations, electoral activities, etc.) that can lead to an improved social condition for black Americans. These figures may also help others to consider in broader fashion how central race is in everyday life, especially for issues that may not immediately appear to many individuals to concern race (e.g., debates on public health and public education). It might also be the case that the attention given to African American public intellectuals may initiate a desire by both black and white Americans to increase their literacy, exposure to literature, or respect for the life of the mind more generally. At bear minimum, elite higher educational institutions (which comprise the institutional base for African American public intellectuals and which shape the form and content of academic knowledge in this country) are being moved further to incorporate the African American context in their dissemination of such knowledge. Although somewhat removed from affecting grass-roots social change, these circumstances do establish a bedrock for broader social changes.

It is important to note, however, that the consequences of too intense a preoccupation with the public figures should be kept in mind. Many of them have been elucidated in a number of works that address the sociological significance of celebrities (Gamson 1994; Gitlin 1980). As this work argues, celebrities can becomes figures who in the end represent little more than themselves as their quest to secure a revered status in the public imagination. Ultimately, this quest may have little or nothing to do with the collective goals and interests of the groups or individuals that they claim to represent. The point of referring to this work is not to assert that such an activity is the motivating force for the current constituency of African American public intellectuals. It is the case, however, that if the public (especially the African American public) expends much time and energy engrossed by such figures then that public minimizes its emphasis on more pragmatic collective interests and goals. The potential for this to occur (if it has not already) is the most grave consequence of the age of the African American intellectual celebrity. In the end, the objectives and efforts of the less public African American scholars leave us with some critical questions about the emergence of the black intellectual celebrity: (1) How do the disadvantaged or disenfranchised people, who are in need of material support and resources, benefit in the age of the African American intellectual celebrity?, and (2) How do non-public black intellectuals get attention, as well as respect, for their effort to meet the needs of those people?

## NOTES

1.   Conservative African American public intellectuals such as Thomas Sowell have been in the public eye for nearly a decade longer period than have the left-of-center scholars that are considered here.

2.   Many African American public intellectuals actually navigate both the culturalist and the public affairs terrain. Thus, the distinction between the two is analytical more so than empirical.

3.   This comment should not imply that the commentary of African American public intellectuals is always void of content that can facilitate or enhance specific political initiatives. However, some of the critics argue that the commentary of these scholars is never subject to such critical interrogation in mass public discourse (see, e.g., Reed 1995).

4.   African American public literary figures, political figures, or even non-African American public intellectuals of the same or earlier eras in American history each can serve as the other half of a potentially provocative comparative inquiry on these matters.

5.   The long-standing commitment of African American scholars to these and other concerns is discussed in the survey-based analysis of African American scholars (Moore and Wagstaff 1974).

6.   My use of the term "organic intellectual" is inspired by, but not altogether identical to, the employment of the term by Cornel West in his "Dilemmas of the Black Intellectual (1985)." In using Antonio Gramsci as a point of departure, West argues that the organic intellectual is involved in grass-roots insurgent activity, but remains committed to "intense intellectual work" as well. Some of this intellectual work is aimed at preserving a critical consideration of one's own allies in social struggle and conflict so that the oppressive demeanor of the opposition is not reproduced by those who are trying to usurp the power of the opposition (thus enabling a more democratic outcome to prevail). Whereas West does not offer any empirical moments to depict how this mode of functioning occurs, the present work attempts to do so, albeit without the umbrella of a social movement or overtly insurgent activism as a location for such a depiction.

7.   The literature on this topic is vast. Some of the most insightful works are among the following: Bourdieu (1985, 1987); Fantasia (1988); Gramsci (1971); Hiller (1975); Sommers (1992, 1993); Thompson (1968).

## REFERENCES

Anderson, J. 1994. "The Public Intellectual." *The New Yorker* 17 (January): 39-
    46.
Baker, H. 1993. *Race, Rap and the Academy*. Chicago: University of Chicago Press.

Berube, M. 1995. "Public Academy." *The New Yorker* 9 (January): 73-80.
Bourdieu, P. 1985. "Social Space and the Genesis of Groups." *Theory and Society* 14.
————. 1987. "What Makes a Class? On the Theoretical and Practical Existence of Groups." *Berkeley Journal of Sociology* 32: 1-18.
Boyton, R.S. 1995. "The New Intellectuals." *The Atlantic Monthly* March: 53-54, 56, 60-62, 64-68, 70.
Dyson, M.E. 1993. *Reflecting Black: African American Cultural Criticism.* Minnesota: University of Minnesota Press.
Fantasia, R. 1988. *Cultures of Solidarity: Consciousness, Action, and Contemporary American Workers.* Berkeley: University of California Press.
Gamson, J. 1994. *Claims to Fame: Celebrity in Contemporary America.* Berkeley: University of California Press.
Gitlin, T. 1988. *The Whole World is Watching; Mass Media in the Making and Unmaking of the New Left.* Berkeley: University of California Press.
Gramsci, A. 1971. *Selections From Prison Notebooks.* London: Lawrence and Wishart.
Hiller, P. 1975. "The Nature and Social Location of Everyday Conceptions of Class." *Sociology* 9 (January): 1-28.
hooks, b. 1992. *Black Looks: Race and Representation.* Boston: South End Press.
————. 1990. *Yearning: Race, Gender, and Cultural Politics.* Boston: South End Press.
————. 1984. *Feminist Theory: From Margins to Center.* Boston: South End Press.
Moore, W., Jr., and L. Wagstaff. 1974. *Black Educators In White Colleges.* San Francisco: Jossey-Bass.
Phillip, M.C. 1995. "Thinking Out Loud; Black Intellectuals Focus on Popular Culture." *Black Issues in Higher Education* 20 (April): 9-12, 14-15.
Reed, A. 1995. "What are the Drums Saying, Booker?: The Current Crisis of the Black Intellectual." *Voice* 11 (April).
Rivers, E. 1992. "On the Responsibility of Intellectuals in the Age of Crack." *Boston Review*, October.
————. 1993 "On the Responsibility of Intellectuals in the Age of Crack." *Boston Review*, January/February.
Rose, T. 1994. *Black Noise: Rap Music and Black Culture in Contemporary America.* Middletown, CT: Wesleyan University Press.
Sommers, M. 1992. "Narrative, Narrative Identity, and Social Action: Rethinking English Working-Class Formation." *Social Science History* 16: 591-630.
————. 1993. "Citizenship and the Place of the Public Sphere: Law, Community, and Political Culture in the Transition to Democracy." *American Sociological Review* 58: 587-620.
Thompson, E.P. 1968. *The Making of the English Working Class.* Harmondsworth: Penguin.
West, C. 1985. "Dilemmas of the Black Intellectual." *Cultural Critique* 1 (1).
————. 1993. *Race Matters.* Boston: Beacon Press.
White, J.E. 1993. "Philosopher With A Mission." *Time* 7 (June): 62.
Wilson, W.J. 1987. *The Truly Disadvantaged: The Inner City, The Underclass, and Public Policy.* Chicago: University of Chicago Press.

_____. 1991. "Studying Inner-City Dislocation: The Challenge of Public Agenda Research." *American Sociological Review* 56: 1-14.

_____. 1996. *When Work Disappears: The World of the New Urban Poor*. New York: Alfred A. Knopf.

# BLACK INTELLECTUALS AND THE POLITICS OF RACE:

## THE AFFIRMATIVE ACTION DEBATE

W. Avon Drake

## INTRODUCTION

Since the Supreme Court overturned the City of Richmond's minority set-aside program in January of 1989[1] the fate of affirmative action has further intensified discussions of race in American life. Not since the Court's decision in Regents of the University of California v. Allan Bakke in 1978 has the policy of affirmative action received so much attention. But six years after the Court's decision in City of Richmond v. J.A. Croson Co., the state of California ignited the latest round of the affirmative action saga. Heated public debates over a new ballot initiative to outlaw the use of minority group preferences, as well as Governor Pete Wilson's overt politicization of the issue, gave new currency to racial politics in America.

In 1954, with Brown v. Board of Education, the high Court began to abolish legal racial segregation in America. A decade later

Research in Race and Ethnic Relations, Volume 10, pages 147-168
Copyright © 1997 by JAI Press Inc.
All rights of reproduction in any form reserved.
ISBN: 0-7623-0275-5

Congress passed the 1964 Civil Rights Bill outlawing racial discrimination in places of public accommodation. Because both of these legal changes made important contributions to expanding racial democracy during the height of the Black Freedom struggle, there was a tendency to equate the objectives of the Civil Rights Movement with all areas of American life. This tendency became especially clear by the late 1960s and early 1970s as the struggle to achieve racial democracy in America was extended from social and political rights to economic progress as well. This effort was revealed incrementally at first and did not receive much public discussion. Following President Kennedy's issuance of Executive Order 10925 outlawing discrimination in federal contracting (Graham 1990, p. 41) and President Johnson's and Nixon's more aggressive initiatives in the area of black economic advancement (Steinberg 1995, pp. 164-167), black civil rights activists and the growing number of black elected officials began to assert the economic demand. One of the most radical voices was that of Dr. Martin Luther King, Jr. who after 1966 began to focus increasingly on the economic underpinnings of blacks and the poor (Garrow 1986).

The purpose of this paper is to frame the ascendant demand for black economic progress within the context of contemporary African American intellectual discourse. The first part of the paper will highlight the central role that the voice of W.E.B. DuBois played in giving intellectual legitimacy to the meaning of race from the perspective of black academics. Key themes from his classic *The Souls of Black Folk* will serve as a preface to the current dialogue on race and American life. The next part of the paper will specify the origins of the contemporary debate by introducing the challenge of Thomas Sowell to black intellectual orthodoxy as it relates to race. It will be argued that the post-civil rights era stagnation of black leaders helped the ideological efficacy of an emergent African American conservative perspective. Next the paper turns to a comparative discourse, signaling the ideological combat going on among black intellectuals in the attempt to provide a vision of racial progress in the post-civil rights era.

The final section of the paper will highlight the policy of affirmative action as a black empowerment strategy. In this regard I will draw on the experience of Richmond, Virginia, a majority black controlled city and the home of former Governor L. Douglas Wilder, the first black elected to that position. The concluding section of the paper will offer an eclectic addendum to the discussion of black progress and why blacks might refocus a preponderance of their energy to better serve their goal.

## PREFACE TO THE RACIAL DIALOGUE

W.E.B. DuBois, perhaps the most significant black intellectual of the nineteenth and twentieth centuries, left a standing scholarship that a wide spectrum of contemporary black academics still are informed by. It can be observed that the majority of notable African American scholars reflect the influence that DuBois' ideas had on their thinking.[2] Following the ascendance of counter-revolutionary forces at the end of Reconstruction, during which both the southern gentry and white racist opinion nearly annihilated black voices seeking equality, DuBois emerged out of that crucible to give intellectual sustenance to a new discourse.

W.E.B. DuBois (1868-1963) got his intellectual grounding at Fisk University, earning a B.A. degree there in 1885. After studying in the graduate school at Harvard University and later the University of Berlin in Germany, DuBois returned to America. Completing his dissertation, *The Suppression of the African Slave Trade* (1896), DuBois became the first black American to earn a Ph.D. from Harvard. In so doing he set out on a life-long journey to employ his talents on behalf of racial uplift.

As noted by the eminent historian John Hope Franklin, DuBois' response to the post-Civil War silence on the topic of race with the publication of his masterpiece on slavery, marked a significant turning point in American history.[3] DuBois continued to use his intellectual skills to usher an assault on American racial ideology and practice. In 1903 he published his classic *The Souls of Black Folk* in which he chronicled the degraded post-Civil War experience of blacks and elevated for national discourse the accommodationist philosophy of Booker T. Washington (Dubois 1961). This publication was a great prelude to the philosophical dynamics among modern black intellectuals. In raising for public consideration the ideological tension between the most powerful black leader and the most accomplished black intellectual, *The Souls of Black Folk* introduced an intra-racial politics to African American progress that never subsided. Fundamentally DuBois and Washington articulated competing visions of black progress strategies, even though a certain general complementarity was evident.

Both Washington and DuBois felt that blacks must play a significant role in their own uplift. Both also felt that white America should play an important role.[4] Besides style, Washington and DuBois differed on the core of racial uplift politics. The former presented a self-help strategy that was not strategically connected to the broad flow of American societal organization. The latter propagated a self-help policy that, as a competing strategy, would be reinforced by the laws and the political system of the dominant society. What lay at the basis of the tension between the two most prominent black leaders of the time? Perhaps, at least partially, the conflict between DuBois and Washington was compounded by the fact that the former was essentially an intellectual and the latter a politician. DuBois, the intellectual, had an expansive mind and had the freedom to use it according to his own standards. Washington, on the other hand, had his world structured by the will of his white financial supporters. Thus, one can imagine a significant difference in the way that DuBois and Washington treated the issue of black oppression and the ideal of racial progress in the late nineteenth and early twentieth centuries.

Following the lead of William M. Banks (1996) it is useful here to draw on the work of Richard Hofstader's conceptual distinction between intellect and intelligence:

> Intellect is the critical, creative, contemplative side of the mind. Whereas intelligence seeks to grasp, manipulate, re-order, adjust, intellect examines, ponders, wonders, theorizes, imagines. Intelligence will seize the immediate meaning in a situation and evaluate it. Intellect evaluates, and looks for the meaning of situations as a whole (Hofstader 1963).

The crucial point is that DuBois the intellectual dealt with the issues of race in a transcendent manner while Washington, though educated and intelligent, dealt with race within the immediacy of late nineteenth and early twentieth century limitations.

DuBois' voice, then, cracked the ideological box of white racial rigidity and ushered forth a new meaning of racial progress. In doing so, he gave lasting meaning to a democratic and equality-seeking racial discourse, one that still informs black thought today.

To illustrate this point, I will introduce and briefly reflect on the four concepts or themes embedded in *The Souls of Black Folk*. In the words of J. Saunders Redding, DuBois' 1903 classic "heralded a new approach to social reform on the part of the American Negro people—an approach of patriotic, non-violent activism which achieved its first success" (DuBois 1961) a decade after World War II. Beginning his militant demand for racial equality, DuBois started by discussing the concept of double-consciousness in which he explains the forced social dilemma and inner emotional turmoil that black Americans experience.

DuBois' concept of double-consciousness reveals an endemic duality in the psyche and behavior of blacks. The dialectic between racial oppression and the simultaneous demand for the expansion of democracy resulted in what DuBois referred to as "our spiritual stirrings." This represented in the black experience a "two-ness—an American, a Negro; two souls, two thoughts, two unreconciled stirrings; two warring ideals in one dark body, whose dogged strength alone keeps it from being torn asunder" (DuBois 1961, p. 17).

In spite of this inner conflict, DuBois argued that blacks were "longing to attain self-conscious manhood, to merge his double self into a better and truer self," both guided by the mutual interaction of the best in both black and white cultures. Yet what DuBois called "the contradictions of double aims," resulting in "the powers of single black men flashing here and there like falling stones, and d[ying] sometimes before the world has rightly gauged their brightness" (DuBois 1961, p. 17), was the explanation for what appeared to be black people's weakness of spirit and ability.

DuBois might assert, this is not the end of the story. For black people's subordinate position in America is not endemic, but socially constructed. And the result of the mutual interaction of black and white people can usher in a new racial equilibrium, "gained through the unifying ideal of race; the ideal of fostering the traits and talents of the Negro, not in opposition to or contempt for the other races, but in large conformity to the greater ideals of the American Republic" (DuBois 1961, p. 22). Thus DuBois asserted, resolving America's racial problem was a concrete test of this nation's underlying principles of a great democracy.

In his competing agenda with Washington regarding black progress, DuBois embraced the full spectrum of democratic rights. Like Washington, DuBois supported manual labor and the teaching of trades. But in opposition to Washington, DuBois was uncompromising in his demand for "higher education" for blacks as well. Besides the hyperbolic conflict between DuBois and Washington over the desired nature of education for blacks, the two adversaries had an equally turbulent conflict over the larger catalog of democratic rights for blacks. In this regard Washington counseled patience and accommodationism. Specifically, Washington exhorted blacks to adjust to the post-Reconstruction social order[5] in exchange for financial support for Tuskegee and other such institutions. Washington argued that blacks could wait for the vote, social equality, and higher education. In return, DuBois would argue the policy of accommodationism had in fifteen years resulted in:

1.  The disenfranchisement of the Negro.
2.  The legal creation of a distinct status of civil inferiority for the Negro.
3.  The steady withdrawal of aid from institutions for the higher training of the Negro (DuBois 1961, pp. 48-49).

In response to Washington's racial politics and the incremental stripping away of Reconstruction gains, DuBois single-handedly asserted the demand—at last from an intellectual perspective—for three things for blacks:

1.  The right to vote.
2.  Civic equality.
3.  The education of youth according to ability (DuBois 1961, p. 50).

While these particulars may seem mundane in the current era they represented the core of the politics of race as reflected in the ideological struggle between the two most dominant black leaders of the late nineteenth and early twentieth centuries.

To fully recapture the exegesis of the moment, at least from the perspective of DuBois, it is necessary to reflect on the meaning and historical place of his often quoted assertion: "the problem of the twentieth century is the problem of the color-line" (DuBois 1961, pp. 23-41). DuBois introduced that theme to open and close "Of the Dawn of Freedom," the second chapter in *The Souls of Black Folk*. That essay, following "Of Our Spiritual Strivings" and preceding "Of Mr. Booker T. Washington and Others," outlined the turbulent socio-economic and political climate immediately following the Civil War and in relationship to Washington, the challenge to accommodationist leadership. DuBois chose for his task here to describe the physical conditions that four million ex-slaves were living in and to offer a minimum program for their human salvation and social development. Having lived through over 30 years of this experience and witnessed the loss of black political rights and brief ownership of land, DuBois was intent on assuring basic democratic rights for the new freedmen. DuBois' intellectual leadership was particularly important as America was in the midst of a transition from agriculture to industrialization. This change in American societal organization combined with white racial hostility, DuBois felt, required that blacks be guaranteed full political rights and opportunities. This was especially necessary in light of the failure of the Freedmen's Bureau of the late 1860s.

The failure of the country to carry out the ideals of the post-Civil War government was related to both the hostility of the South and the indifference of the North. The failure to significantly obliterate the most resolvable obstacles to black progress was the clear predicate for DuBois' conclusion that "the problem of the twentieth century is the problem of the color line." And, at least from the perspective of contemporary black intellectuals, the unresolved problems of race give currency to DuBois' strategic thesis. The immediate challenge for African American intellectuals is to update and clarify the black progress discourse and target its substantive objectives.

## ORIGINS OF THE CONTEMPORARY DEBATE

In *The Crisis of the Negro Intellectual*, Harold Cruse wrote rather poignantly:

> In order to get down to the roots of this racial crisis in America one must excavate every established factional creed and conformism; whether black or white, that has blocked the analysis and re-evaluation of the American mythology. In this pursuit all intellectual superficiality on the American race question, coming from either side of the racial fence, must be shattered with the most rigorous critical assault the collective intelligence can muster (Cruse 1976, p. 402).

Even though written in 1967 during an emergent Black Power Movement, this advice has critical significance for the present topic.

It points to the view that post-civil rights liberal black thought must be re-examined, and alternative views of competing black intellectuals need to be analyzed. Peter Steinfels, in *The Neo-Conservatives*, makes the point more succinctly. He noted:

> A distinct and powerful political outlook has recently emerged in the United States. It's outlook has produced telling critiques of contending political views and provocative analysis of specific political proposals; it has devoted its attention to fundamental questions its rivals have frequently overlooked; and it deserves, accordingly a thoughtful, extensive and careful evaluation (Steinfels 1979, p. 1).

In proper context, this refers to a group of well published black thinkers led by Thomas Sowell, Walter Williams, and Glenn C. Loury. These writers have challenged the analysis and policy prescriptions of the dominant, liberal wing of black social opinion and, perhaps inadvertently, opened up the black public policy discourse far beyond the pale of black conservative thought. This is evidenced by the entrance into the Public Intellectual's foray by black social democratic thinkers such as William Julius Wilson and Adolph Reed, Jr.

It has long been established that competing strategies for social group progress in situations of politico-economic conflict often lend themselves to intense ideological debate. In *Ideology and Utopia*, Karl Mannheim noted that his book is concerned with the problem of how men actually think. The aim of these studies, he said, is to investigate not how thinking appears in textbooks on logic, but how it really functions in public life and in politics (Mannheim 1936, p. 1). He later noted that "when measured by the standards of practical conduct, mere thinking, or reflection on a given situation turns out to be trivial" (Mannheim 1936, p. 72). The aim of intellectual work then, especially in the context of post-civil rights black life, ought to have a public policy or community enhancement dimension to it.

Long before contemporary black intellectuals acknowledged the arrival of competing ideas as it relates to racial progress, a thoughtful black academic introduced an ideological alternative to the hegemony of liberal black opinion. Thomas Sowell, formerly of the Brookings Institute and now a Senior Fellow at the Hoover Institution, Stanford University, published *Black Education: Myths and Tragedies* (1972). This conservative and provocative exposition was followed by a flood-tide of other works by Sowell. An economist with degrees from Harvard, Columbia, and the University of Chicago, Sowell published *Classical Economics Reconsidered* (1974), *Race and Economics* (1975), *Markets and Minorities* and *Ethnic America* (1981), *Civil Rights: Rhetoric or Reality* (1984), and *Race and Culture: A World View* (1994). Numerous articles were published in academic journals and daily newspapers. These were supplemented by high visibility lectures.

Sowell's emergence as a prolific writer and indomitable thinker provided a worrisome challenge to mainstream black thought. His ideological underpinnings were a broadside attack on the sanctity of black liberalism. Sowell's overriding theme is that black Americans must attempt more individual tenacity and self-sufficiency and there must be a corresponding disengagement of the state from cumbersome regulations of economy and society.

The politics of race in the current era should be conceptualized as having its intellectual genesis in the writings of Thomas Sowell, the leading challenge to black liberal orthodoxy in the post-civil rights period. But Sowell would quickly be followed by a growing number of black conservative thinkers. Speaking about this new development, Markin Kilson noted that it "marks an important crossroads in the life cycle of the Afro-American intelligentsia" ("Breaking the Code" 1985). Kilson is referring to this post-civil rights tendency in black thought, played out in journals such as the *New Republic*, *The Public Interest*, and *The Wall Street Journal*.

The writers identified with this movement are highly trained, strategically placed and often combative. They have successfully mounted a sustained attack on what is called "the civil rights strategy" of alleviating the deteriorating socio-economic condition of rank-and-file blacks ("Breaking the Code" 1985). Embedded in the conservatives challenge to black liberal thought is the former's view that socio-economic disparity is not necessarily caused by racial discrimination. Secondly, this position cautions on the commonly held belief that mechanisms of the courts and government can be meaningful tools for racial group advancement in the post-civil rights era. This position argues that the old line civil rights agenda was useful as a tool against overt forms of discrimination such as poll taxes, restrictive housing covenants, and segregated places of public accommodation.

However, black conservative thinkers argue that the civil rights strategy of the 1960s has very limited utility when confronted with disparities created by social class differences. Worse, they say, is the black liberal's view that discrimination is to blame for the expanding black underclass which constitutes a problematic sector of post-civil rights black America. From the perspective of black conservative thinkers, dominant liberal opinion refuses to boldly tackle current social pathology in the black community.

## IDEOLOGICAL STAKES AND VISION OF BLACK PROGRESS

While the writings of Thomas Sowell generated a clear dialectic of post-civil rights black thought, it is the work of William Julius Wilson that expanded the boundaries of the racial discourse. After the publication of *The Declining Significance of Race* in 1978, Wilson eclipsed Sowell as the major focus of black liberalism's attack. The stage is now set for the intensification of ideological warfare among the dominant black intellectual camps: black liberalism, conservatism and social democracy. In the post-civil rights era the ideological stakes are high because the African American community, for the first time since the collapse of racial segregation, is being offered competing visions of black progress. It was within this context that the politics of race among black intellectuals became salient. The mere idea that Sowell or Wilson could offer an ideological alternative to black liberalism was unacceptable to much of the African American intelligentsia and the civil rights leadership.

Following the historic gains of the 1960s and, to a less extent, the early 1970s, black leaders had to continue pursuing the unfinished business of desegregation. With the passage of the 1964 Civil Rights Bill, the 1965 Voting Rights Act, the 1968 Open Housing Ordinance and economic opportunity initiatives like Nixon's "black capitalism" agenda (Byrne and Edsall 1991, esp. Chap. 5) in 1969, it was inevitable that the commonality of race unity would begin to crack. For obvious reasons, this could first be observed among black intellectuals.

Going as far back as the early writings of W.E.B. DuBois, black liberalism's vision of racial progress was shaped by its faith in piece-meal reform measures and enlightened white elites. The goal of this movement was to open up American institutions so that blacks could have greater access to American opportunities. During World War I, DuBois again reflected this view with an article, "Close Ranks" published in the *Crisis Magazine*. In that article blacks were asked to lay down their legitimate complaints regarding racial discrimination and unite with the larger project of fighting the war. For this, DuBois thought, the nation would reward blacks by removing obstacles to their inclusion as full citizens.

In addition to DuBois' *The Souls of Black Folk*, Dr. Kenneth B. Clark's *Dark Ghetto* published over a half century later offered a similar analytical caveat regarding black progress. In his 1965 volume Clarke, like DuBois in his 1903 classic, put his faith in the good will of white political and economic elites. In this regard both the early DuBois and Clark operated on the assumptions of black liberalism, which follows American liberalism without its racial particularities.

In the more recent era, the black liberal perspective is given sustenance by works like *The Illusion of Black Progress* (1978), *The Black Underclass* (1981), *The New Black Middle Class* (1987), and *The Color Line and the Quality of Life* (1987). These works represent an updated version of its antecedents which is an evolving black liberal position shaped by the early DuBois and Kenneth B. Clark.

To a less extent, a vigorous voice of black studies scholars support the liberal position. They include the founders and leadership of the National Council for Black Studies and most of it's board members. Some in this core, at first glance, might not appear to be so clearly within the black liberal camp. Upon close examination, however, one will note a striking similarity between established black liberalism and its more rhetorical bedfellows.

In spite of varying degrees of racial acrimony, a broad spectrum of black academic opinion, including its Afrocentric derivation, shares a similar ideological profile with the liberal vision of black progress.

The overriding unifying thread binding this entire core of black intellectuals is their hostile opposition to any view that does not unconditionally support the primacy of race thesis. A corollary of this perspective is black liberalism's position that advances an uncompromising emphasis on the obligation of the government to the furtherance of black progress.

A striking example of the liberal position is found in Glasgow's *The Black Underclass*. In discussing the occupational obsolescence of the black underclass, the author argues that the phenomenon is rooted in "the large-scale rejection of black youth by white-controlled institutions of employment, education, and training" (Glasgow 1981, p. 160).

Closely following Glasgow is the work of Alphonso Pinkey. In *The Myth of Black Middle Class*, the writer asserts:

> Black people are the victims of oppression because of their racial heritage, not because they are separated by whites by class differences. Indeed, in matters involving the two races upperclass blacks fare no better than do poor blacks.

The tendency to deny the significance of intra-racial class differences is a poignant dimension of black liberalism. Furthermore, when comparing black and white family status, Farley and Allen argue that race is the critical explanatory variable (Farley and Allen 1987, pp. 185-187, 410-411). Clearly Sowell and those not wedded to the liberal paradigm would insist that other non-racial factors help explain the differential socio-economic condition of blacks and whites.

In the current era, several widely read works have been published supporting the black liberal paradigm.[6] Scholars such as Henry Louis Gates, Jr., Michael Eric Dyson, Lani Guinier, and even Cornel West are proponents of the black liberal position. The intellectual motif inherent in their writing is the almost unilateral concentration on the racial factor as the key explicator of African American life chances.

Historically, black liberalism has been quite successful in charting a course for racial progress. It has maintained a legitimate and aggressive presence in discussions of the race problem in America, insisting that the government play a rigorous role in resolving black/white inequities. Unfortunately, black liberalism has not kept pace with changes in American societal organization. Consequently, its impact on black progress has diminished considerably in the current period.

For most of the twentieth century, liberalism has been the dominant position in black thought. Even though from time to time it has been confronted with alternative nationalist and Marxist perspectives, the black liberal stance has remained hegemonic in African American intellectual circles.

As previously noted, during the early phase of the post-civil rights era a black free-market economist began to expand the racial discourse relating to black progress. Furthermore, Thomas Sowell's vitriolic and systematic challenge to black liberalism was joined by increasing African American intellectuals who supported his basic argument. But by the late 1970s another emergent view entered the foray. Before black intellectuals of a liberal bent could mount an effective response to a quickening conservative challenge, University of Chicago sociologist William Julius Wilson entered the debate concerning the status of blacks and its redress.

Wilson, like Sowell and his ideological cohorts, think that race is assigned too much salience by black liberal intellectuals. Unlike Sowell, Shelby Steele, Stephen Carter and other black conservatives, Wilson associates the subordinate status of contemporary blacks with the structure and functioning of the modern American economy. But like black liberals Wilson is acutely aware that race must be factored into any meaningful solutions designed to positively impact the life chances of African Americans. Yet, in the context of post-civil rights changes in American societal organization,[7] Wilson does not embrace the black liberal's position on the across the board salience of race in explaining the current state of black disadvantage. Consequently, Wilson enters the politics of race discourse as an intellectual alternative to both black liberalism and black conservatism.

During the past 20 years William Julius Wilson has pioneered a new approach to the study of social relations, with special attention to its racial component. Though controversial and a bit misunderstood, Wilson provided a new theoretical architecture for the study of the black experience. He provided, of course, a competing analysis of post-civil rights black life. In so doing, Wilson signaled the need for alternative black progress strategies.

Following the publication of *The Truly Disadvantaged* in 1987, Wilson gained uncontested ascendancy in urban poverty research and social policy discourse. He became the dominant voice in both the national print and the electronic media. He published in the *New York Times*, *Washington Post*, *Democratic Left*, *Black Scholar*, and *Dissent* among others. From April 1964 to March 1992, Wilson presented 63 papers at professional conferences including the American Sociological Association, World Congress of Sociology, National Urban League Convention, the Annual Congress Association for Sociology in Southern Africa (in Lesotho), Socialist Scholars Conference, National Association of Social Workers, New York Summit on Black and Hispanic Children, American Economic Association, British Sociological Association, and the Association for the Study of Afro-American Life and History.

This brief catalog of Wilson's professional activities highlight how widely spread his views have been disseminated. The overwhelming purpose was to illuminate the post-civil rights nature of race in America and especially intra-black class changes. Also, I wanted to note Wilson's contributions to a wide range of audiences as the nation discussed race and black progress in the post-civil rights era.

Wilson's ideas first burst on the public scene in a major way following the 1978 publication of a very controversial book, *The Declining Significance of Race: Blacks and Changing American Institutions.* Wilson meet immediate and widespread attack, especially by mainstream black academics and civil rights leadership. False repetition became the order of the day, especially by many who apparently had not even read his book. This was in large measure related to Wilson's attempt to de-emphasize the power of race in social analysis at a time when many African Americans felt that the country was moving towards a more racist stance. In reality, Wilson had a different objective, in terms of public policy and internal racial improvement strategies, than black liberalism was willing to accommodate. Wilson questioned the political efficacy and economic meaning of affirmative action.

As one can surmise, as it related to the future of the African American community, black intellectual combat was extremely dynamic during the decade of the 1980s. Piercing jabs emerged from both black liberal and black conservative camps, while William Julius Wilson attempted to sharpen and sustain his position. Writings from each of the three major perspectives among black intellectuals were competing for influence. Each wanted to have significant influence in shaping race-related public opinion, public policy, and the post-civil rights black agenda.

It was in this atmosphere that a few black academics endeavored to present an alternative interpretation of *The Declining Significance of Race* and Wilson's later writings. I, for example, argued that Wilson's de-emphasis of race in contemporary America is not in itself a conservative stance. One had to look at Wilson's empirical data and the efficacy of his theoretical formulations about black life in post-civil rights America. One also needed to study the public policy implications of his work. Only then could a fair assessment of Wilson's thesis in *The Declining Significance of Race* be executed. Wilson's argument that "many important features of black and white relations in America are not captured when the issue is defined as majority versus minority and that a pre-occupation with race and racial conflict obscures fundamental problems that derive from the intersection of race with class" (Wilson 1978, p. ix), was the foundation for the gross misinterpretation of his analysis. Wilson's view that "it is difficult to speak of a uniform black experience when the black population can be meaningfully stratified into groups whose members range from those who are affluent to those who are impoverished" (Wilson 1978, p. x) was rejected because, his critics argued, it deflected attention away from white racism and concurrently exaggerated the progress of middle class African Americans. The repetitive ring was that all blacks are essentially in the same boat because middle class African Americans are only one paycheck from poverty.

An alternative interpretation of Wilson's analysis, more clearly elaborated on in *The Truly Disadvantage* associated his efforts to describe the contemporary black experience within the context of structural, social democratic and political changes in American societal organization.

Wilson does not treat the black community as a monolith. Instead, he has demonstrated empirically that in the current era the black experience is best understood by taking note of the worrisome class differences that have become increasingly sharp over the past twenty five years. By concentrating on this development, Wilson has been able to shift attention to the dialectical link between dramatic improvements in the black middle class and the expansive nature of poverty in low income black inner-city neighborhoods.

Here, it should be recognized that the contradictory nature of the black economic experience is not new; black America has long had various class or socio-economic sectors. This was even true during the slavery and Jim Crow eras when blacks lived under state-imposed racial-caste and racial segregation situations. Today, however, the economic condition of blacks reflects an exaggeration of those earlier experiences, so much so until one can now speak of an intra-racial economic dialectic. It is this post-civil rights phenomenon, born of the liberal and democratic changes in the modern American economy and polity, that helped shape the ideological contours and policy agenda of Wilson's writings.

## AFFIRMATIVE ACTION AND BLACK INTELLECTUALS

Beginning with the Supreme Court's ruling in University of California, Davis v. Bakke, civil rights leaders and many black intellectuals proclaimed that this would undermine many of the hard won gains of the 1960s. Black liberal academics seemed unanimous in their view that a judicial challenge to racial preferment programs would halt the pace of black progress. And because black liberal opinion on race-related matters is so influential in the African American community, it first appeared as though that view would go unchallenged.

For many blacks affirmative action is automatically interchanged, at least conceptually, with black progress. This is related to the domination of black public opinion by civil rights leaders and liberal intellectuals. Consequently, the interest of middle class blacks is often represented as the interest of all blacks and because of the memory of segregation, this assumption usually goes unchallenged. But with the emergent views of black conservatism, later joined by Wilson, Adolph Reed and others, the class bias of black liberalism was noted.

It is from an understanding of how black intellectuals deal with the issue of race in post-civil rights America that illuminates the current discourse on African American progress. This essay will conclude with a summary of the black liberal perspective on the policy of affirmative action, after which competing views of Thomas Sowell and William Julius Wilson will be considered.

Most contemporary black intellectuals embrace the liberal perspective. The primacy of race is usually at the center of their writings. In the current era affirmative action is the first line of defense. Any criticism of the policy is considered to be in opposition to the interest of the black community. Rarely is the question asked, "Do lower income, unemployed blacks benefit from the center-piece of post-civil rights racial advancement strategies?" Black liberal intellectuals along with the civil rights leaders seem to think that affirmative action is sacrosanct, never admitting that the masses of African Americans do not benefit at all from a policy built on the political capital of the entire race. Richmond, Virginia, a majority black city, is a case in point. Beginning in 1977, African American voters succeeded in electing a black majority to city council. Because Richmond has a ward-based council with power to choose the mayor, that position is usually occupied by an African American also.

Since the emergence of black political control of city politics, African Americans have been appointed to increasing numbers of high level jobs. Currently, Richmond politics are driven by a black majority city council, a black mayor, a powerful black city manager, black police chief, and black superintendent of schools. Still politics and black leadership follow the traditional liberal philosophy guided by voter registration efforts and affirmative action concerns. Hardly is there ever advanced a demand for increased black self-help, community accountability, race-based economic nationalism, or strategies to target benefits of racial redistribution to the inner-city poor. But, as was the case in Atlanta and other cities under black political control, affirmative action soon became in Richmond the focus of black leadership. A few years after the black majority came to power, Richmond's center-piece of black progress initiatives was passed by city council. In 1983, the Richmond City Council passed a resolution requiring that minority contractors receive 30 percent of the total dollar value of the total contract whenever the prime contractor was white (Drake and Holsworth 1996, p. 37). This case ultimately lead in 1989 to the Supreme Court's ruling in Richmond v. J.A. Croson, which overturned the city's set-aside plan and further increased the volatility of affirmative action.

The main proof of African American progress in Richmond since the emergence of black political control in 1977 has been the city's minority set-aside plan. During a two year period of the plan's existence, 47 companies received construction monies for an average of $248,786 per company. But, illuminating the economic constriction of affirmative action, two contractors received a majority of the money that went to minority firms. In 1985, the most situated, Dwight Snead's company, earned $1,971,880 while Quail Oak Company received $828,000, out of a total of $5,446,291 earned by minority firms. In 1986 Quail Oak received $1,731,297 and Snead earned $1,529,833 out of the $6,276,667 that went to minority contractors (Drake and Holsworth 1996, p. 40).

Since the political takeover of Richmond politics by black leaders, much has been made about the significance of the city's set-aside program for African American development. Rarely does a civil rights leader or black academic question the substance of the claim or the efficacy of affirmative action as the foundation of racial advancement initiatives. The repetition of the value of the set-aside program for Richmond's black community serves as proof of its validity.

Perhaps the main reason for the lack of competing interpretations of urban black progress strategies is because of the straight and narrow focus on dismantling racial disadvantage. In the post-civil rights era, black leaders and black liberal intellectuals remain wedded to the primacy of race thesis, not taking into account the changed nature of American societal organization or the emergent black economic dialectic. The primacy of race thesis is the political and intellectual predicate for the current sterility in black thought today.

One way of understanding this phenomenon is to conceptualize the efficacy of competing schools of black thought in the African American community. Since the days of the early DuBois, liberalism has been a significant and often dominant strain in the racial progress discourse, and for understandable reasons. But in the post-civil rights era, objective conditions warrant a broader and more rigorous discourse regarding the black experience. This necessitates a closer analysis of intra-black class differences and how public policy might be crafted to respond to the competing needs of the African American community. Investing the political capital of the entire black community in a policy that only benefits a small sector of African Americans demands reconsideration. But because of narrow electoral reasons, this need will not likely come from black politicians.

As early as the mid-1970s and especially during the past 15 years, an expanded black intellectual voice has begun to be recognized in the African American community. The tendency of unilaterly placing race as the primary factor in black life is being increasingly contested. This is particularly important as it relates to the development of public policy initiatives that are designed to be the centerpiece of black advancement.

In *Civil Rights: Rhetoric or Reality*, Thomas Sowell calls into question the entire affirmative action agenda. Not only is it misguided, according to the author, but the policy has a decided class bias. In *The Truly Disadvantaged: The Inner City, the Underclass, and Public Policy*, Wilson moves towards a framework for addressing the post-civil rights heterogenous character of the black community. That framework, informed by the increasing economic bifurcation of the black community, calls on elected officials and policy makers to alter the standard racial progress agenda to include a comprehensive program of economic and social reform that would include targeted programs, both means tested and race-specific. The object is to create programs that would be attentive to both race and class, thus having the potential to draw political support from a wide spectrum of American people. Also, Wilson's framework would prevent the redistribution of racial benefits from going primarily to middle class blacks, a key limitation of affirmative action politics.

While Wilson's entrance into the post-civil rights racial discourse has largely been concerned with the changing racial situation and intra-black class divisions, his recent work focuses more specifically on the roots of current black disadvantages. In concluding this section of the topic, it is necessary to highlight the direction that government officials, policymakers, and black leaders should give increased attention.

"Many of today's problems in the inner-city ghetto neighborhoods—crime, family dissolution, welfare, low levels of social organization, and so on—are fundamentally a consequence of the disappearance of work"(Wilson 1996, p. xiii). For black intellectuals who are searching for an alternative to the politics of race through affirmative action demands, more concentration on the widespread and long term rate of black joblessness is required. It is the phenomenon of joblessness, especially black male joblessness, that has fueled problems of social organization in inner-city ghetto neighborhoods. And the consequences of social isolation of the black poor and the simultaneous social demographic shifts of the black middle-class are now clear. The continuing rise of crime and violence, a proliferation of negative behavior patterns, and the increased alienation of the ghetto poor from white institutions and the black middle-class are not being addressed with current affirmative action politics.

Therefore, it seems incumbent on black intellectuals who are concerned about African American uplift to broaden their conception of black progress.

Following the lead of William Julius Wilson, I believe that "a comprehensive race-neutral initiative to address economic and social inequality should be viewed as an extension of—not a replacement for—opportunity-enhancing programs that include race-based criteria to fight social inequality" (Wilson 1996, p. 205). But in this effort there would need to be built-in oversight mechanisms to ensure the implementation of race-neutral programs to benefit the black disadvantaged in a non-discriminatory manner.

As we move into the twenty-first century, black intellectuals ought to be driven by the need to place more attention on the most disadvantaged sector of the African American community. This effort should be multi-dimensional with a strategic focus on the economic, social, and educational. The main objective must be to craft policies...both government-assisted and community self-help...that will have a clear utilitarian impact on the life chances of the most disadvantaged in the black community. In this regard affirmative action must be relegated as a black middle-class enhancing strategy. The political capital of the African American community ought now be targeted on the special needs of the black poor and working class.

## CONCLUSIONS

Black public intellectuals emerged in the context of the racial and political turmoil of the late 1960s and early 1970s. Their goal was to help shape the black community discourse about the direction of struggle against racist oppression. Some in this earlier group of black public intellectuals were associated with the rise of Afro-American Studies Programs or the Black Power Movement. Most notably were James Turner of the Africana Studies and Research Center of Cornell University, Maulana Karenga and Angela Davis, both of Los Angeles, Howard Fuller of Malcolm X Liberation University in Durham, North Carolina and Stokely Carmichael (now Kwame Toure), a leading advocate of black self-determination.

Following the demise of the Black Freedom struggle in the late 1970s new voices of black public intellectuals emerged. Generally the new writers and thinkers were associated with traditional academic institutions; their voices regarding racial conflict were rather muted. They did, however, publish significant scholarly works. Their product, however, was geared primarily towards middle-class blacks and to white society. Whereas the first wave of black public intellectuals spoke directly to the anger of blacks and attempted to instill a strong racial identity concept, this more widely known group spoke to academics, hoping to influence the racial discourse relating to the construction of public policy.

The third wave of black public intellectuals to emerge does not offer either the racial identity or substantive policy contribution of the first two. This third group has achieved significant notoriety for its populist treatment of racial matters. Examples in this younger group include Henry Louis Gates, Jr. and Cornel West, co-authors of *The Future of the Race*, Michael Eric Dyson, author of *Race Rules: Navigating the Color Line*, and journalist Ellis Cose, author of *The Rage of a Privileged Class.*

On the right of these younger black liberal intellectuals are their conservative foes. Shelby Steele's *The Content of Our Character* and Stephen Carter's *Reflections on an Affirmative Action Baby* represent the racial thought of this group.

But what is needed now from black intellectuals is a creative supplement to the writings of the likes of William Julius Wilson. Coalition and race-specific politics, along with formulations of models of black economic nationalism, a rejuvenated cultural integrity valuation, and a concentration on making public education for black inner-city youth employment-specific need to be the primary focus of any discourse on African American progress in the immediate future.

Historically, black intellectuals have made a very important contribution to the struggle for racial uplift. They attacked and analyzed overt discrimination against blacks and even helped to advance the post-civil rights demands for affirmative action. But in doing so the black community was too often viewed as monolithic. Black intellectuals now need to use the memory of race to argue for the creation of life-opportunity enhancing strategies that target the black disadvantaged, particularly the inner-city ghetto poor.

## NOTES

1. For a detailed review of this case see Drake and Holsworth (1996), especially Chapter Five.

2. Black scholars of all intellectual persuasions reflect this position. One will often see references in the writings of many black intellectuals to the work of W.E.B. DuBois.

3. See John Hope Franklin's forward in the reissue of W.E.B. DuBois' *The Suppression of the African Slave Trade* (1965).

4. For Washington's position on this point see his "Atlanta Exposition Address" of 1895 in Brotz (1966).

5. See Booker T. Washington's "Atlanta Exposition Address" in Brotz (1966).

6. See current works such as *Race Matters* by Cornel West, *Race Rules* by Michael Eric Dyson, *The Tyranny of the Majority* by Lani Guinier, *Faces at the Bottom of the Well* by Derrick Bell, and *The Rage of a Privileged Class* by Ellis Cose.

7.  See Wilson's perspective on this phenomenon in *The Declining Significance of Race*, (1978), especially Chapter Seven. Also, see Wilson (1996), Chapters Two and Three.

# REFERENCES

Banks, W.M. 1996. *Black Intellectuals: Race and Responsibility in American Life*. New York and London: W.W. Norton and Company.

"Breaking the Code." 1985. *Newsweek* (October 21), pp. 84-87.

Brotz, H. 1966. *Negro Social and Political Thought: 1850-1920*. New York and London: Basic Books, Inc.

Byrne, T., and M.D. Edsall. 1991. *Chain Reaction: The Impact of Race, Rights, and Taxes on American Politics*. New York and London: W.W. Norton and Company.

Carter, S. n.d. *Reflections of an Affirmative Action Baby*.

Cruse, H. 1967. *The Crisis of the Negro Intellectual*. New York: William Morrow and Company, Inc.

Drake , W.A., and R.D. Holsworth. 1996. *Affirmative Action and the Stalled Quest for Black Progress*. Urbana and Chicago: University of Illinois Press.

DuBois, W.E.B. 1961. *The Souls of Black Folk*. New York: Fawcett Publications.

Farley, R., and W.R. Allen. 1987. *The Color Line and the Quality of Life in America*. New York: Russell Sage Foundation.

Franklin, J.H. 1965. *The Suppression of the African Slave Trade*. Baton Rouge, LA: Louisiana State University Press.

Garrow, D.J. 1986. *Bearing the Cross*. New York: William Morrow and Company.

Glasgow, D.G. 1981. *The Black Underclass*. New York: Vintage Books.

Graham, H. 1990. *The Civil Rights Era: Origins and Development of National Policy, 1960-1972*. New York: Oxford University Press.

Hill, R.B. 1978. *The Illusion of Black Progress*. New York: National Urban League.

Hofstadter, R. 1963. *Anti-Intellectualism in American Life*. New York: Vintage Books.

Landry, B. 1987. *The New Black Middle Class*. Berkeley, Los Angeles, and London: University of California Press.

Mannheim, K. 1936. *Ideology and Utopia*. New York: Harcourt, Brace and World, Inc.

Pinkney, A. 1984. *The Myth of the Black Middle Class*. New York: Cambridge University Press.

Steele, S. 1990. *The Contempt of Our Character*. New York: St. Martin's Press.

Steinberg, S. 1995. *Turning Back: The Retreat from Racial Justice in American Thought and Policy*. Boston: Beacon Press.

Steinfels, P. 1979. *The Neo-Conservatives: The Men Who Are Changing American Politics*. New York: Simon and Schuster.

Wilson, W.J. 1978. *The Declining Significance of Race*. Chicago and London: The University of Chicago Press.

Wilson, W.J. 1996. *When Work Disappears: The World of the New Urban Poor*. New York: Alfred A. Knopf.

# DEMOCRACY AND INTELLECTUAL RESPONSIBILITY:

## THE CASE OF POLITICAL SCIENCE IN NIGERIA

L. Adele Jinadu

---

*Experts, advisers, counsellors-how many of them I have seen in my life-mostly nice, intelligent people caught in an inherently frustrating role.....*

(Kurczewski 1990, p. 77)

*... The succession of the military usurpations aggravated the alienation of academic intellectuals- the largest body of intellectuals in nearly every African country- and reduced them to a sense of impotence and despondence.*

(Shil, 1990, p. 300)

## I

I want to problematize and illustrate the issue of intellectual responsibility through an examination of the opportunities, problems

Research in Race and Ethnic Relations, Volume 10, pages 169-195
Copyright © 1997 by JAI Press Inc.
All rights of reproduction in any form reserved.
ISBN: 0-7623-0275-5

and dilemmas which the antinomies of democracy and military rule pose for academic political scientists in Nigeria. My purpose, in other words, my aim is to examine the universal problem of intellectual responsibility in the specific context of the responses of Nigerian academic political scientists to the antinomic relationships between democracy and military rule in their country.

It has often been claimed that intellectuals in developing countries have a special responsibility to their societies. But what is "special" about this responsibility, and how do we even begin to define the notion of "responsibility," as applied specifically to the intellectual vocation, as such? What does the experience of Nigeria academic political scientists indicate about the nature of this responsibility, or about how it has been or can be pursued?

I shall attempt to illustrate various dimensions of these questions through a discussion of the impact or effect of the recurring, albeit so far ill-fated democratic project in Nigeria on the development of political science and its practice by academic political scientists in the country.

If we are to begin to talk about intellectual responsibility, we must have some idea of who intellectuals are and of what we mean by responsibility, in the special and specific sense in which it applies to intellectuals in society.

## II

Who is an intellectual? An intellectual is a person who cherishes and pursues truth and knowledge for their own sake. It is in this sense, for example, that Montefiore (1990, p. 201) affirmed that, "by an intellectual" I mean here to refer to anyone who takes a committed interest in the validity and truth of ideas for their own sake." But this definition is only a starting-point; it refers basically to a particular attitude of mind or disposition to truth and knowledge. Indeed, as Montefiore (1990, p. 202) further observed, this definition commits one to agreeing "...that everyone must be considered, to some small extent at least, to have something of the intellectual in them."

For my purpose, we need to go beyond this attitudinal definition to a functional or practical, problem-solving definition of the intellectual. It is in this latter or functional sense of an intellectual that Shils (1990, p. 259) refers to "intellectual-practical activities." I shall, therefore, use the term, "intellectual" in this practical or functional sense. But in doing so, I shall also keep in mind that the distinction which Gramsci makes between traditional intellectuals ("teachers, priests, and administrators") and organic intellectuals, those "...directly connected to classes or enterprises that used intellectual to organize interests, gain more power, get more control" (Said 1994, p. 3). So functionally defined, intellectuals are those engaged in the production and distribution of knowledge (Said 1994, p. 7).

It is in this Gramscian twin-functional sense of traditional and organic intellectuals that I refer here to Nigerian academic political scientists as intellectuals. As teachers in the various departments of political science in Nigerian Universities, they are traditional intellectuals. In so far as they collectively provide a pool of "specialist experts" from whose ranks various interests, including the state, source for advice and legitimisation, Nigerian academic political scientsts are also organic intellectuals.

## III

What is intellectual responsibility? It seems to me that there are at least two senses in which one can talk of intellectual responsibility. The first sense is intellectual responsibility to and for the pursuit and defense of truth and of the conditions that make them possible. This view, the cultural view of intellectual responsibility also demands, indeed presupposes respect for as well as commitment and adherence to the canonical rules of scholarship and intellectual traditions.

The point here is the claim that there are certain values that define not only the intellectual vocation but also the identity of the intellectual. The extreme version of this view denies any public, that is, political role or responsibility for the intellectual other than that of defending, and *ipso facto* opposing threats to, conditions that make the pursuit of the intellectual vocation possible.

The second sense of intellectual responsibility and one which I shall use largely in this paper is political or social responsibility. As Szacki (1990, p. 235) has observed, this notion of intellectual responsibility "...is essentially identical with *political involvement*, with coming out of 'laboratories and libraries'..."

Let me elaborate on this notion of political responsibility. I shall use it to describe and assess how Nigerian academic political scientists have performed the function or role of traditional and/or organic intellectuals, especially in the face of their problematic relationships or encounters with various social forces, including the state and the powers-that-be. Although the term is descriptive, it is also fundamentally morally prescriptive and evaluative. It enjoins intellectuals to be "other-worldly," to get involved in political matters, while it also provides a basis for passing moral judgements on how they perform this public function.

This evaluative or moral judgmental dimension of the term is brought out in accusations about "betrayal of the intellectual vocation" that one hears again and again with reference to some intellectuals who are occupying or have occupied political positions.

But my use of this notion of intellectual responsibility is not limited to Nigerian academic political scientists who have served the state in one capacity or the other. I use it also to refer to how, as traditional intellectuals, in the Gramscian sense, they have confronted or sought to interpret Nigerian and international society and to their participation in the public discussion of national and international issues.

Nigerian academic political scientists, like other academic intellectuals in Africa, have a special responsibility to put their expert knowledge and training at the diposal of their country, to be concerned about the direction in which the powers-that-be, the world of power are shaping and moving their country. Their responsibility in this respect is also to define their role in so "politicizing" the intellectual vocation.

In the case of Nigerian academic political scientists, this responsibility is all the more acute and "special." This is because the antinomies of democracy and military rule bear directly on their discipline and its professionalization, as well as on their academic training. In other words, their "special" responsibility derives from the opportunities and challenges provided by military rule for them to offer directly or indirectly expert advice or to conjecture policy scenarios and measures for institutional designs and structural reforms necessary to reconstruct the Nigerian polity and to enthrone democracy and the culture of democracy in the country. As I have indicated earlier on, an examination of the impact or effect of the country's ill-fated but on-going democratic project on the development of political science in the country and its practice by Nigerian academic political scientists should throw some light on the problematic nature of intellectual responsibility in a country like Nigeria in transition to democracy.

## IV

Let me now indicate briefly the nature of the democratic project in Nigeria. My point of departure is the immediate post-World War II period when, under the influence of constitutional and political developments in the colonies in the Far East and the Indian subcontinent, and of liberal and social democratic ideas, Nigerian nationalists more aggressively than before began to define the democratic project they were pursuing in terms of decolonization. They linked democracy to self-determination and self-rule, both of which presumed participatory politics, although the emergent nationalist politics was elitist and narrow-based.

This democratic project drew, as indicated above, on liberal and social democratic sources and placed emphasis on economic development and the long-term indigenisation of the country's economy. Supervised and closely superintended by the British colonial administration, and in response to pressures from Nigerian nationalists for constitutional devolution of power to Nigerians, the democratic project was premised on the development of competitive, multiparty electoral politics and a parliamentary system of government based on the Westminister model.

The democratic project began to assume concrete institutional and constitutional shape from the late 1940s and the 1950s. The multiparty system emerged between 1946 and 1951. Representative government was introduced in 1951, and was followed by responsible government in 1954, self-government for the Eastern and Western regions in 1956 and for the Northern region in 1959, and independence for the country in 1960. Competitive multiparty parliamentary and local government elections, based on the gradual adoption and extension of universal adult suffrage, were conducted at various times between 1951 and 1959.

A central aspect of this democratic project was the adoption of a federal (initially under the 1954 constitution a quasi-federal) system of government, based on a theory of segmental autonomy for the major ethnic groups in the country.

The pursuit of this democratic project in practice thew up contradictions that exposed the fragility of the political inheritance at independence: serious systemic-threatening disequilibrium emerged in the operation of the multiparty system, parliamentarism and constitutional government, and federalism. In other words, by 1966 the democratic project had revealed institutional and structural weaknesses and psychocultural dissonance in the practice of liberal democracy in the country. Added to this was a fundamentally flawed and ethnostructurally imbalanced federalism.

Failure to resolve these contradictions was a major reason for the collapse of parliamentary rule and constitutional government on January 15, 1966 and the subsequent imposition of military rule. Nigeria has since then experienced the following alternations between democratic (civil) rule and military rule:

> 1 October 1960-15 January 1966: democratic (civil) rule;
> 16 January 1966-1 October 1979: military rule;
> 1 October 1979-31 December 1983: democratic (civil) rule; and
> 1 January 1984 to date: military rule (with Interim National Government, under a non-elected civilian as head from June-November 1993).

These alternations have been characterised by programmes of transition to democratic civil rule. Between July 1975 and October 1979, the military administrations of Murtala Muhammed and Olusegun Obasanjo faithfully pursued and successfully concluded a transition program which led to the transfer of power to democratically elected civilian chief executives (Governors and President) and legislatures at the state and federal levels, under a presidential system.

The military again took over power by force in December 1983. Another transition program to democratic civil rule was begin in late 1985 by the military administration of Ibrahim Babangida. This program which led to the emergence of democratically elected civilian chief executives and legislatures at the local government and state levels and of the federal legislature, under a presidential system, was aborted at its terminal phase with the annulment of the presidential elections of June 12, 1993 which Chief M.K.O. Abiola of the Social Democratic Party had apparently won with a clear margin.

As a way out and bowing to popular pressures, Babangida stepped down as President. Elected civilian chief executives and legislatures at the local government and state levels and the federal legislature were retained. However, at the federal level a new executive, called the Interim National Government, and with a non-elected civilian as head, but which was later pronounced by the courts as unconstitutional and illegal, was formed. But it was short-lived. It was overthrown by the military, with General Sani Abacha becoming head of state and government. The new military government has in turn announced another transition program to democratic civil rule, with October 1998 as the terminal date.

## V

The foregoing is on outline of the democratic project in Nigeria since the late 1950s. The alternations between democratic civil rule and military rule and the paradox of military-induced or engineered transitions to democratic civil rule must be situation, as I have attempted to do in summary form here, in the historical conjectures and the deepening contradictions of the Nigerian state.

In the rest of this paper, I attempt to illustrate some aspects of these conjectures and contradictions through an examination the reaction to them by, or their effect on Nigerian academic political scientists and of the role they have played in the unfolding of the antinomies of democracy and military rule in the rule.

## VI

I have traced the development of academic teaching and research in Nigeria elsewhere (Jinadu 1987). But it is pertinent here to make the following observation. At its onset, the democratic project did not produce an atmosphere conducive to the development of political science as an academic discipline at the then University Colege, Ibadan which was founded in 1948. This was partly due to the antipathy, even hostility of the colonial administration which feared the radicalizing impact of academic political science. There were also elements, as Eme Awa (1972, p. 2) has argued, among the emergent indigenous political class, the leadership of the nationalist movement in the country, who, from their own objective class position, were afraid that university teaching in political science would expose their class positions and raise the political, if not the class consciousness of the common man.

However, the logic of the anticolonial struggle and of the democratic project on the nationalist agenda, especially its welfarist emphasis on economic development, gave rise, in due course, to the view that political science and the other social sciences were relevant to national development and should, therefore, be constituted into autonomous academic departments in the country's university system, then about to be increased on the basis of the Ashby Commission Report with the establishment of more universities in the country. As Mabogunje (1973, p. 173) has observed, "by 1957, the birth of an independent Nigeria was already in sight and two of the three regions...had already achieved a high degree of internal self-government. These developments...had their impact on University College [Ibadan] and were clearly reflected in the new programs contemplated in the humanities and the social sciences."

From small beginnings, which saw it serve "apprenticeships" in other departments, political science has emerged as a major academic discipline in its own right in several Nigerian universities. Student enrollment has expanded in geometric proportions as has the size of academic political scientists, in spite of threatened rationalizations and reductions in subventions to social sciences in the 1980s.

An important feature of this development is the fact that Nigerian academic political scientists are employed the the state and are regarded as public servants, with all the privileges and legal obligations that go with that status. This is because all universities in the country are owned by and receive annual subventions from the state, either state governments, in respect of state-owned universities or the federal government, in respect of federal universities. The implications of this for intellectual responsibility shall be discussed later.

## VII

Let me now begin to indicate how Nigerian academic political scientists have reacted to the developmental trajectories of the country's democratic agenda. I begin with their role as traditional intellectuals, that is as teachers and researchers.

The democratization processes, in the form of the gradual devolution of power which began in the late 1940s through the 1950s, had an impact of a non-institutional character on the development of academic political science in the country. The devolution agenda and the socio-economic and political institutions and proceses it generated provided research agenda and data source for the country's first generation of academic political scientists and the type of subjects they introduced into their syllabuses. For example, the political science major textbooks produced by them, arising out of their doctoral dissertations, generally reflected concern with the formal, legal, constitutional processes of government: the role of parliaments, political parties, constitutionalism and constitutional law, federal government and national integration, to take a random survey (Awa 1960; Ezera 1962; Dudley 1968).

The turbulence which the democratic project experienced from the mid-1960s onwards had similar impact on the teaching and research agenda of academic political scientists in the country. The earlier focus on formal parliamentary institutions and governmental processes gave way to a new focus on three important issues: electoral violence and politics, federalism and party politics, and military rule.

With these substantive issues as new points of departure, Nigerian academic political scientists became more overtly critical and policy-oriented. Some of them began to explore the material forces at work with emphasis on the pathologies and contradictions of the democratic project: What has wrong? What needs to be done now? What structural changes and consequential institutional reforms are needed to get the democratic agenda on track? Can democratic transitions from mility rule be engineered?

What have been the major contributions of Nigerian academic political scientists, as they attempted to unscramble the antinomies of democracy and military rule in their country? First, they have advanced our understanding of the relationship between federalism and ethnicity as fundamentally involving the politics of elite accommodation and class formation in the country (Nnoli 1978; Jinadu 1985). Other aspects of federalism, including federal finance, party politics and federalism and foreign policy and federalism have been well-explored by Rafiu Akindele, Bolaji Akinyemi, Issawa Elaigwu, Gordon Isang, Eghosa Osaghae, and Rotimi Suberu who have built on the seminal, if descriptive work of Eme Awa and Kalu Ezera.

Secondly, the local government reforms of 1976, 1987 and 1989 which were intended to ensure participatory politics at the grassroots level and to extend the home rule notion inherent in federalism to the local government as a third tier of government, have been the subject of critical searchlight by Nigerian academic political scientists to this level of government, which had hitherto been neglected in the study of Nigerian politics, with good results, as in the writings of Ladi Adamolekun, Alex Gboyega, Dele Olowu, and Oyeleye Oyediran.

Thirdly, Nigerian academic political scientists have added greatly to our understanding of the nature of military rule, of militarism, demilitarization and transitions to democracy. Substantial contribution in this area has been made by Bayo Adekanye.

Fourthly, there is the general theoretical reinterpretation of the structural crises of the Nigerian state and of the democratic project in the country from a new political economy perspective offered by Claude Ake, Eme Ekekwe, Julius Ihonvbere, Okwudiba Nnoli, and such younger generation academic political scientists like Said Adejumobi, Sam Egwu, and Abubakar Momoh.

There are some of the areas in which Nigerian academic political scientists have attempted to come to grips with and interpret the democratic agenda in their country. The ensuing political science that their writings spawned was a much more critical one than was the case with the thrust and focus of the initial political science of the early 1960s in the country.

Its emergence was no doubt influenced by radical historiographical revisions and paradigmatic shifts in international political science, such as the Marxist and Neo-Marxist challenge to the mainstream orthodoxies represented by structural-functionalist and pluralist theories in the study of politics. But a much more powerful source of influence was the radical political science of Claude Ake and Okwudiba Nnoli who returned to the country in the late 1970s and early 1980s, especially in terms of their influence on younger academic political scientists in the country.

To conclude this examination of the ways in which the antinomies of democracy and military rule have impacted the teaching and research of Nigerian academic political scientists, a word is appropriate about the character of the environment in which they pursued their vocation as traditional intellectuals.

First, there is the ill-fated course of the democratic project itself. The overthrow of the democratically elected civilian regime in 1966 has meant that historically there has been an inadequate data source or base for Nigerian academic political scientists undertake synchronic and diachronic studies of parliamentary institutions and democratic processes in the country. Moreover, military rule has been diversionary of even any attempt to undertake such studies on the politics of the country between 1960 and 1966, about which much remains to study: the nature of cabinet government; legislative and judicial behavior, intergovernmental relations; electoral behavior; and bureaucratic behavior.

Secondly, Nigerian academic political scientists have had difficulty or have shown little interest in studying the policymaking process under military rule because of problems inherent in the nature of military rule itself: access to the such policymaking institutions like the military high command itself. How did issues get on the policy agenda? What options were considered? What did the issues indicate about factions within the military? What civilian inputs have there been to the policy process and how are they sifted? What role is played by the civil service in the policy process under the military and how does it differ under democratic civilian administration? What role does the cabinet play in the policy processs? What military-created institution under military rule serves as the functional equivalent of the legislature, and how is it organized for the lawmaking function?

The problem Nigerian academic political scientists apparently have faced in this area, as I have already suggested, is one of access to such key military policymaking institutions as the Armed Forces Ruling Council or the Provisional Ruling Council. The problem is also due to the undemocratic nature of military rule and the consequential political "irresponsibility" and lack of accountability on the part of the military.

The study of the public policy process under the military is an important lacuna or missing link in the study of military rule by Nigerian academic political scientists. This is a serious lacuna, if only because the military, in power for over 26 years of Nigeria's 37-year independent nationhood, have taken critical decisions, including the preservation of Nigeria as an indissoluble, independent sovereign state and the decision to wage the civil war, and the annulment of the June 1993 presidential elections, which have had serious and lasting consequences for the democratic project in the country.

Let me relate the foregoing discussion to the issue of intellectual responsibility. Nigerian academic political scientists as traditional intellectuals, in the Gramscian sense, in other words as teachers and researchers, have been faithful by and large to the intellectual traditions of their discipline, through their research and publications.

Peer review and assessment, especially in respect of appointments and promotions and publications, have served to ensure their adherence to these traditions.

Another point to make is that Nigerian academic political scientists have been active in interpreting their society, more often than not in a critical matter, holding up a mirror within which the rest of the society can view societal developments, and in doing so, also speaking the truth to power. The cumulative effect of this is that they have significantly added to the stock of knowledge about Nigerian politics.

A further observation is that the earlier generation of Nigerian academic political scientists who started their academic careers in Nigerian universities in the 1960s and 1970s have succeeded in reproducing themselves in the form of the emergence of a new generation of academic political scientists who were trained by them and who are now establishing their own reputation as academics, even under harsh conditions that are most hostile to academic work.

A final observation is that, through their research and publications, Nigerian academic political scientists, have contributed to our understanding of the nature of military rule in the country, not for its own sake but with a view to transcending it and exploring conditions for enduring democratic transitions in the country.

## VIII

Let me now examine the issue of intellectual responsibility of Nigerian academic political scientists from the perspective of the professionalization of the discipline in the country. Professionalization offers academics and other professionals the opportunity to organize themselves into a network to promote and protect their individual as well as collective interests, to advance their discipline, to develop a code of ethics to guide their professional or academic conduct and to ensure accountability among them for their professional conduct, and to influence public policy.

It was not until 1972/1973 that Nigerian academic political scientists organized themselves into a professional body, the Nigerian Political Science Association (NPSA), although some of them were members of extra-Nigerian professional bodies like the British Political Science Association, the American Political Science Association, and the International Political Science Association.

Prior to 1972/1973, many Nigerian academic political scientists pursued and sought to advance their professional interests through membership in the Nigerian Economic Society (NES), whose conferences and related activities served the "brokerage" or networking function of providing various forums for academic social scientists to interact with top civil servants and top private sector functionaries to discuss national and international issues.

The professionalization of academic political science must also be set against trends and developments between 1970 and 1975 in the antinomic relationship between democracy and military rule in the country. These trends, to be elaborated below, threatened the integrity of Nigerian academic political scientists at a time when the discipline itself had come of age in the organization of academic programmes in Nigerian universities and was in the process of consolidating itself and establishing its relevance.

The combination of affluence and poverty brought about by the oil boom in the country after the end of the civil war, coupled with the strain and bottlenecks created by the uncontrolled expansion in public sector expenditures and investments provided a challenge to Nigerian academic social scientists who had gradually begun to view their academic discipline as a development-and policy-oriented social science. By 1972 and 1983, chronic shortages were commonplace in the country, public service delivery was shoddy and inefficient and had virtually been paralyzed, inflation was spiralling at uncontrolled pace, corruption was rampant and blatant and, worse of all, government was apparently helpless and seemed to have no credible agenda to stem the tide of these socioeconomic problems to bring them under control.

Added to this confusion was the suspicion that the military government was preparing to go back on its promise to hand over power to a democratically elected civilian administration in 1976. Rather, it seemed the military government was behind the kite about diarchy, a combination of military and civilian rule with a military veto, that was then being flown in public discussions. The political atmosphere was also tainted by the offensive which the military government mounted against university lecturers when in 1973 it gave them the option of calling off a threatened strike action or vacating government housing allocated to them.

It was against the background of these social and political trends in the country that the founding of the Nigerian Political Science

Association (NPSA) in 1973 must be located. A number of Nigerian academic political scientists had become uncomfortable with the pro-military government posture of the Nigerian Economic Society (NES) on several important national issues. They were also worried about the close links of the NES with the military government.

For example, in his address at the 1973 Annual Conference of the NES, its President, a top government functionary, argued for a one-party state in the country, which at the time was viewed as a euphemism for continued military rule. He followed this up soon after with a statement at a seminar at the University of Ibadan to the effect that there was no need for a change in the military administration of the country, except through a military coup. The same view, suspected to be the official government view or thinking, was expressed by the military governors of Bendel State and the Western State to the effect that since the essence of governance was "to deliver the goods," then there was no need to canvass for a return to democratic civilian rule since the military government was satisfying that condition.

The contrary position of prominent Nigerian academic political scientists like Billy J. Dudley, Eme Awa, and Babs Williams to the mainstream position within the NES on military rule was that the problem of Nigeria was primarily political and not economic and should not therefore be reduced to that of "delivering [economic] goods."

It was with a view to providing an independent intellectual forum for academic political scientists to address and promote this view of the primacy of democratic political development in the country and to advance their academic and professional interests as well that a meeting of heads of departments of political science in the country's universities was convened in 1973 to inaugurate the NPSA, with Billy J. Dudley and Omo Omoruyi as Secretary.

The NPSA convened its 1st annual conference at the University of Nigeria, Nsukka amidst rumors and expectations that the military administration was about to issue a policy statement on democracy and a program of demilitarization or transition to democratic rule. The theme of the conference was Agenda For The Nation, 1976, in an obvious reference to the earlier commitment by the military to hand-over power to a democratically elected civilian government in 1976.

The conference was unequivocal in its opposition to military rule, to the diarchy option as well as to the suggestion on socialist grounds by Eme Awa, one of its members, for one-party rule. The presidential address of Billy J. Dudley and the closing speech by the new president, Babs A. Williams reflected the mood of the general membership in their defence of the primacy of politics and the call of a speedy return to democratic rule under a multiparty system.

Less than three months after this conference, the military government issued the long-suspected policy statement, announcing the indefinite postponement of the 1976 date for its return to the barracks. Barely a year after this, it was overthrown on July 25, 1995 in a military coup by a new military administration that promptly announced a programme of transition to democratic (civil) rule in 1979.

As the concrete, positive steps the new military administration took to implement its transition program unfolded, the NPSA became more and more self-conscious and self-assertive about its role in setting or in influencing the public debate on the transition. The military government appeared to have appreciated the positive contribution which academic political scientists as "specialists" could make to the democratic project in the country. As a result it began to provide subvention on a regular basis for the NPSA to hold its annual conferences.

The NPSA was, however, careful to protect and preserve its autonomy as well as the professional integrity of its members. Although it was not averse to receiving subvention, which it actively solicited sometimes from the military government, the NPSA neither became a mouthpiece of government nor served as its apologist. A watershed in this assertion of its professional integrity was the 1977 NPSA annual conference which was virtually bankrolled by the federal cabinet office. The theme of the conference was that Draft Constitution submitted to the military government by the Constitution Drafting Committee.

The NPSA resisted and rebuffed attempts by federal cabinet office functionaries to dictate the agenda, tone, and direction of the conference. This independent posture has since been maintained and has indeed assumed consensual proportions.

This tradition of independence and professional integrity has been sustained and reflected in another way. This is the tradition begun by Billy J. Dudley of using the Presidential Address at the NPSA annual conference not only to focus on and address in a critical matter national issues and government policies, even when military governors who were usually invited to open these annual conferences were in attendance, but also to suggest broad patterns along which the democratic project should proceed.

Sometimes, these presidential addresses were accompanied by high drama. For example at the 1984 annual conference of the NPSA held in Ilorin, Kwara State, the NPSA presidential address by Sam Oyovbaire was so critical of the military administration that the military governor of Kwara State who had earlier on delivered an Opening Address on behalf of the Head of State insisted on giving on-the-spot rebuttal to Oyovbaire's presidential address, contrary to the usual practice at NPSA's annual conferences. The importance attached to these NPSA presidential addresses is reflected in the wide coverage in the print and electronic media that they usually get.

This independent posture of the NPSA is a nationalist one, similar to that which informed the philosophy and editorial opinions of the now defunct THE NIGERIAN OPINION, edited by Billy J. Dudley in the 1960s. It is a posture grounded in an intellectualized and principled opposition to military rule and militarist solutions to problems of democratic and good governance in the country. While not agitational, it is based and anchored on a realism and pragmatism arising out of the historical conjuctures which have made military rule possible in the country.

What the NPSA sseks to do is to provide a forum for its members to engage in the Socratic dialectics of the national debate on the country's democratic agenda, within the framework provided by the reality of military rule and the social forces in contention for hegemony in the country. In doing so, the NPSA has defined professionalism in terms of the intellectual responsibility of the Nigerian academic political scientist to promote and advance the cause of the democratic project in the country. What the NPSA has refused to do in effect is to be used to legitimize military rule.

If it has established this general and principled attitude or position, the NPSA is yet to address itself to the issue of a code of ethics and the enforceability of accountability among its members, especially those who have been coopted into public (political) service. This is in spite of the fact that the theme of its 1979 annual conference at the University of Benin was "Commitment and the Social Responsibility of the Political Scientist."

The adoption of such a code of conduct which will also spell out modalities for enforcing accountability is all the more desirable becausee all too often in the recent past, the annual conference of the NPSA has provided the launching pad for some of its members to make serious allegations of unprincipled behavior, or professional misconduct or betrayal of the intellectual vocation against other members who are serving the government. The NPSA, perhaps, need to establish machinery for investing the allegations, if formally brought before it and must establish sanctions not only against those who are culpable but also against those who bring false or unsubstantiated allegations which border on libel.

This is not to deny that the problem of professional misconduct is a serious and real one. The temptation for professional misconduct is an all-too-common one; but so also is the temptation for others to jump too quickly and too readily to the conclusion that an academic political scientist holding public or political office has compromised himself or herself. This latter temptation smacks of intellectual irresponsibility, a departure from the canonical demand of the intellectual tradition to "suspend judgement" and come to conclusions only on the basis of the facts. Invariably, those who make the allegations too readily assume or combine the role of accuser, judge, jury and executioner.

It is to the vexed issue of the cooptation or recruitment of Nigerian academic scientists to serve public authorities or governments as political or quasi-political functionaries that I now turn.

## IX

Nigerian academic political scientists have not been immune to the now-common practice all over the world of inviting or appointing academic and other intellectuals to serve as cabinet ministers, as advisers, as experts and as members of commissions and boards of public and private sector corporations. In nearly all countries, the tendency is to regard such appointments as illustrative of the public service functions of universities, as necessary for the enrichment of the intellectual vocation and as providing unique opportunities for intellectuals to merge theory and practice in the service of their society.

If this is the theory to explain this practice, it must, however, be placed in perspective of the fundamental love-hate relationship between the world of power and the world of learning, academia.

As some have argued, academic intellectuals only stand to lose, to be used and dumped thereafter, they risk being corrupted and debased, with their professional integrity a casualty, if they cohabit with the world of power. In spite of this, as others have pointed out, the lure of power, their fascination with it and the advantages which proximity to it confers on them are all too tempting for academic intellectuals to rests. As Shils (1990, pp. 226-227) has put it, "...intellectuals despite their tradition of distrust [of power] have been gratified by the prospect and the realities of the proximity to power...[They] are preoccupied with the political centre; they want to be near it and to influence it."

Another perspective from which to view this practice is the commodization of the intellectual vocation in the twentieth century and its implications for the intellectual responsibility and the independence of the intellectual. This is particularly relevant in the highly statist societies of Africa where the possibilities and prospects for academic intellectuals to have independent means of livelihood or secured employment outside of the public sector are very slim. As I have indicated earlier here, Nigerian academic political scientists, like other university teachers in the country, are, by law, public servants, enjoying the privileges and subject to the obligations attaching to that status.

What has been the Nigerian experience with the involvement of academic political scientists in the service of their government? It is useful in answering this question to make a distinction between those who went into partisan politics and those who were appointed to serve as cabinet ministers, as advisers and as members of commissions in their own right and not as members of political parties.

Nigerian academic political scientists have generally not entered partisan politics, even though they may have been active on the sidelines as "closet" politicians. This is not unconnected with their legal status as public servants, their lack of independent means of livelihood, the financial requirements or outlay necessary to go into partisan politics and running for elective public office, and their general aversion to the uncertainties and rough and tumble of partisan politics.

However, some of them have entered into partisan politics. Prominent among them were Kalu Ezera, Omo Omoruyi, Ali D. Yahaya, Asikpo Essien-Ibok, Bala Takaya, John Zwingina, and Emeka Enejere. Some of them, like Dunmoye and Amdi, also ran for elective office at the local government level on a non-party basis, during the local government elections of 1987. Others like Claude Ake and Moyibi Amoda, who were both active in some of the unregistered political associations that sought registration as political parties in 1989-1990, abandoned partisan politics out of disappointment with the registration exercise, and what they thought it portended for the transition program.

Military regimes in the country have tended to draw on the services of Nigerian academic political scientists, among other academics so appointed, in larger numbers than civilian regimes have done. This is due to the fact that the country has been under military rule much longer than it has been under civil rule. It is also due to the practice of the military administrations to seek a wider and constituencies within civil society to legitimize themselves and to look beyond the civil service for inputs into the administrative and policymaking machinery at the executive branch level.

Prominent Nigerian academic political scientists who have been appointed to serve as federal ministers or as commissioners [ministers] at the state government level have included Babs Williams, Odenigwe, Gordon Idang, Ibrahim Gambari, Bolaji Akinyemi, Tunji Olagunju, Sam Oyovbaire, Kimse Okoko, and Humphrey Mwosu. Ukpabi Asika was appointed the Administrator [Governor] of the East Central State while Essien-Udom served as the Secretary to the Government of South Eastern State and Head of Service.

Academic political scientists who served as Special Advisers include Professor Odenigwe [to President Shagari], Tunji Olagunju [to President Babangida], Sam Oyovbaire [to Vice-President Aikhomu], George Obiozor [to Vice President Aikhomu], Tunde Adeniran [to Governor Bola Ige], and Femi Otubanjo [to General Diya, Chief of General Staff]. Those who served or are serving as non-career ambassadors include Larry Ekpebu (Ivory Coast), Ibrahim Gambari (United Nations) and Alaba Ogunsanwo (Botswana).

Those who have served in other political positions include the following: Issawa Elaigwu and Ali D. Yahaya [members of the President Advisory Committee]; Eme Awa, Ali D. Yahaya, Haroun Adamu, Oyeleye Oyediran, Tunde Adeniran, and Bala Takaya [members of the Political Bureau that drew up the report that served as the transition blueprint of the military administration of President Babangida]; Billy Dudley and Oyeleye Oyediran [members of the

Constitution Drafting Committee that prepared the 1979 Nigerian Constitution]; Oyeleye Oyediran [member of the Constitution Review Committee that prepared the 1989 Nigerian Constitution]; Moyibi Amoda and Rafiu Akindele [members of the 1989-90 Constituent Assembly]; and Haroun Adamu, [Member, National Economic Intelligence Committee].

Those who served on other bodies include, Eme Awa [Chairman and Member, National Electoral Commission, 1987-89], Humphrey Nwosu [Chairman and Member, National Electoral Commission, 1989-93]; L. Adele Jinadu [Member, National Electoral Commission]; Omo Omoruyi, [Director-General, Centre for Democratic Studies]; Tunde Adeniran [Executive Secretary and later Chairman, National Mobilisation Agency, MAMSER]; Elo Amucheazi [Director-General, National Orientation Agency, successor to MAMSER].

Other Nigerian academic political scientists who have held important public offices include Bolaji Akinyemi, Ibrahim Gambari, and George Obiozor, all as Director-General of the Nigerian Institute of International Affairs at different times; Issawa Elaigwu as Director-General of the Centre for Inter-Governmental Relations; and Ali D. Yahaya and L. Adele Jinadu as Director-General of the Administrative Staff College of Nigeria at different times.

It is unclear what criteria were used for these appointments or what considerations other than professional competence and attainment informed them. Personal recommendations from friends, relations, power brokers, traditional rulers, religious leaders as well as considerations of ethnic diversity were important. Of central importance under President Babangida was the proximity to the "center" or the innermost recesses of power which a number of academic political scientists had by virtue of the close personal relationships they had developed with President Babangida and some members of the military high command over the years.

# X

How is this movement, transformation from the classroom to the center of power to be viewed? What has been the reaction to it? What do these academic political scientists have to show for their "sabbatical"? What has been their experience?

The movement, especially during the Babangida years (1985-1993) was criticized on the ground that it had led to the depletion of academic staff strength, particularly at the senior level, in departments of political science in the affected universities. The argument that the discipline stood to gain in the long run, since those who had left on this "sabbatical" would eventually return, as better teacher in view of the richness of their "field experiences," was countered with the argument that they would not likely return to their teaching posts at the end of their "sabbatical," preferring and using their strategic positions and connections to look instead for greener pastures.

There is some force to this counterargument, as many academic political scientists, and indeed other academic intellectuals who have gone on this kind of "sabbatical" rarely return to the universities. But, there has also been a general depletion of university staff strength in recent years because of the deterioration of university facilities, poor remuneration and the attraction of alternative career opportunities elsewhere in the public sector, in the private sector and in international organizations. It should be added that some of those who returned to the university at the end of their political appointments were exposed to ridicule, hostility and in some cases physical assault by their colleagues. This experience has discouraged others from returning to their universities at the end of their "sabbatical."

A more problematic aspect is the accusation that these academic political scientists or some of them were used to legitimise military regimes and that in the process they might have compromised their professional integrity, playing the role of military apologists and vicariously, if not morally or even criminally responsible for the perpetuation of military rule in the country.

This problem goes to the heart of the long-standing aversion of the NPSA to too close an association with military regimes in the country. It was raised at the annual conferences of the NPSA in 1988 at the University of Ibadan, in 1989 at the University of Calabar, in 1992 at the Administrative Staff College of Nigeria, and in 1993 at the University of Ife.

A pertinent comment in this respect is the following one made by Bayo Adekanye, in his inaugural lecture as Professor of Political Science at the University of Ibadan: "In recent years, the political science profession nationally has come under considerable attack not just from other academic professions, but also from fellow and much younger members from within the profession itself. The worry has been over too close identification of many of the country's professors of political science with the major aspects of the Babangida military presidency, raising the question, "Have the Professors of Political Science Lost Their Science and Gained the Political?"

Indeed, "have the professors…lost their science, and gained the political?" This seems to me to be a generalized indictment. There are various dimensions to the indictment. First, there is the accusation of collusion with President Babangida in what was alleged to be his dishonourable "hidden agenda" to perpetuate himself in office, in spite of his public pronouncements to the contrary and the elaborate transition program he had introduced. The accusation against the academic political scientists involved in his administration was either that they had taken part in preparing the "hidden agenda," the other transition program, and were active in implementing it; or that, through their naivety, they were vicariously responsible by providing intellectual cover for it by defending his commitment to handing over power to a democratically elected civilian regime.

If there was any evidence of President Babangida's "hidden agenda," the accusation claims, it was provided by his annulment of the popular June 12, 1993 presidential elections. Those academic political scientists who served in his administration "lost their science" in not seeing through his subterfuges.

Secondly, there is the imputation, sometimes at the NPSA annual conference of 1993 at the University of Ife the explicit accusation that some academic political scientists in President Babangida's administration had corruptly enriched themselves, have "gained the political," while in office and should have place within the NPSA.

These two allegations, of complicity and corrupt enrichment, have never been substantiated. Nor have those who made the allegations distinguished between those who served in government as ministers or in similar positions; and those who were not strictly speaking part of the administration but served in independent or quasi-independent institutions or transition agencies under President Babangida.

What is the force of the allegations, anyway? The more difficult problem is to determine whether President Babangida did have a hidden agenda, and if so, whether some academic political scientists were privy to it, master-minded it, or whether not being privy to it, they should have seen through it and resigned.

These are difficult questions, the more so since it is not clear what would constitute evidence to substantiate or deny the allegation. Even then, the question whether there was a hidden agenda should be separated from the issue, rarely posed, of whether academic political scientists being accused acted in good faith, even if mistaken or if they exhibited poor judgement, and whether, in their naivety, they did their best to make the transition succeed.

The allegation of collusion, it seems to me, is indicative of the failure of many Nigerian academic political scientists to situate their own "science" in a theory of transitions to democracy which seeks the explanation to the course of the Babangida administration's transition in terms of the inherently endangered nature of transitions. As theoretical work on Latin American and South European transitions (Przeworksi 1991; O'Donnell 1989) have shown, transitions to democracy under military rule should not be taken for granted and are full of "positive paradoxes." According to O'Donnell, "the main factor of uncertainty is obvious: during the transition, as the democratic opposition becomes more assertive and civil society unfolds, the reasons that both induce and deter a regressive coup grow together. One of the archtypical dramas of these transitions is the possibility of a coup-a coup that all the actors (except, of course, the hardliners and the maximalists) have as their paramount goal to avoid, which in certain circumstances seem imminent...and which does not happen."

What this requires but which proponents of a hidden agenda do not seem to understand, is the need to go beyond psychological reductionist explanations of General Babangida's annulment to explanations grounded concretely in an examination of the various social forces and actors in contention to save or abort the transition. To attribute the annulment to a hidden agenda begs the question. Even if there was such an agenda, there is need to bridge the gap between intention, process, structure, action and outcome.

# XI

What do Nigerian academic political scientists who have served in government have to show for it? The first point to make is that academic political scientists who served on the Political Bureau, on the National Electoral Commission, on MAMSER, in the CDS, and other transition agencies under the Babangida administration, as well as their colleagues who served as Special Advisers to the President and Vice President played major, even crucial roles in bringing their professional expertise as political scientists to bear on, to influence and to direct the course of the political processes that led to the successful reestablishment of democratic institutions under the transition program. I refer here to elections that led to the assumption of office by popularly elected civilian chairmen and councillors of local government councils in 1990, by popularly elected Governors and legislators in the various states of the federation in 1991, and by popularly elected members of the National Assembly (House of Representatives and Senate) at the federal level in 1992. To this must be added the success of the two party system in ensuring the emergence of national as opposed to tribal or ethnic parties.

Although the annuled presidential elections of June 1993 has provided the post facto justification and substance for the allegation of a hidden agenda and connivance by academic political scientists involved with the transition, the fact of its success, that it was acclaimed the best elections so far conducted in the country's postcolonial history is due to the central role played in organizing and conducting them by academic political scientists who were in command at such critical transition agencies as the National Electoral Commission and the CDS. Without them and their colleagues June 12 would not have been possible. This speaks a great deal for their commitment to democratic transitions. It was beyond their powers to prevent the annulment and some of them, Omo Omoruyi, for example spoke out publicly and boldly against it.

Another point to make is that the two academic political scientists who served as the Special Adviser to President Babangida and the Special Adviser to the then Chief of General Staff, Aikhomu worked hard behind-the-scene to ensure that the proscription on the National Association of Nigeria Students (NANS) and other civil associations was lifted, as a good faith demonstration of the administration's commitment to open up the political space. Through the efforts of these two academic political scientists and a number of their colleagues in government, the NPSA itself received substantial subvention from the administration for its annual conferences and other activities, to encourage research by its members, to set up research outfits and to ensure that NPSA as a professional association was given official place on some transition agencies, such as the nomination of the President of the NPSA as an unelected member of the Constituent Assembly.

## XII

To conclude, what can be said of the experience of these Nigerian academic political scientists? Is it one of frustration and despondency, of powerlessness and impotence? This is true to some extent, although it varies from one individual academic political scientists to the other, and in what capacity they served. On the other hand, there is also reason to believe that some of them found fulfillment in their assignments, exercised influence over public policy in certain situations and were not frustrated, even if things did not work out as well as they had expected.

Life involves give and take, and it is not all the time that one gets one's way or that one is fortunate to strike it lucky. If this is true of one's personal life, it is even more so when one moves into the public sphere, where the stakes are high, with protagonists ready to destroy one's career, and where contending perspectives and view points on the course of public policy are in contention and the final authority does not lie with one. Luck also plays its part in these things.

It may well be that academic political scientists were not, by training and outlook, prepared for the complexities and tortuous, even treacherous terrains of the public sphere, of its dog-eat-dog character and might have gone into it with high, starry-eyed expectations, only to find that there were serious limitations and impediments in their way.

For example, Professor Essien-Udom who served as the Secretary to the government of the South-Eastern State and as Head of Service has related to colleagues, on the basis of his own experience in government, how the discipline had ill-prepared him for what he had to deal with in office.

Eme Awa has complained of the difficulties he had with the military administration, especially with some military governors and a number of high federal government functionaries, in performing his duties as chairman of the National Electoral Commission. Humphrey Nwosu who succeeded him would probably have the same story to tell, especially in respect of the circumstances surrounding the annuled presidential elections of June 12, 1993.

But these experiences are not common or unique to academic political scientists. It seems to be an inherent aspect of the policy process which all who are engaged in it at the highest level of policy initiation have to battle with. And nowhere is this more so than in a developing country and especially one like Nigeria which has experienced military rule for much of its postcolonial existence, where arbitrary and personalized rule has tended to be the norm and where capricious behavior by the powers-that-be is all too common and, perhaps the norm.

There is reason to believe, however, that Nigerian academic political scientists who served in publis positions did exert influence and power of a positive nature and did make a difference for good, under certain situations. This is clear from situations where they were involved in regulatory and independent institutions like the National Electoral Commission.

The decisions of the commission under Eme Awa to prohibit inter-local government movement during elections and to limit voting to the daytime, from 8 a.m. to 4 p.m., the controversial open-ballot voting system, and the similarly controversial Option A4 used in the presidential primaries that preceded the annuled presidential elections, both of which were introduced under Humphrey Nwosu's chairmanship of the commission, fundamentally altered the structure of elections in the country.

I have used these examples because I am familiar with them, having played critical roles in the processes that led to the decisions. But other cases of the success of policy initiatives of academic political scientists in government could be cited. For example, Bolaji Akinyemi used his position as Minister of External Affairs under President Babangida to see to it that his vision of a Nigerian equivalent of the peace corps was translated into concrete form as Nigeria's Technical Aid Corps.

The experience of Nigerian academic political scientists who have served their country as political functionaries has not been only a tale of woes, of despondency and frustration, of powerlessness and impotence. It has been that. But it has also been a positive one which has seen them make important, even if unacknowledged contribution to their country's development.

## REFERENCES

Adekanye, J.B. 1993. *Military Occupation and Social Stratification.* Inaugural lecture, University of Ibadan.

Awa, E. 1960. *Federal Government in Nigeria.* Berkeley, CA: University of California Press.

Dudley, B.J. 1968. *Parties and Politics in Northern Nigeria.* London: Frank Cass.

Ezera, K. 1961. *Constitutional Development in Nigeria.* Cambridge, England: Cambridge University Press.

Jinadu, L.A. 1987. "The Institutional Development of Political Science in Nigeria: Trends, Problems and Prospects." *International Political Science Review* 8(1).

_____. 1985. "Federalism, the Consociational State and Ethnic Conflict in Nigeria." *Publius: The Journal of Federalism* 15(2).

Kurczewski, J. 1990. "Power and Wisdom: The Expert as Mediating Figure in Contemporary Polish History." Chap 5 *Political responsibility of intellectuals,* edited by I. Maclean, A. Montefiore, and Peter Winch. Cambridge: Cambridge University Press.

Mabogunje, A. 1973. "The Humanities and the Social Sciences." In *The University of Ibadan, 1948-1973: A History of the First Twenty-Five Years,* edited by J.F. Ade Ajayi and Tekena Tamuno. Ibadan: University of Ibadan Press.

Maclean, I., A. Montefiore, and P. Winch. (eds.). 1990. *The Political Responsibility of Intellectuals.* Cambridge, England: Cambridge University Press.

Montefiore, A. 1990. "The Political Responsibility of Intellectuals." Chap. 11 in *The Political Responsibilty of Intellectuals,* edited by I. Maclean, A. Montefiore, and P. Winch. Cambridge, England. Cambridge University Press.

O'Donnell, G. 1989. "Transitions to Democracy: Some Navigational Instruments." In *Democracy in the Americas, Democracy in the Americas: Stopping the Pendulum,* edited by Robert A. Pastor. New York: Holmes and Meier.

Nnoli, O. 1978. *Ethnic Politics in Nigeria.* Enugu, Nigeria: Fourth Dimension Press.

Przeworski, A. 1991. *Democracy and the Market: Political and Economic Reform in Europe and Latin America.* Cambridge University Press.

Said, G.W. 1994. *Representations of the Intellectual,* 1993 Reith Lectures. London: Viking Press.

Shils, E. 1990. "Intellectuals and Responsibility." Chap. 14 in *The Political Responsibility of Intellectuals,* edited by I. Maclean, A. Montefiore, and P. Winch. Cambridge, England. Cambridge University Press.

Szacki, J. 1990. "Intellectuals Between Politics and Culture." Chap. 12 in *The Political Responsibility of Intellectuals,* edited by I. Maclean, A. Montefiore, and P. Winch. Cambridge, England. Cambridge University Press.

**J**

**A**

**I**

**P**

**R**

**E**

**S**

**S**

# Research in Race and Ethnic Relations

Edited by **Rutledge M. Dennis,** *Department of Sociology, Virginia Commonwealth University*

**Volume 9, W.E.B. Du Bois:**
**The Scholar As Activist**
1996, 239 pp.                                    $73.25
ISBN 0-7623-0045-0

**CONTENTS:** PART I. INTRODUCTION. Continuities and Discontinuities in Du Bois's Social and Political Thought, *Rutledge M. Dennis*. PART II. THE INTERVIEW. Personal Reflections on W.E.B. Du Bois: The Person, Scholar, and Activist, By Herbert and Fay Aptheker, *Benjamin Bowser and Deborah Whittle*. PART III. DOUBLE CONSCIOUSNESS. Du Bois's Concept of Double Consciousness: Myth or Reality, *Rutledge M. Dennis*. Double Consciousness and the Politics of the Elite, *Toni-Michelle C. Travis*. PART IV. THE SOCIOLOGY OF KNOWLEDGE AND EDUCATION. Present at the Creation: Rethinking Du Bois's Practice Theory, *Paul Jefferson*. W.E.B. Du Bois: His Evolving Theory of Education, *Myrtle G. Glascoe*. PART V. RACE, CLASS, AND GENDER. Race, Class, and Gender in the Work of W.E.B. Du Bois: An Exploratory Study, *Betsy Lucal*. Race, Class, and Power: The Impact of Du Bois's Scholarship and Revolutionary Agenda, *Rodney D. Coates, Sandra Lee Browning, and Beenah Moshay Brown*.

Also Available:
**Volumes 1-8** (1979-1995)                      $73.25 each

**JAI PRESS INC.**
55 Old Post Road No. 2 - P.O. Box 1678
Greenwich, Connecticut 06836-1678
Tel: (203) 661- 7602    Fax: (203) 661-0792

# Research in Economic Anthropology

Edited by **Barry L. Isaac,**
*Department of Anthropology,*
*University of Cincinnati*

**Volume 17,** 1996, 400 pp.                    $82.50
ISBN 0-7623-0151-1

Also Available:
**Volumes 1-16** (1978-1995)
 **+ Supplements 1-7** (1980-1993)                    $73.25 each

J
A
I

P
R
E
S
S

**JAI PRESS INC.**
55 Old Post Road No. 2 - P.O. Box 1678
Greenwich, Connecticut 06836-1678
Tel: (203) 661- 7602    Fax: (203) 661-0792

# Cultural Studies

Edited by **Norman K. Denzin,** *Institute of Communications Research, University of Illinois at Urbana-Champaign*

*Cultural Studies* is an interdisciplinary series, drawing on contemporary scholarship in such fields as speech communication, education, anthropology, sociology, history, and English. Manuscripts focus on the intersection of interpretive critical theory, qualitative inquiry, culture, media, history, biography and social structure. This new international research publication creates a space for the study of those global cultural practices and cultural forms that shape the meanings of race, ethnicity, class, nationality, and gender in the contemporary world.

**Volume 1,** 1996, 372 pp.                    $73.25
ISBN 1-55938-951-6

# Knowledge and Society

Edited by **Shirley Gorenstein,**
*Department of Science and Technology Studies,*
*Rensselaer Polytechnic Institute*

**Volume 10, Research in Science and**
**Technology Studies: Material Culture**
1996, 224 pp.                    $73.25
ISBN 1-55938-000-4

**CONTENTS:** Introduction: Material Culture, *Shirley Goren-*
*stein.* Progress in Separate Spheres: Selling Nineteenth-Cen-
tury Technologies, *Pamela Walker Laird.* "Excavating" the
Present: The Computer as Gendered Material Culture, *Merete*
*Lie.* The Electric Fridge and Other Recollections—On Things
as Memory Objects, *Liv Emma Thorsen.* Technologies and Interpretations: The Case of the Telephone, *John W. Bakke.*
The Culture of Instrument: A Case from the Engineering Sciences, *Lusin Babla-Gökalp.* Toward a Grammar of Artifacts,
*Russell Mills.* Separate from the "World": The Use of Material
Culture in Shaker Social Reproduction, *Kenneth D. Croes.*
Reflections in a Mechanical Mirror: Automata as Doubles and
as Tools, *Linda M. Strauss.*

Also Available:
**Volumes 1-9** (1978-1992)                    $73.25 each

**JAI PRESS INC.**
55 Old Post Road No. 2 - P.O. Box 1678
Greenwich, Connecticut 06836-1678
Tel: (203) 661- 7602    Fax: (203) 661-0792

J
A
I

P
R
E
S
S

# J A I  P R E S S

## Research in
## Social Stratification and Mobility

Edited by **Kevin Leicht,**
*Department of Sociology, University of Iowa*

**Volume 15,** 1997, 259 pp.                    $73.25
ISBN 0-7623-0048-5

Also Available:
**Volumes 1-14** (1981-1995)                    $73.25 each

**JAI PRESS INC.**
55 Old Post Road No. 2 - P.O. Box 1678
Greenwich, Connecticut 06836-1678
Tel: (203) 661- 7602    Fax: (203) 661-0792